BLU

WINCHESTER
FIREARMS & VALUES
BY S.P. FJESTAD

Publisher's Suggested List Price
$14.95

This book is the result of nonstop and continuous firearms research obtained by attending and/or participating in trade shows, gun shows, auctions, and also communicating with contributing editors, gun dealers, collectors, company historians, and other knowledgeable industry professionals worldwide each year. This book represents an analysis of prices for which collectible firearms have actually been selling during that period at an average retail level. Although every reasonable effort has been made to compile an accurate and reliable guide, gun prices may vary significantly (especially auction prices) depending on such factors as the locality of the sale, the number of sales we were able to consider, and economic conditions. Accordingly, no representation can be made that the guns listed may be bought or sold at prices indicated, nor shall the author or publisher be responsible for any error made in compiling and recording such prices and related information.

Content Disclaimer:

Due to space considerations, this book does not contain information or values on machine guns, select fire, NFA classified firearms, firearms accessories (scopes, bayonets, etc.), airguns, modern black powder reproductions and replicas. For current information on airguns and modern black powder replicas, please refer to the *Blue Book of Airguns* and the *Blue Book of Modern Black Powder Arms*. Visit www.bluebookofgunvalues.com for more info on how to order either online or in print.

Blue Book Publications, Inc.
8009 34th Avenue South, Suite 250
Minneapolis, MN 55425 U.S.A.
Customer Service: 800-877-4867, ext. 3 (domestic only)
Phone No.: 952-854-5229 (International)
Fax No.: 952-853-1486
General Email: support@bluebookinc.com
Website: www.bluebookofgunvalues.com
Published and printed in the United States of America

ISBN 10: 1-936120-82-8
ISBN 13: 978-1-936120-82-6

Distributed in part to the book trade by Ingram Book Company and Baker & Taylor.

Table of Contents

The author/publisher would like to thank the following individuals for their contributions to this Fourth Edition *Blue Book Pocket Guide for Winchester Firearms & Values*:

Ashley Hlebinsky and her capable staff – Buffalo Bill Center of the West, Cody Firearms Museum

Jessica Bennet – Firearms Records Specialist at Buffalo Bill Center of the West

Jackie Love, Cindy Jensen, Kirk Jensen - Browning

Randy Shuman

The Great White LeRoy of the North

Michael Salisbury

Ron Lough

Orvin Olson

Gene Leopold

Alvin Olson

Greg Martin

John Lacy

Larry Orr

Don "Duck" Combs

R.L. Wilson

Kevin Cherry

Don Herigstad

Steve Engleson

Steve Hamilton

Dennis Dawson

CREDITS:

Cover artwork: Clint H. Schmidt

Printing: POD by BR Printers located in East Windsor, NJ.

How to Use This Book

The values listed in this Fourth Edition *Blue Book Pocket Guide for Winchester Firearms & Values* are based on national average retail prices for both modern and antique firearms, and some accessories/accoutrements. This is not a firearms wholesale pricing guide. More importantly, do not expect to walk into a gun/pawn shop or gun show and think that the proprietor/dealer/collector should pay you the retail values listed within this text for your gun(s). Resale offers on many models could be anywhere from near retail to 20%-50% less than the values listed, depending upon locality, desirability, dealer inventory, and profitability. In other words, if you want to receive 100% of the retail value, then you have to do 100% of the work (become the retailer, which also includes assuming 100% of the risk).

Percentages of original condition (with corresponding values) are listed between 10%-100% for most antiques (unless configuration, rarity, and age preclude upper conditions). 60%-100% condition factors are listed on most modern firearms since condition below 60% is seldom encountered (or purchased). Please consult our revised Photo Percentage Grading System™ (PPGS) available on our website: www.bluebookofgunvalues.com to learn more about the condition of your firearm(s). Since condition is the overriding factor in price evaluation, study these photos and captions carefully to learn more about the condition of your specimen(s).

A copy of NRA Condition Standards and Grading Criteria have been included to help make the conversion to percentages easier.

To find a Winchester model in this text, first look under the correct category name, then find the model, sub-model, or variation you are looking for. Winchester Commemoratives will appear last in this text. When applicable, antiques will appear before modern guns, and are typically listed in chronological sequence.

Trademarks are listed alphabetically in uppercase bold typeface, like this:

WINCHESTER

Manufacturer/trademark information is listed directly beneath the trademark heading:

Mfg. in Japan since circa 1992, Herstal, Belgium (O/U shotguns since 2004), and in Columbia, SC (Model 70 only beginning 2008). Previously manufactured in New Haven, CT, 1866-2006, and by U.S. Repeating Arms from 1981-2006 through a licensing agreement from Olin Corp. to manufacture shotguns and rifles domestically using the Winchester Trademark.

Manufacturer notes may appear next under individual heading descriptions and can be differentiated by the following typeface:

For more information and current pricing on both new and used Winchester airguns and current black powder models, please refer to the Blue Book of Airguns by Dr. Robert D. Beeman & John B. Allen, and the Blue Book of Modern Black Powder Arms by John B. Allen (also online).

The next classification is the category name (normally, in alphabetical sequence) in uppercase lettering (inside a screened gray box) which primarily refers to a firearm's configuration. Category names can be differentiated by the following typeface.

PISTOLS: SINGLE SHOT

A further sub-classification may appear under a category name, as depicted below. These sub-categories of a major category name appear in both upper and lower case type, and typically appear in alphabetical order. Sub-category names can be differentiated by the following typeface:

Shotguns: Single Barrel, 1968-1980 mfg.

A category note may follow a category or sub-category name to help explain the category, and/or provide limited information on the models and values listed within the category. This appears as follows:

Values by percentages are not listed on the Models Henry and 1866, as original condition over 30% is seldom encountered.

Model names appear flush left, are bold faced, and are in uppercase lettering either in chronological order (normally) or alphabetical order (sometimes, the previous model name and/or close sub-variation will appear at the end in parentheses) and are listed under the individual category and sub-category names. Examples include:

MODEL 70 ULTIMATE SHADOW

Model descriptions are denoted by the following typeface and usually include the following information:

- calibers, gauges/bore, action type, barrel length(s), finish(es), weight, and other descriptive data are provided adjacent to model names in this typeface. This is where most of the information is listed for each specific model, including identifiable features and possibly some production data, including quantity, date of manufacture, and discontinuance date, if known.

Variations (and possible production periods) within a model appear as sub-models - they are differentiated from model names by an asterisk (*), are italicized and indented, and appear in upper and lowercase type, as follows:

    * ***Model 1866 First Model Rifle***

This is usually followed by a short description of that sub-model. These sub-model descriptions have the same typeface as the model descriptions:

- additional sub-model information could include finishes, calibers, barrel lengths, special order features, or other production data specific for that sub-model.

Also included is yet another layer of model/information nomenclature differentiating sub-models from variations of sub-models or a lower hierarchy of sub-model information. These items are indented from the sub-models, and have the icon graphic », for example:

    » ***Model 42 Slide Action Deluxe Grade Solid Rib***

A description for this level of sub-model information may appear next to the sub-entry, and uses the same typeface as model and sub-model descriptions shown above.

Model notes and information appear in smaller type, generally after the price line, and should be read since they contain important, critical, and interesting facts/information. In some cases, factory recalls (some include serialization) are also provided. Examples include:

During the first year of manufacture (2008), this model featured an engraved custom one-piece floorplate marked "2008 Model 70 Limited Edition".

This model was also available with left-hand action, except in WSM cals.

Extra features/special orders which can add or subtract value are placed either under category names, model/sub-model descriptions, or pricing lines. On current models that don't have a price line, the MSR will also appear in this typeface, in addition to other pricing information regarding that model. These individual lines appear bolder than other descriptive typeface, such as the following:

Add approx. 10% for Mag. cals.

Subtract $100 if without stainless barrel.

On many discontinued models/variations after 1985, the following line may appear under the price line, indicating the last manufacturer's suggested retail price flush right on the page, like this:

Last MSR was $1,750.
Last MSR in 2006 was $850.

Grading lines normally appear at the top of each page, and in the middle if price lines change. If you are uncertain as to how to properly grade a particular firearm, please refer to the digital color Photo Percentage Grading System (PPGS) at www.bluebookofgunvalues.com for more assistance. The most commonly encountered grading line (shown with a typical price line underneath) in this text is for 100%-60% condition factors:

MSR	100%	98%	95%	90%	80%	70%	60%

Price line formats are as follows - when the price line shown below (with proper grading line) is encountered, it automatically indicates the gun is currently manufactured, and the MSR is shown left of the 100% column. Following this are the 100%-60% values. This 100% value is the national average price a consumer will typically expect to pay for that model in NIB unfired condition. 100% specimens without boxes, warranties, etc., which are currently manufactured may be discounted (5%-20%, depending on the desirability of make and model). This 100% price on currently manufactured guns also assumes not previously sold at retail.

MSR $1,150	$925	$795	$675	$600	$475	$375	$325
	$895	$775	$675	$575	$500	$450	$400
	$2,050	$1,795	$1,550	N/A	N/A	N/A	N/A

When "N/A" (Not Applicable) is listed instead of a value, this indicates that this particular model is not encountered enough in those condition factors to warrant a value - especially true on antiques in upper condition factors and with commemoratives and special/limited editions under 95%.

Values for conditions under 60% will typically be no less than 50% (1/2) of the 60% price, unless the gun has been shot to a point where the action may be loose or questionable. Obviously, no "MSR" will appear in the left margin, but a last manufacturer's suggested retail price may appear flush right below the price line, automatically indicating a discontinued gun, like this:

Last MSR was $975.

On older Winchester lever actions grading and values are provided from 100%-10%, and an example of this grading line is as follows:

100%	98%	95%	90%	80%	70%	60%	50%	40%	30%	20%	10%

Typically, 100%-10% values are listed for these older firearms and a few examples of the price lines are as follows:

$800	$675	$575	$500	$425	$375	$325	$275	$225	$175	$150	$125
N/A	N/A	$21,750	$18,150	$14,575	$12,000	$9,600	$7,700	$5,950	$4,675	$3,700	$2,850

Again, N/A's are abbreviations for not applicable, which indicates this model is not encountered enough in those upper condition factors to warrant a value.

Some antiques listed will not have price lines, but rather value ranges for Above Average, Average, and Below Average condition factors. These value range price lines with corresponding grading line will appear as follows:

Above Average	Average	Below Average
$75,000 - $150,000	$50,000 - $75,000	$25,000 - $50,000

Included for your convenience at the end of this pocket guide is an Index of all category names, Abbreviations listings, company contact information, Serialization and a Serialization Index.

Most dealers and collectors are now utilizing what is essentially an objective method for deciding the condition of a gun: THE PERCENTAGE OF ORIGINAL FACTORY FINISH(ES) REMAINING ON THE GUN. After looking critically at a variety of firearms and carefully studying the Photo Percentage Grading System™ (available online at www.bluebookofgunvalues.com), it will soon become evident if a specific gun has 98%, 90%, 70% or less finish remaining. Remember, sometimes an older unfired gun described as NIB can actually be 98% or less condition, simply because of the wear accumulated by taking it in and out of the box and excessive handling. Commemoratives are especially prone to this problem. Of course, factors such as quality of finish(es), engraving (and other embellishments), special orders/features, historical significance and/or provenance, etc. can and do affect prices immensely. Also, it seems that every year bore condition (especially on antiques) becomes more important in the overall grading factor (and price) of both collectible and desirable Winchester models. Because of this, bore condition must be listed separately for those guns where it makes a difference in value.

Every gun's unique condition factor – and therefore the price – is best determined by the percentage of original finish(es) remaining, with the key consideration being the overall frame/receiver finish. The key word here is "original", for if anyone other than the factory has refinished the gun, its value as a collector's item has been diminished. The exceptions would be rare and historical guns that have been properly restored. Every year, top quality restorations have become more accepted, and prices have gone up proportionately with the quality of the workmanship. Also popular now are antique finishes, and a new question has come up, "What is 100% antique finish on new reproductions?" Answer – a gun that started out as new, and then has been aged to a lower condition factor to duplicate natural wear and tear.

When examining a gun's condition, note where the finishes of a firearm typically wear off first. These are usually places where the gun accumulates wear from holster/case rubbing, and contact with the hands or body over an extended period of time.

It should be noted that the older a collectible firearm is, the smaller the percentage of original finish one can expect to find. Some very old and/or very rare firearms are sought by collectors in almost any condition!

PHOTO PERCENTAGE GRADING SYSTEM CONVERSION GUIDELINES

New/Perfect – 100% condition with or without box. 100% on currently manufactured firearms assumes NIB (New In Box) condition and not sold previously at retail.

Mint – typically 98%-99% condition with almost no observable wear. Probably sold previously at retail, and may have been shot occasionally.

Excellent – 95%+ - 98% condition.

Very Good – 80% - 95% condition (all parts/finish should be original).

Good - 60% – 80% condition (all parts/finish should be original).

Fair – 20% - 60% condition (all parts/finish may or may not be original, but must function properly and shoot).

Poor – under 20% condition (shooting not a factor).

NRA CONDITION STANDARDS

The NRA conditions listed below have been provided as guidelines to assist the reader in converting and comparing condition factors. Once the gun's condition has been accurately assessed, only then can values be accurately ascertained. Please refer to the Photo Percentage Grading System (PPGS) available online at www.bluebookofgunvalues.com to learn more about condition factors. Why guess when you can be sure?

NRA MODERN CONDITION DESCRIPTIONS

New - not previously sold at retail, in same condition as current factory production.

Perfect - in new condition in every respect, may have previously been sold at retail.

Excellent - near new condition, used but little to no noticeable marring of wood or metal, bluing near perfect (except at muzzle or sharp edges).

Very Good - in perfect working condition, no appreciable wear on working surfaces, no corrosion or pitting, only minor surface dents or scratches.

Good - in safe working condition, minor wear on working surfaces, no broken parts, no corrosion or pitting that will interfere with proper functioning.

Fair - in safe working condition, but well worn, perhaps requiring replacement of minor parts or adjustments which should be indicated in advertisement, no rust, but may have corrosion pits which do not render article unsafe or inoperable.

NRA ANTIQUE CONDITION DESCRIPTIONS

Factory New - all original parts; 100% original finish; in perfect condition in every respect, inside and out.

Excellent - all original parts; over 80% original finish; sharp lettering, numerals and design on metal and wood; unmarred wood; fine bore.

Fine - all original parts; over 30% original finish; sharp lettering, numerals and design on metal and wood; minor marks in wood; good bore.

Very Good - all original parts; none to 30% original finish; original metal surfaces smooth with all edges sharp; clear lettering, numerals and design on metal; wood slightly scratched or bruised; bore disregarded for collectors firearms.

Good - less than 20% original finish, some minor replacement parts; metal smoothly rusted or lightly pitted in places, cleaned or reblued; principal lettering, numerals and design on metal legible; wood refinished, scratched, bruised or minor cracks repaired; in good working order.

Fair - less than 10% original finish, some major parts replaced; minor replacement parts may be required; metal rusted, may be lightly pitted all over, vigorously cleaned or reblued; rounded edges of metal and wood; principal lettering, numerals and design on metal partly obliterated; wood scratched, bruised, cracked or repaired where broken; in fair working order or can be easily repaired and placed in working order.

Poor - little or no original finish remaining, major and minor parts replaced; major replacement parts required and extensive restoration needed; metal deeply pitted; principal lettering, numerals and design obliterated, wood badly scratched, bruised, cracked or broken; mechanically inoperative, generally undesirable as a collector's firearm.

WINCHESTER

Current trademark established in 1866 in New Haven, CT. Currently manufactured by Miroku of Japan since circa 1992, Herstal, Belgium (O/U shotguns since 2004), and in Columbia, SC (Model 70 only beginning 2008). Previously manufactured in New Haven, CT, 1866-2006, and by U.S. Repeating Arms from 1981-2006 through a licensing agreement from Olin Corp. to manufacture shotguns and rifles domestically using the Winchester Trademark. Corporate offices are located in Morgan, UT. Olin Corp. previously manufactured shotguns and rifles bearing the Winchester Hallmark at the Olin Kodensha Plant (closed 1989) located in Tochigi, Japan, Cobourg, Ontario, Canada, and also in European countries. In 1992, U.S. Repeating Arms was acquired by GIAT located in France. In late 1997, the Walloon region of Belgium acquired controlling interest of both Browning and U.S. Repeating Arms.

For more information and current pricing on both new and used Winchester airguns and current black powder models, please refer to the *Blue Book of Airguns* by Dr. Robert D. Beeman & John B. Allen, and the *Blue Book of Modern Black Powder Arms* by John Allen (also online).

In addition to the models listed within this section, Winchester also offered various models/variations that were available only at the annual SHOT SHOW beginning 2004. More research is underway to identify these models, in addition to their original MSRs (if listed).

WINCHESTER TIMELINE 1855-TO DATE

1855 - Horace Smith and Daniel Wesson form Volcanic Repeating Arms Co. in Norwich, CT.

1856 - Volcanic Repeating Arms Co. moves to New Haven, CT. Oliver Winchester purchases majority of company stock.

1857 - Volcanic Repeating Arms Co. becomes insolvent, Smith & Wesson sell remaining stock to Oliver Winchester. Winchester reorganizes as New Haven Arms Co.

1866 - New Haven Arms Co. is renamed Winchester Repeating Arms Co.

1919 - Company releases Winchester branded consumer products that are sold at Winchester stores and independent retailers.

1923 - The first Winchester 3 in. Magnum is released.

1931 - Winchester Repeating Arms Co. is sold to Olin Industries. Olin merges Winchester with its Western Cartridge Co., forming the Winchester-Western Division of Olin Industries.

1936 - Winchester releases the legendary Model 70 centerfire bolt action rifle.

1941 - Winchester engineers develop an M1 Carbine working model and the .30 M1 Carbine cartridge in thirteen days for government testing.

1964 - Winchester releases its first Commemorative, the Wyoming Diamond Jubilee Model 1894.

1969 - Winchester introduces the Winchoke on some of its shotguns.

1980 - Olin sells New Haven manufacturing plant to employees. Manufacturing of firearms continues under license with the name of U.S. Repeating Arms Co. (USRAC).

1992 - U.S. Repeating Arms bought by GIAT (Groupement des Industries de l' Amree de Terre), a French owned arms conglomerate.

1997 - Belgian Walloon Region government acquires U.S. Repeating Arms Co., Browning Arms Co., and Fabrique Nationale.

2006 - U.S. Repeating Arms Co. plant in New Haven, CT closes.

2007 - Winchester Repeating Arms Co. formed by FN/Browning.

2008 - Winchester Model 70s begin production in FN's Columbia, SC plant.

2009 - Winchester Model 1892s made by Miroku.

2010 - Winchester Model 1894s re-introduced.

2013 - Winchester Model 1873 re-introduced mfg. by Miroku Corp. in Japan.

2016 - Winchester's 150th Anniversary - Commemorative Sesquicentennial Models 1866, 1873, 94, 70, and 101 released.

WINCHESTER OVERVIEW

Note: Winchester Rifles are a field in themselves. Models Henry, 1866, 1873, 1876, 1885, 1886, 1892, 1894, and 1895 all were produced with a multitude of special order options. Special orders included front and rear special sights, half or 2/3 magazines, takedown, various barrel lengths (barrel lengths from 14 to 36 inches could be special ordered for many models), configurations, and weights, special metal finishes, deluxe wood (either checkered or carved) in a variety of finishes, an impressive range of engraving options, different butt plates, etc. All of these special orders act independently and interdependently to determine the correct value of a particular Winchester. Some of the finest rifles ever made are special order Winchesters engraved by the Ulrichs, G. Young, L.D. Nimschke, and others. For these reasons, a Model 1886 Winchester can range in price from $1,000 to over $500,000 - quite a price range for one model alone! When contemplating a purchase on the higher dollar range, qualified and professional opinions should be secured, preferably from at least 2 sources. Unfortunately many fakes and upgraded (non-original) guns have surfaced in the last 10 years with the sudden increase in prices. Winchesters shown in this section are priced assuming a standard model with no special orders. Any special orders will further add to the prices shown. Caliber rarities must also be considered. Many of the early Winchesters are broken down by year of manufacture. Refer to the "Model Serialization" section in this book.

A factory letter specifying original shipping information by serial number will certainly help solidify values shown on older out of production Winchester rifles and shotguns. A listing has been provided by model number with serialization range which can be historically researched by the Winchester Museum now located in Cody, WY. To use this outstanding service, make sure the model and its serial number fall within the ranges listed. Simply mail in your informational request with serial number, model, and caliber to the Cody Firearms Museum, 720 Sheridan Ave. in Cody, WY, 82414. There is a $70 charge for lever action models, and $85 for Model 21 SxS shotguns. Research results will include (if available) specimen caliber, barrel length, any special orders or finishes, return(s) to the factory, as well as any additional provenance contained by interpolating existing factory shipping ledgers. I would recommend a trip to the Buffalo Bill Historical Center as it contains the most comprehensive collection of projectile arms (including Chinese specimens that date back 2,000 years) and Americana housed under one roof in this country.

With the recent price appreciation of most upper condition Winchester rifles, excellent original condition has become so expensive that the many special order features

Winchester offered do not cost that much more. However, on lesser condition guns that are much less expensive, these same special order features will cost more percentage-wise since the condition factor does not cost a premium.

Model 1866 Lever Action Rifle - ser. no. range 125,000-170,101.

Approx. 33 specimens have been researched outside of this ser. no. range.

Model 1873 Lever Action Rifle - ser. no. range 1-720,496.

Approx. 160 specimens have been researched outside of this ser. no. range.

Model 1876 Lever Action Rifle - ser. no. range 1-63,871.

Model 1883 Bolt Action Rifle (Hotchkiss Repeater) - ser. no. range 1-84,555.

May be referred to as Model 1879, 1880, or 1883.

Model 1885 Single Shot Rifle or Shotgun - ser. no. range 1-109,999.

Not available in ser. nos. 74,459-74,556. Also known as High and Low Wall.

Model 1886 Lever Action Rifle - ser. no. range 1-156,599.

Not available in ser. nos. 135,125-135,144 and 146,000-150,799.

Model 1887 & 1901 Lever Action Shotguns - ser. no. range 1-72,999.

Model 1890 Slide Action Rifle - ser. no. range 1-329,999.

Not available in ser. nos. 10,809-10,884, 20,000-29,999, 32,629-32,698, 37,599-37,627, 234,061- 234,140, and 234,142-234,160.

Model 1892 Lever Action Rifle - ser. no. range 1-379,999.

Not available in ser. nos. 374,851-376,100.

Model 1893 Slide Action Shotgun - ser. no. range 1-34,050.

Model 1894 Lever Action Rifle - ser. no. range 1-353,999.

Model 1895 Lever Action Rifle - ser. no. range 1-59,999.

Model "Lee" Bolt Action Rifle - ser. no. range 1-19,999.

Model 1897 Slide Action Shotgun - ser. no. range 34,051-377,999.

Model 1903 Semi-Auto .22 Cal. Rifle - ser. no. range 1-39,999.

Model 1905 Semi-Auto Rifle - ser. no. range 1-29,078.

Model 1906 Slide Action Rifle - ser. no. range 1-79,999.

Model 1907 Semi-Auto Rifle - ser. no. range 1-9,999.

Winchester factory data on models produced between approx. 1907-1961 is almost non-existent (except Custom Shop mfg.) since there was a fire at the Winchester factory in 1961.

A NOTE ON WINCHESTER FINISHES: It is very important to understand that there is a big value difference between a Model 1873 with 90% bright blue as opposed to a gun that has patina finish (turning brown). A bright blue specimen might bring several times more, because it is closer to the way it originally left the factory - with bright bluing. "Brown" guns are simply not as desirable as guns that show little or no use and retain bright blue finish.

GRADING EXPLANATION FOR WINCHESTER LEVER ACTIONS

A combination of grading systems is being used exclusively for Winchester Models 1873 and 1876 in this section to assist the reader in ascertaining the value of a particular specimen more accurately. They work as follows - the top pricing line contains three value ranges (Above Average, Average, or Below Average) which have been created to encompass most of the specimens commonly encountered within these models.

Since there is a drastic value difference between 95%-50% bright blue and 30% dull patina/fading finish on older Winchesters, a traditional grading/value line has been included to give you examples of values from 100% down to 10% providing you a better perspective of the top end of the marketplace.

The three value groupings include "Below Average," "Average," and "Above Average" condition factors. These value ranges indicate the following conditions:

BELOW AVERAGE VALUE RANGE - a specimen with no finish remaining, perhaps some parts have been replaced, deteriorated metal may be lightly pitted with faint barrel/frame markings, rounded edges of wood and metal, wood showing much wear with possible repairs or cracks, must be in working order.

AVERAGE VALUE RANGE - a specimen with all original parts, exhibits gun metal patina finish, metal mostly smooth (perhaps lightly pitted), principal lettering and markings legible throughout, wood showing honest wear with little finish remaining (may have small cracks and other imperfections), good working order.

ABOVE AVERAGE VALUE RANGE - a specimen featuring unpolished brass (on Henrys and Model 1866s) or plum brown patina with traces of bluing in protected areas (on all steel frame models), sharp corners, crisp barrel markings, traces of original finish remaining, metal should exhibit nice patina or older flaking finish, wood should have some original stock varnish remaining and minor handling marks and dings, good bore, perfect working order with no replacement parts.

VALUES FOR 10%-100% CONDITION FACTORS - this includes the entire range of condition factors from 10% - 100% in many cases. N/As indicate that the condition factor is so infrequently encountered, it does not have a value. Normally, below average value ranges will approximately correspond to the 0%-10% pricing line values, average value range represents 10%-20%, and above average can range from 20%-40%, depending on the model. Typically, over 50% refers to a rifle which exhibits over 30% bright bluing/case colors or unpolished brass on the frame. See PPGS for percentage grading examples.

PISTOLS: SINGLE SHOT

SINGLE SHOT PISTOL - .22 LR cal., bolt action, walnut, brass, or pot metal grips, 9 in. barrel with open sights, no two are exactly alike, and quality can run from very good to crude, ser. nos. under 20.

Prices on this model typically range from $3,750 - $4,950, depending on original condition.

RIFLES: LEVER ACTIONS - 1860-1964

Values by percentages are not listed on the Models Henry and 1866, as original condition over 30% is seldom encountered.

Volcanic pistols and carbines may be found under the Volcanic listing.

For the following lever action rifles, multiple special order features that add value are not cumulative (i.e., do not add 30% for an octagon barrel to the premium for a Deluxe rifle). Also, as a general rule, premiums for calibers, options, and special order features become less important on the following lever action models in under 90% original condition (i.e., do not add a 50% premium for .44-40 WCF on a Model 1892 rifle if original condition is under 90%).

Subtract 20%-40% on the following models if metal is pitted or poorly refinished (i.e., rounded edges on metal because of over buffing, and/or wood has been excessively sanded).

	Above Average	Average	Below Average

HENRY RIFLE - .44 Henry Flat (rimfire) cal., 15 shot, 24 in. barrel with integral slotted tube mag. and loading lever, blue barrel, brass or iron frame. Approx. 13,000 total production, mfg. 1860-1866.

Because almost all Henrys have little or no original finish remaining, values are in ranges rather than listed by separate condition factors.

* *Henry Rifle Iron Frame Model* – frame made of iron, round type buttplate, without lever latch, adj. sporting type rear leaf sight, serial numbers are in three digits only. Total production is believed to be less than 300.

$75,000 - $150,000	$50,000 - $75,000	$25,000 - $50,000

* *Henry Rifle First Model* – approx. 3,500 mfg., generally serialized below 3,500, with or without lever latch, perch belly stock and slotted receiver for rear sight.

$50,000 - $100,000	$25,000 - $50,000	$12,000 - $25,000

* *Henry Rifle Martial Marked* – contracted by U.S. military for Civil War use, denoted by "C.G.C." inspector markings on upper barrel breech and stock, approx. 1,900 with serialization scattered.

$60,000 - $120,000	$35,000 - $60,000	$20,000 - $35,000

This rifle was the most revolutionary shoulder weapon introduced in the Civil War.

* *Henry Rifle Late Model* – similar to first model, except buttplate heel has pointed profile, lever latch became standard and receiver is not slotted for rear sight, serial numbers over approx. 3,500, most commonly encountered Henry with approx. 8,000 mfg.

$40,000 - $75,000	$20,000 - $40,000	$10,000 - $20,000

MODEL 1866 – .44 rimfire or centerfire (4th Model only), 24 in. barrel, blue barrel with brass frame, differs from Henry in that it has a wood forearm, frame cartridge loading port, and separate tube mag. Total production reached 170,101 for all models, mfg. 1866-98.

Because almost all Model 1866s have little or no original finish remaining, values are in ranges rather than listed by separate condition factors.

* *Model 1866 First Model Rifle* – "Improved Henry" action, .44 cal. rimfire, without forend cap, serialization is concealed on lower tang inside buttstock, serial range is from mid-12,000 to mid-15,000 (in Henry serial range sequence).

$40,000 - $85,000	$20,000 - $40,000	$7,500 - $20,000

Buyer beware - watch for fakes!

* *Model 1866 Carbine First Model* – same action as Rifle, only with 20 in. barrel, 2 barrel bands and saddle ring.

$25,000 - $40,000	$10,000 - $25,000	$4,000 - $10,000

* *Model 1866 Rifle Second Model* – "New Model" with redesigned frame, with Henry barrel markings, serial number inside on the earlier guns after ser. no. 19,000, outside lower tang beneath lever (approx. after ser. no. 20,000).

$25,000 - $45,000	$12,500 - $25,000	$5,000 - $12,500

	Above Average	Average	Below Average

* *Model 1866 Carbine Second Model* – frame and other changes similar to Second Model Rifle.

$20,000 - $35,000	$8,000 - $20,000	$3,000 - $8,000

* *Model 1866 Rifle Third Model* – block style serial numbers usually located behind trigger, improved frame. Serial numbered approx. 25,000-149,000.

$20,000 - $35,000	$8,000 - $20,000	$3,000 - $8,000

* *Model 1866 Carbine Third Model* – same changes as Model 1866 Third Model Rifle, 20 in. barrel with 2 bands.

$20,000 - $35,000	$8,000 - $20,000	$3,000 - $8,000

* *Model 1866 Musket Third Model* – 27 in. round barrel, 24 in. magazine, 3 barrel bands.

$20,000 - $35,000	$8,000 - $20,000	$3,000 - $8,000

* *Model 1866 Rifle/Carbine/Musket Fourth Model* – .44 cal., twin rimfire and centerfire, script style serial number on lower tang near lever latch, improved frame, serial range approx. 149,000-170,101.

$20,000 - $35,000	$8,000 - $20,000	$3,000 - $8,000

Subtract 20% for steel buttplate and forend cap on rifle.

This rifle is usually found with steel buttplate and forend cap.

100%	98%	95%	90%	80%	70%	60%	50%	40%	30%	20%	10%

MODEL 1873 – .32-20 WCF, .38-40 WCF, or .44-40 WCF cal., iron frame with sideplates, frame loading port, 20 or 24 in. round or octagon barrel, rifles have forearm caps and carbines have forearm bands, tube mag., blue finish with case hardened parts, oil finished stock, serial numbered on lower tang, 720,610 mfg. between 1873-1919.

Since early Model 1873s were only made in .44 cal., no caliber markings are present. With the introduction of additional calibers, barrels (just in front of the receiver) and the brass elevator were stamped with the caliber.

Model 1873s are serial numbered sequentially on the lower tang. On guns serial numbered 80,000 to 170,000, an "A" followed the number. From 170,000 to 190,000, either "A" or "B" may be found, while after 200,000, usually "B" was used. The letter does not seem to have any definite meaning. The earliest guns had no marking on the upper tang, but were marked "Model 1873" on the lower tang next to the ser. no. up to number 350, after which "Model 1873" is marked on the upper tang, where it remained through the model run.

* *Model 1873 First Model Rifle* – serial numbers approx. 1-30,000, sliding thumbprint dust cover on 2 guides which are an integral part of upper frame, absence of any cal. marking.

N/A	N/A	$22,000	$18,000	$16,000	$12,000	$10,000	$6,000	$4,000	$2,500	$1,500	$1,000

A below average Model 1873 First Model Rifle is currently valued in the $900-$1,650 range.

An average Model 1873 First Model Rifle is currently valued in the $1,650-$2,500 range.

100% 98% 95% 90% 80% 70% 60% 50% 40% 30% 20% 10%

An above average Model 1873 First Model Rifle is currently valued in the $2,500-$4,950 range.

Percentage values listed above are for original guns with corresponding percentages of bright blue finish remaining (refer to PPGS for accurate grading).

* ***Model 1873 Carbine First Model*** – 20 in. round barrel with carbine style forearm band. Distinctive curved buttplate, with saddle ring.

N/A N/A $30,000 $25,000 $20,000 $15,000 $10,000 $7,000 $5,500 $4,000 $2,500 $1,500

A below average Model 1873 Carbine First Model is currently valued in the $1,100-$2,100 range.

An average Model 1873 Carbine First Model is currently valued in the $2,500-$3,500 range.

An above average Model 1873 Carbine First Model is currently valued in the $3,500-$5,000 range.

Percentage values listed above are for original guns with corresponding percentages of bright blue finish remaining (refer to PPGS for accurate grading).

* ***Model 1873 Musket First Model*** – 30 in. round barrel, 27 in. mag. with 3 barrel bands, approx. 500 mfg.

N/A N/A $17,000 $15,000 $13,000 $11,000 $9,000 $7,000 $5,500 $3,600 $2,200 $1,500

A below average Model 1873 Musket First Model is currently valued in the $1,100-$2,150 range.

An average Model 1873 Musket First Model is currently valued in the $2,150-$2,650 range.

An above average Model 1873 Musket First Model is currently valued in the $2,650-$3,750 range.

Percentage values listed above are for original guns with corresponding percentages of bright blue finish remaining (refer to PPGS for accurate grading).

* ***Model 1873 Rifle Second Model*** – improved dust cover which slides on center rail on rear section of frame top which is held in place by two screws, serial range 31,000-90,000.

N/A N/A $12,000 $11,000 $9,000 $8,700 $6,600 $4,500 $3,300 $2,250 $1,300 $800

A below average Model 1873 Rifle Second Model is currently valued in the $675-$1,325 range.

An average Model 1873 Rifle Second Model is currently valued in the $1,325-$1,825 range.

An above average Model 1873 Rifle Second Model is currently valued in the $1,825-$2,750 range.

Percentage values listed above are for original guns with corresponding percentages of bright blue finish remaining (refer to PPGS for accurate grading).

* ***Model 1873 Carbine Second Model*** – changes similar to 1873 Second Model Rifle, with 20 in. round barrel and 2 barrel bands.

N/A N/A $22,500 $19,500 $17,500 $13,000 $11,000 $9,000 $6,800 $4,500 $2,500 $1,200

A below average Model 1873 Carbine Second Model is currently valued in the $875-$1,550 range.

An average Model 1873 Carbine Second Model is currently valued in the $2,000-$2,500 range.

An above average Model 1873 Carbine Second Model is currently valued in the $2,500-$3,500 range.

Percentage values listed above are for original guns with corresponding percentages of bright blue finish remaining (refer to PPGS for accurate grading).

* ***Model 1873 Musket Second Model*** – changes similar to 1873 Second Model Rifle, with 30 in. barrel and 3 barrel bands.

N/A N/A $6,250 $5,600 $5,000 $4,200 $3,500 $3,000 $2,500 $1,800 $1,400 $1,200

A below average Model 1873 Musket Second Model is currently valued in the $1,000-$1,400 range.

An average Model 1873 Musket Second Model is currently valued in the $1,400-$1,800 range.

An above average Model 1873 Musket Second Model is currently valued in the $1,800-$2,500 range.

Percentage values listed above are for original guns with corresponding percentages of bright blue finish remaining (refer to PPGS for accurate grading).

* ***Model 1873 Rifle Third Model*** – dust cover rail integral with frame, serial 90,000-end of production.

N/A N/A $7,500 $6,300 $5,500 $4,500 $3,750 $3,250 $3,000 $1,700 $1,500 $800

Add 20% for .44-40 WCF cal.

Add 30% for octagon barrel for .44-40 WCF cal. only.

A below average Model 1873 Rifle Third Model is currently valued in the $750-$1,000 range.

An average Model 1873 Rifle Third Model is currently valued in the $1,000-$1,650 range.

An above average Model 1873 Rifle Third Model is currently valued in the $1,650-$2,300 range.

Percentage values listed above are for original guns with corresponding percentages of bright blue finish remaining (refer to PPGS for accurate grading).

* ***Model 1873 Carbine Third Model*** – changes similar to 1873 Rifle Third Model, with 20 in. barrel and 2 barrel bands.

N/A N/A $19,000 $16,000 $12,000 $11,000 $10,000 $7,500 $5,600 $3,400 $2,300 $1,200

Add 10% for .32-20 WCF cal.

A below average Model 1873 Carbine Third Model is currently valued in the $1,200-$1,800 range.

An average Model 1873 Carbine Third Model is currently valued in the $1,800-$2,200 range.

An above average Model 1873 Carbine Third Model is currently valued in the $2,500-$3,500 range.

Percentage values listed above are for original guns with corresponding percentages of bright blue finish remaining (refer to PPGS for accurate grading).

100%	98%	95%	90%	80%	70%	60%	50%	40%	30%	20%	10%

* ***Model 1873 Musket Third Model*** – 30 in. round barrel and 3 barrel bands.

100%	98%	95%	90%	80%	70%	60%	50%	40%	30%	20%	10%
N/A	N/A	$5,100	$4,500	$4,000	$3,400	$2,900	$2,400	$1,850	$1,300	$1,000	$850

A below average Model 1873 Musket Third Model is currently valued in the $800-$1,200 range.

An average Model 1873 Musket Third Model is currently valued in the $1,200-$1,500 range.

An above average Model 1873 Musket Third Model is currently valued in the $1,500-$2,000 range.

Percentage values listed above are for original guns with corresponding percentages of bright blue finish remaining (refer to PPGS for accurate grading).

* ***Model 1873 .22 Rimfire Rifle*** – .22 S, L, or Extra L (very rare) cal., 24 in. barrel, no loading gate, the first .22 caliber repeater, 19,552 produced, mfg. 1884-1904. Made in rifle configuration only.

100%	98%	95%	90%	80%	70%	60%	50%	40%	30%	20%	10%
N/A	N/A	$11,250	$9,500	$8,500	$7,500	$5,800	$4,750	$3,600	$2,400	$1,200	$800

Add 30% for takedown model.

A below average Model 1873 .22 Rimfire Rifle is currently valued in the $725-$1,375 range.

An average Model 1873 .22 Rimfire Rifle is currently valued in the $1,375-$1,875 range.

An above average Model 1873 .22 Rimfire Rifle is currently valued in the $1,875-$2,500 range.

The takedown mechanism is unique in that a pin is driven out of the receiver, and is very prone to wear.

Percentage values listed above are for original guns with corresponding percentages of bright blue finish remaining (refer to PPGS for accurate grading).

* ***Model 1873 Deluxe Rifle*** – distinguishable by color case hardened frame and deluxe checkered stock and forearm, this model was special order only with many features and options available at an extra cost.

100%	98%	95%	90%	80%	70%	60%	50%	40%	30%	20%	10%
N/A	N/A	N/A	$55,000	$47,500	$40,000	$32,500	$25,000	$17,500	$10,000	$7,500	$5,000

A below average Model 1873 Deluxe Rifle is currently valued in the $2,750-$4,500 range.

An average Model 1873 Deluxe Rifle is currently valued in the $4,500-$7,500 range.

An above average Model 1873 Deluxe Rifle is currently valued in the $7,500-$10,000 range.

Values are for standard deluxe gun, w/o any special orders.

Percentage values listed above are for original guns with corresponding percentages of bright blue finish remaining (refer to PPGS for accurate grading).

* ***Model 1873 Trapper's Carbine*** – all features similar to .22 rimfire model, except available with 14, 15, or 16 in. barrel.

100%	98%	95%	90%	80%	70%	60%	50%	40%	30%	20%	10%
N/A	N/A	$34,000	$31,500	$27,000	$23,000	$20,500	$17,000	$12,250	$8,500	$6,500	$4,000

100%	98%	95%	90%	80%	70%	60%	50%	40%	30%	20%	10%

A below average Model 1873 Trapper's Carbine is currently valued in the $2,250-$3,500 range.

An average Model 1873 Trapper's Carbine is currently valued in the $3,500-$4,500 range.

An above average Model 1873 Trapper's Carbine is currently valued in the $4,500-$6,000 range.

Other barrel lengths were also available on this model, but are much rarer.

Percentage values listed above are for original guns with corresponding percentages of bright blue finish remaining (refer to PPGS for accurate grading).

* *Model 1873 "One of One Thousand "* – special care taken during assembly and testing to guarantee better accuracy, markings on top of breech designate model, deluxe walnut, extremely rare, barrel marked "One of One Thousand" in most cases, 136 mfg. Original cost was $100.

Values can range from $75,000 - $500,000, depending on condition.

A factory letter is a must for any "One of One Thousand" Winchester. Watch for fake letters. Note: Rarity of the "One of One Thousand" and the "One of One Hundred" models has made unethical upgrading of this model fairly common. Use extreme caution in purchasing.

* *Model 1873 "One of One Hundred "* – similar to "One of One Thousand" only rarer, 8 known. Sold new for $20 over the list price of a similarly equipped Model 1873.

Values can range from $75,000 - $500,000, depending on condition.

A factory letter is a must for any "One of One Hundred" Winchester. Watch for fake letters.

MODEL 1876 – .40-60 WCF, .45-60 WCF, .45-75 WCF (first caliber offered), or .50-95 Express cal., 22, 26, or 28 in. round or octagon barrel, similar but larger frame than Model 1873, tube mag., rifles have forearm caps while carbines and muskets have forearm bands and caps, crescent butt, blue finish, straight grip stock, 63,871 mfg. between 1876-1897.

The Model 1876 was also called the Centennial Model since its introduction coincided with the U.S. Centennial Exposition held in Philadelphia, PA in 1876. Popularity for this model decreased ten years later when the more powerful and advanced Model 1886 was introduced.

1876 Deluxe Models with 90%+ original case colors are extremely rare.

* *Model 1876 Rifle First Model* – serial numbered approx. 1-5,000, distinguishable by no dust cover on frame top.

N/A	N/A	$22,750	$20,125	$17,750	$15,275	$12,750	$10,625	$8,400	$6,200	$3,950	$2,700

A below average Model 1876 Rifle First Model is currently valued in the $1,875-$2,525 range.

An average Model 1876 First Model is currently valued in the $2,525-$3,600 range.

An above average Model 1876 First Model is currently valued in the $3,600-$4,400 range.

100%	98%	95%	90%	80%	70%	60%	50%	40%	30%	20%	10%

Percentage values listed above are for original guns with corresponding percentages of bright blue finish remaining (refer to PPGS for accurate grading).

* ***Model 1876 Carbine First Model*** – 22 in. round barrel, one barrel band, saddle ring, full-length forearm giving a musket appearance.

N/A N/A $21,500 $19,000 $16,750 $14,500 $12,000 $10,000 $7,900 $5,800 $3,600 $2,500

A below average Model 1876 Carbine First Model is currently valued in the $2,000-$2,500 range.

An average Model 1876 Carbine First Model is currently valued in the $2,500-$3,250 range.

An above average Model 1876 Carbine First Model is currently valued in the $3,250-$4,500 range.

Percentage values listed above are for original guns with corresponding percentages of bright blue finish remaining (refer to PPGS for accurate grading).

* ***Model 1876 Musket First Model*** – 32 in. round barrel with 1 band, scarce model because no foreign military contracts.

N/A N/A $30,000 $25,250 $21,350 $19,250 $16,450 $12,600 $9,800 $6,800 $4,600 $3,300

A below average Model 1876 Musket First Model is currently valued in the $2,500-$3,750 range.

An average Model 1876 Musket First Model is currently valued in the $3,750-$5,500 range.

An above average Model 1876 Musket First Model is currently valued in the $5,500-$6,200 range.

Percentage values listed above are for original guns with corresponding percentages of bright blue finish remaining (refer to PPGS for accurate grading).

* ***Model 1876 Rifle Second Model*** – "Thumbprint" dust cover rail held on by screw, serial range 5,000-30,000.

N/A N/A $16,250 $13,750 $11,500 $9,500 $7,750 $6,000 $4,750 $3,750 $2,250 $1,500

Add 35% for .50-95 WCF cal.

A below average Model 1876 Rifle Second Model is currently valued in the $1,000-$1,600 range.

An average Model 1876 Rifle Second Model is currently valued in the $1,750-$2,500 range.

An above average Model 1876 Rifle Second Model is currently valued in the $2,750-$3,750 range.

Percentage values listed above are for original guns with corresponding percentages of bright blue finish remaining (refer to PPGS for accurate grading).

* ***Model 1876 Carbine Second Model*** – changes similar to Model 1876 Rifle Early Second Model, with 22 in. round barrel and full length forearm giving a musket appearance.

N/A N/A $24,500 $19,500 $14,000 $11,000 $8,750 $6,750 $5,000 $3,250 $2,400 $1,650

A below average Model 1876 Carbine Second Model is currently valued in the

100%	98%	95%	90%	80%	70%	60%	50%	40%	30%	20%	10%

$1,200-$1,500 range.

An average Model 1876 Carbine Second Model is currently valued in the $1,500-$2,500 range.

An above average Model 1876 Carbine Second Model is currently valued in the $2,500-3,500 range.

Percentage values listed above are for original guns with corresponding percentages of bright blue finish remaining (refer to PPGS for accurate grading).

* ***Model 1876 Musket Second Model*** – changes similar to Model 1876 Rifle Early Second Model, with 32 in. round barrel and carbine forend tip.

N/A	N/A	$19,500	$17,500	$14,000	$12,750	$11,250	$10,500	$8,500	$5,750	$3,250	$2,000

A below average Model 1876 Musket Second Model is currently valued in the $1,200-$2,500 range.

An average Model 1876 Musket Second Model is currently valued in the $2,500-$3,750 range.

An above average Model 1876 Musket Second Model is currently valued in the $3,750-$5,000 range.

Percentage values listed above are for original guns with corresponding percentages of bright blue finish remaining (refer to PPGS for accurate grading).

* ***Model 1876 Rifle Third Model*** – dust cover rail integral with frame, serial range 30,000-end of production.

N/A	N/A	$15,000	$12,750	$10,750	$9,000	$7,500	$6,000	$4,750	$3,750	$2,250	$1,500

Add 25% for .50-95 WCF cal.

A below average Model 1876 Rifle Third Model is currently valued in the $1,000-$1,600 range.

An average Model 1876 Rifle Third Model is currently valued in the $1,600-$2,500 range.

An above average Model 1876 Rifle Third Model is currently valued in the $2,750-$3,750 range.

Percentage values listed above are for original guns with corresponding percentages of bright blue finish remaining (refer to PPGS for accurate grading).

* ***Model 1876 Carbine Third Model*** – frame similar to Model 1876 Rifle Third Model, with 22 in. round barrel and full-length forearm giving a musket appearance.

N/A	N/A	$22,500	$18,000	$13,000	$10,500	$8,500	$6,750	$5,000	$3,250	$2,400	$1,650

A below average Model 1876 Carbine Third Model is currently valued in the $1,200-$1,500 range.

An average Model 1876 Carbine Third Model is currently valued in the $1,500-$2,500 range.

An above average Model 1876 Carbine Third Model is currently valued in the $2,500-$3,500 range.

Percentage values listed above are for original guns with corresponding percentages of bright blue finish remaining (refer to PPGS for accurate grading).

100%	98%	95%	90%	80%	70%	60%	50%	40%	30%	20%	10%

* ***Model 1876 Musket Third Model*** – frame similar to Model 1876 Rifle Third Model, with 32 in. round barrel.

N/A	N/A	$17,000	$15,000	$13,000	$11,000	$9,500	$8,250	$6,500	$4,500	$3,000	$2,000

A below average Model 1876 Musket Third Model is currently valued in the $1,500-$2,000 range.

An average Model 1876 Musket Third Model is currently valued in the $2,000-$3,000 range.

An above average Model 1876 Musket Third Model is currently valued in the $3,000-$4,500 range.

Percentage values listed above are for original guns with corresponding percentages of bright blue finish remaining (refer to PPGS for accurate grading).

* ***Model 1876 Deluxe Rifle*** – distinguishable by color case hardened frame and deluxe checkered stock and forearm, this model was special order only with many features and options available at extra cost.

N/A	N/A	N/A	$80,000	$72,500	$65,000	$55,000	$45,000	$35,000	$25,000	$17,500	$10,500

Values are for standard deluxe gun.

A below average Model 1876 Deluxe Rifle is currently valued in the $4,400-$11,000 range.

An average Model 1876 Deluxe Rifle is currently valued in the $11,000-$16,500 range.

An above average Model 1876 Deluxe Rifle is currently valued in the $16,500-$30,000 range.

Percentage values listed above are for original guns with corresponding percentages of bright blue finish remaining (refer to PPGS for accurate grading).

* ***Model 1876 "One of One Thousand"*** – special care taken in manufacture to guarantee better accuracy, markings on top of breech designate model, deluxe walnut, extremely rare, 54 mfg. Original cost was $100.

Values can range from $75,000 - $500,000, depending on condition.

A factory letter is a must for any "One of One Thousand" Winchester. Watch for fake letters. Values are not listed because too few original specimens are bought or sold to accurately establish pricing.

Note: Rarity of the "One of One Thousand" and the "One of One Hundred" models has made unethical upgrading of this model fairly common. Use extreme caution in purchasing.

* ***Model 1876 "One of One Hundred"*** – similar to "One of One Thousand" only rarer, 8 mfg. Sold new for $20 over the list price of a similarly equipped Model 1876.

Values can range from $75,000 - $500,000, depending on condition.

A factory letter is a must for any "One of One Hundred" Winchester. Believe it or not, watch for fake letters. Values are not listed because too few original specimens are bought or sold to accurately establish pricing.

100%	98%	95%	90%	80%	70%	60%	50%	40%	30%	20%	10%

* ***Model 1876 Northwest Mounted Police Carbine*** – .45-75 WCF cal. only, 22 in. barrel, "NWMP" or "MP" marking may appear on stock (with wear, this cartouche may not be visible - the majority were not marked) approx. 1,600 mfg., factory records can only verify 150.

N/A	N/A	$16,500	$13,750	$11,000	$9,000	$7,750	$6,250	$5,250	$4,250	$3,500	$2,750

A below average Model 1876 Northwest Mounted Police Carbine is currently valued in the $2,500-$4,150 range.

An average Model 1876 Northwest Mounted Police Carbine is currently valued in the $4,150-$5,250 range.

An above average Model 1876 Northwest Mounted Police Carbine is currently valued in the $5,250-$6,500 range.

Above average specimens in this model should have traces of blue. Be very wary of the stock cartouche since these buttstocks were sold as surplus back in the 1920s. A letter of authenticity is a good idea on this model.

Percentage values listed above are for original guns with corresponding percentages of bright blue finish remaining (refer to PPGS for accurate grading).

MODEL 1886 – .33 WCF, .38-56 WCF, .38-70 WCF (830 mfg.), .40-65 WCF, .40-70 WCF (629 mfg.), .40-82 WCF, .45-70 Govt., .45-90, .50-110 Express, or .50-100-450 (234 mfg.) cal. available, Browning's first high power lever action design distinguishable by vertical locking bars, .45-70 Govt. most popular cal., 26 in. round or octagon barrel, tube mag., steel forend cap, straight grip stock. Case colored receiver was standard finish until 1901, then blue became the standard finish. Approx. 159,990 mfg. between 1886-1935.

On the following Model 1886 variations add the percentages non-cumulative for special order features and/or configuration.

Add 20% for octagon barrel.

Add 30% for octagon barrel with takedown (not on Lightweight).

Add 25% for .45-70 Govt. or .45-90 cal.

Add 100% for .50-110 or 200% for .50-100-450 cal.

Add 100%-150% for case colored receivers on standard guns only (pre-1902 mfg.), depending on original condition.

* ***Model 1886 Standard Rifle*** – various cals., color case hardening was standard on the frame, buttplate, and forend cap until 1901 (approx. 122,000 ser. no. range), when the standard finish became blue.

N/A	N/A	$9,250	$8,250	$7,000	$6,150	$5,125	$4,000	$2,975	$2,000	$1,625	$1,250

* ***Model 1886 Carbine*** – same general specifications as Rifle, except 22 in. round barrel and saddle ring, solid frame only.

N/A	N/A	$21,500	$18,000	$15,250	$12,250	$10,000	$8,250	$6,300	$5,000	$3,600	$2,400

Add 40% for full stock carbine (very rare).

.33 WCF cal. is the rarest caliber in this model.

100%	98%	95%	90%	80%	70%	60%	50%	40%	30%	20%	10%

* ***Model 1886 Musket*** – almost all are chambered in .45-70 Govt. cal., 30 in. round barrel, full-length military style forearm, military sights, only 350 mfg., very rare.

N/A	N/A	$20,000	$17,000	$14,500	$12,000	$10,000	$8,250	$6,300	$5,000	$3,600	$2,400

Most specimens encountered in this variation are in very good condition. A pitted musket is almost never encountered.

* ***Model 1886 Deluxe Rifle*** – distinguishable by deluxe checkered pistol grip walnut stock and forearm, color case hardened frame, this model was special order only with many features and options available at an extra cost.

N/A	N/A	N/A	$39,500	$34,500	$29,500	$25,000	$20,000	$15,500	$11,500	$7,500	$4,000

Values are for standard deluxe gun, w/o any special orders.

* ***Model 1886 Lightweight Rifle*** – .45-70 Govt. or .33 WCF cal. only, 22 (.45-70 Govt. cal.) or 24 (.33 WCF cal.) in. round nickel steel tapered barrel, half mag., rubber shotgun buttplate.

» ***Model 1886 Lightweight .33 cal.***

N/A	N/A	$4,500	$4,000	$3,200	$2,600	$2,200	$1,800	$1,500	$1,250	$1,000	$600

» ***Model 1886 Lightweight .45-70 Govt. cal.***

N/A	N/A	$6,500	$5,750	$5,000	$4,200	$3,625	$3,150	$2,725	$2,000	$1,650	$1,200

Since lightweight rifles were fairly late production, all specimens are blue and in very good condition usually.

* ***Model 1886 Deluxe Lightweight Rifle*** – distinguishable by fancy checkered wood stock.

N/A	N/A	$19,500	$16,700	$13,250	$11,000	$9,500	$7,100	$5,600	$4,500	$3,300	$2,500

Since lightweight rifles were fairly late production, all specimens are blue and in very good condition usually.

MODEL 1892 RIFLE – .25-20 WCF, .32-20 WCF, .38-40 WCF, or .44-40 WCF cal., 24 in. round or octagon barrel, blue, tube mag., forend cap, crescent butt. Approx. 1,000,000 mfg. between 1892-1941.

N/A	N/A	$3,750	$3,000	$2,350	$1,850	$1,475	$1,150	$925	$750	$600	$500

Add 75% for .44-40 WCF cal.

Add 25% for .38-40 WCF cal.

Add 25% for Takedown Model.

A short rifle configuration was available in this model with special order barrels under 16 inches, 12 in. being the rarest. These guns are very rare (most went to South America) and prices typically range $2,750-$8,000, depending on original condition.

* ***Model 1892 Rifle Antique*** – .25-20 WCF, .32-20 WCF, .38-40 WCF, or .44-40 WCF cal., 24 in. round or octagon barrel, blue, tube mag., forend cap, crescent butt, ser. no. range under 168,000. Mfg. 1892-1898.

N/A	N/A	$5,400	$3,950	$3,150	$2,650	$2,000	$1,750	$1,500	$1,200	$950	$750

Add 100% for .44-40 WCF cal.

Add 25% for .38-40 WCF cal.

Add 25% for Takedown Model.

* ***Model 1892 Deluxe Rifle*** – distinguishable by fancy pistol grip checkered wood. Mfg. 1892-1941.

N/A N/A $15,250 $13,500 $11,500 $9,500 $8,250 $6,850 $5,350 $3,850 $2,600 $1,875

MODEL 1892 CARBINE – 20 in. round barrel, 2 barrel bands, and saddle ring, except one barrel band and one rifle style mag. tube retainer on cals. .25-20 WCF and .32-20 WCF.

N/A N/A $5,400 $4,475 $3,450 $2,650 $2,175 $1,575 $1,150 $1,000 $825 $725

Add 50% for .44-40 WCF cal. or 25% for .38-40 WCF cal.

MODEL 1892 TRAPPER'S CARBINE – all features similar to standard SRC, except has a 12, 14, 15, 16, or 18 in. barrel, so called Trapper's Model because it was handy for trappers who had to carry a powerful but lightweight repeating rifle.

N/A N/A $14,250 $11,750 $8,950 $7,400 $6,350 $4,225 $3,350 $2,400 $1,875 $1,250

Most 1892 Trapper's Carbines are in the 15 in., .44-40 WCF cal. configuration. Most of the 1892 Trapper's Carbine were shipped to South America or Australia. This variation is almost never encountered over 30% condition - most are brown guns. Check federal laws regarding 12, 14 and 15 inch barrels.

MODEL 1892 MUSKET – most are chambered in .44-40 WCF cal., 30 in. round, full length military style forearm with military style rear sight.

N/A N/A $21,750 $18,150 $14,575 $12,000 $9,600 $7,700 $5,950 $4,675 $3,700 $2,850

Add $1,500 - $2,000 for correct bayonet.

MODEL 1894 RIFLE – .25-35 WCF, .30-30 Win. (.30 WCF), .32-40 WCF, .32 Spl., or .38-55 WCF cal., most common (and popular) is .30-30 Win. cal., tube mag., 24 or 26 in. round or octagon barrel was standard, blue, straight grip stock, Model 1894 barrel marking changed just before ser. no. 500,000 circa 1908, tang marking changed after ser. no. 500,000, "18" was removed around ser. no. 1,000,000 circa 1927. Over 5,000,000, mfg. 1894-2006.

Newer Model 94 mfg. may be found in the RIFLES: MODEL 94 LEVER ACTION - POST 1964 PRODUCTION section. The Model 1894 rifle configuration (forearm stock with forearm cap) was discontinued circa 1925 at approx. ser. no. 950,000-995,000. The Model 1894 rifle was replaced by the Model 55 (mfg. 1924-1932), and the Model 64 (mfg. 1933-1957 and 1972-1973).

* ***Model 1894 Rifle 1894-1898 Mfg.*** – antique mfg., pre-148,000 ser. no.

N/A $7,000 $6,000 $5,000 $4,250 $3,125 $2,150 $1,650 $1,275 $1,100 $900 $750

Add 20% for takedown variation.

Add approx. 25% for cals. other than .30-30 Win. or .32 Spl.

The Model 1894 Winchester has the distinction of being the world's most popular rifle.

100% 98% 95% 90% 80% 70% 60% 50% 40% 30% 20% 10%

* ***Model 1894 Rifle 1899-1929 Mfg.*** – Model 94s built 1899-1929. After 1929, only the Model 1894 carbine was produced up until 1940.

N/A $4,750 $4,175 $3,250 $2,550 $1,950 $1,300 $975 $800 $675 $550 $475

Add 25% for takedown variation.

Add approx. 50% for cals. other than .30-30 Win. or .32 Spl.

The Model 1894 Winchester has the distinction of being the world's most popular sporting rifle.

* ***Model 1894 Deluxe Rifle*** – distinguishable by fancy pistol grip checkered wood. Mfg. 1894-1929.

N/A N/A $13,750 $11,750 $9,750 $8,000 $7,500 $6,000 $4,500 $3,000 $2,250 $1,250

MODEL 1894 TRAPPER'S CARBINE – all features similar to the standard SRC, except with a 14, 15, or 16 in. barrel.

N/A N/A $7,750 $6,550 $5,250 $4,350 $3,550 $2,850 $2,200 $1,650 $1,350 $1,000

The large majority of this variation are encountered in .30-30 Win. cal. with 15 in. barrel. Any other caliber or barrel length will create a premium. Most of these carbines are brown and rusty. Rarely, if ever, encountered with very much finish remaining.

Note: Check federal laws on legality of 14 and 15 in. barrels.

MODEL 1894 SADDLE RING CARBINE – 20 in. round barrel.

N/A N/A $3,150 $2,550 $1,975 $1,450 $1,075 $925 $775 $625 $500 $450

Add 40% for any cal. other than .30-30 Win. or .32 Spl.

Carbines with special order features such as pistol grip, deluxe wood, checkering, etc. can bring even greater premiums than the rifle.

* ***Model 1894 Saddle Ring Carbine Antique*** – 20 in. round barrel, antique mfg., pre-148,000 ser. no.

N/A N/A $5,150 $4,350 $3,650 $2,650 $1,700 $1,550 $1,300 $1,000 $825 $750

Add 40% for any cal. other than .30-30 Win. or .32 Spl.

Carbines with special order features such as pistol grip, deluxe wood, checkering, etc. can bring even greater premiums than the rifle.

* ***Model 1894 Saddle Ring Carbine Eastern*** – features long forearm, early stock design, early style carbine post or hooded ramp (later mfg.) front sight, and without saddle ring, mfg. late 1920s-early 1930s.

N/A N/A $2,250 $1,975 $1,750 $1,500 $1,300 $1,100 $925 $775 $650 $495

MODEL 1894 1940-1964 PRODUCTION CARBINE – 1940-1964 mfg. without saddle ring, barrel is marked Model 94.

$1,100 $900 $750 $650 $500 $425 $375 $325 $275 $250 $225 $200

Add 100% for .25-35 WCF cal.

Some WWII carbines with special U.S. markings will bring a premium over prices listed.

100% 98% 95% 90% 80% 70% 60% 50% 40% 30% 20% 10%

MODEL 1895 RIFLE FLATSIDE – .30 US (most common), .38-72, or .40-72 cal., early model, distinguishable in that frame does not have fluting or ridge contouring, serial range approx. 1-5000. Mfg. 1895-1896.

N/A N/A $9,250 $8,100 $6,750 $6,000 $4,950 $4,100 $3,400 $2,450 $1,700 $1,250

Add 30% for octagon barrel on cals. .38-72 or .40-72.

MODEL 1895 RIFLE – .30-03, .30-06, .30-40 Krag, .303 Brit., .35 Win., .38-72, .40- 72, .405 Win., or 7.62mm Russian cal., 24-28 in. barrel, blue action, box mag., straight grip stock, 425,881 mfg. from 1896-1931.

N/A N/A $4,900 $4,300 $3,750 $3,250 $2,825 $2,350 $1,925 $1,450 $1,000 $750

Add 25% for octagon barrel.

Add 75% for .405 Win. cal.

Add 20% for takedown model.

The Model 1895 was a Browning design incorporating the first box type mag. in a lever action repeating rifle. .30 US is the most commonly encountered cal. in this model. A large Russian military contract was secured in 1915 with chambering for the 7.62mm Russian cartridge (over 293,000 mfg. or over 66% of total production).

* ***Model 1895 Deluxe Rifle*** – distinguishable by fancy pistol grip checkered wood. Mfg. 1894-1929.

N/A N/A $13,500 $11,500 $10,000 $8,000 $6,850 $5,350 $4,500 $3,500 $2,200 $1,150

MODEL 1895 CARBINE – .30 US (.30-40 Krag Army - most common cal.), .30-03, .30-06, or .303 Brit. cal., 22 in. round barrel, military style top handguard wood and military sights, with or without saddle ring.

N/A N/A $4,625 $4,175 $3,650 $3,175 $2,800 $2,300 $1,850 $1,375 $1,000 $825

Add 20% for caliber other than .30 U.S.

Add 50% for U.S. government marked.

MODEL 1895 FLATSIDE MUSKET – early models have serial range under 5,000, no flutes on frame, .30-40 Krag only.

Rarity on this model means only a few specimens in several museums.

MODEL 1895 MUSKET – .30-03, .30-06, or .30-40 Krag cal., 28 in. round barrel with handguard over barrel, military sights.

N/A N/A $6,000 $5,250 $4,750 $4,200 $3,600 $3,150 $2,650 $2,125 $1,600 $1,100

Add 10%-15% if U.S. Govt. marked.

MODEL 1895 NRA MUSKET – .30-03, .30-06, or .30-40 Krag cal., similar to Standard Musket grade with 24 or 30 in. barrel, 1901 Krag style rear sight. NRA approved for official NRA competition.

N/A N/A $5,275 $4,725 $4,125 $3,475 $2,975 $2,375 $2,000 $1,550 $1,100 $825

Add 30% if U.S. government marked.

MODEL 1895 RUSSIAN MUSKET – 7.62mm Russian cal., over 293,000 mfg. for Imperial Russian Govt., mfg. 1915-16, various Russian Ordnance stamps should be present.

N/A N/A $4,400 $3,950 $3,475 $3,000 $2,575 $2,100 $1,700 $1,400 $1,150 $950

100%	98%	95%	90%	80%	70%	60%	50%	40%	30%	20%	10%

MODEL 53 RIFLE – .25-20 WCF, .32-20 WCF, or .44-40 WCF cal., 22 in. round barrel, 1/2 tube mag. holding 6 cartridges, solid frame or takedown, blue finish, pistol grip or straight grip stock, serial numbered both separately and within the Model 92 range. Mfg. 24,916 between 1924-32.

N/A	N/A	$2,100	$1,875	$1,625	$1,350	$1,175	$900	$725	$600	$500	$375

Add 75% for .44-40 WCF cal.

Add 25% for Takedown Model.

* *Model 53 Deluxe Rifle* – distinguishable by fancy pistol grip checkered wood.

N/A	N/A	$4,000	$3,650	$3,350	$3,000	$2,600	$2,300	$1,950	$1,650	$1,350	$995

MODEL 55 RIFLE – .25-35 WCF (rare), .30-30 Win. (takedown only), or .32 Win. Spl. cal., lever action design, solid frame (less common) and takedown (more common), 24 in. lightweight rapid taper round barrel, shotgun style buttstock with serrated steel buttplate, tube mag., holds 3 cartridges. Approx. 20,500 mfg. between 1924-1932. Serial numbered independently to approx. 2,865, then serialized with Model 1894 production on underside of receiver. Simply could not compete with the Model 1894. Note that a small number of rifles were made during a parts clean-up from 1933-1942.

* *Model 55 Rifle Standard Cals.* – .30-30 Win. or .32 Win. Spl. cal.

N/A	$2,425	$2,150	$1,775	$1,425	$1,175	$995	$825	$725	$600	$475	$375

Add 20% for solid frame model.

* *Model 55 Rifle .25-35 WCF Cal.*

N/A	$6,750	$5,750	$4,550	$3,675	$2,950	$2,500	$2,100	$1,825	$1,500	$1,200	$950

MODEL 64 RIFLE – .219 Zipper (very rare), .25-35 WCF (rare), .30-30 Win., or .32 Win. Spl. cal., 20 (may be referred to as carbine) or 24 in. round barrel, with standard 26 in. on the .219 Zipper, blue metal, pistol grip stock, revamped Model 55 action with increased mag. capacity, 66,783 mfg. between 1933-1957 and 1972-73 (over 8,250 mfg. in .30-30 Win. cal. only - these last two years with minor changes).

N/A	$1,350	$1,200	$1,000	$900	$850	$750	$650	$550	$500	$450	$400

Add 150% for 20 in. barrel (sometimes referred to as Carbine).

Add 300% for .25-35 WCF cal. (rare).

Add 500% for .219 Zipper cal. (very rare).

Many of this variation now have extra holes drilled on the top of the receiver to accept scope mounts - subtract 50% for this alteration. The Model 64 is usually found in excellent condition.

Model 64 1972-73 mfg. may be found in the post-'64 section.

* *Model 64 Deluxe Rifle* – distinguishable by fancy checkered wood stock with pistol grip.

N/A	N/A	$2,750	$2,375	$2,100	$1,875	$1,700	$1,475	$1,275	$1,050	$900	$800

100%	98%	95%	90%	80%	70%	60%	50%	40%	30%	20%	10%

MODEL 65 RIFLE - .218 Bee (introduced 1939), .25-20 WCF, or .32-20 WCF cal., 22 in. round barrel (except .218 Bee - 24 in.), 1/2 tube mag. holding 7 cartridges, blue with pistol grip stock. Mfg. 5,704 between 1933-1947.

N/A	$5,450	$4,650	$4,000	$3,450	$2,950	$2,425	$2,100	$1,750	$1,425	$1,125	$950

While the .25-20 WCF cal. is the rarest, the .218 Bee has the most demand.

The Model 65 was a design evolved from the Model 53. The Model 65 was not tapped on receiver side for scope mounts. As a rule, most specimens are in either pretty nice or refinished condition.

* ***Model 65 Deluxe Rifle*** - distinguishable by fancy pistol grip checkered wood.

N/A	$8,750	$7,750	$6,850	$6,000	$5,000	$4,275	$3,750	$3,200	$2,500	$2,000	$1,500

MODEL 71 RIFLE - .348 Win. cal., 2/3 tube mag. holding 4 cartridges, improved Model 1886 frame, blue metal with pistol grip stock, 20 or 24 in. barrel, short or long tang. Mfg. 47,254 between 1935-1957.

N/A	$2,000	$1,800	$1,675	$1,500	$1,300	$1,100	$975	$875	$800	$725	$650

Add 30%-40% for early variation long tang, depending on condition.
Add 150% for short rifle with 20 in. barrel.
Add $250 for bolt peep sight.

* ***Model 71 Deluxe Rifle*** - distinguishable by fancy pistol grip cap, sling swivel studs, checkered wood.

N/A	$4,400	$3,800	$3,450	$3,400	$2,600	$2,300	$1,950	$1,650	$1,350	$995	$800

Add 20% for long tang.

MSR	100%	98%	95%	90%	80%	70%	60%

MODEL 88 RIFLE - pre-'64 version with diamond cut checkering, no barrel band, 22 in. barrel. Mfg. 1955-63. Total production for all varieties of the Model 88 Lever Action was approx. 284,000 units. Mfg. 1955-1963.

	100%	98%	95%	90%	80%	70%	60%
.308 Win. (1955-1963)	$1,150	$975	$725	$500	$400	$325	$275
.243 Win. (1956-1963)	$1,795	$1,525	$1,275	$1,000	$850	$750	$550
.358 Win. (1956-1962)	$4,350	$3,700	$2,950	$2,100	$1,625	$1,300	$995
.284 Win. (Intro-1963)	$3,200	$2,750	$2,300	$1,800	$1,425	$1,150	$850

RIFLES: SINGLE SHOT

MODEL 1885 - available in most popular rimfire and centerfire cals. between .22 S-L-LR and .50, falling block trigger guard activated action, John Browning's first high power single shot rifle design, many variations were made and we will list the standard types. Over 139,725 mfg. between 1885-1920.

This design was originally mfg. as the Model 1878 by the Browning Brothers in Ogden, UT, in the early 1880s. Fewer than 600 were mfg. - see the Browning section for values.

100%	98%	95%	90%	80%	70%	60%	50%	40%	30%	20%	10%

* ***Model 1885 Sporting Rifle Low Wall*** – 24 or 26 in. round or octagon barrel was standard, open sights, solid frame, standard trigger.

N/A N/A $1,650 $1,450 $1,275 $1,150 $975 $825 $700 $550 $400 $300

Add 30% for centerfire cal.

Add 50% for case colored frame, if in 95%+ original condition.

* ***Model 1885 Sporting Rifle High Wall*** – 30 in. barrel, standard trigger, open sights, solid frame. Available in various size and weight barrels numbered (in front of forearm) from lightest to heaviest: 1, 2, 3, 3 1/2 (introduced 1910), 4, and 5. Case hardened frames standard until 1901 when bluing became standard, three different frames depending on caliber. Heavier barrels in rare calibers will bring a premium.

N/A N/A $5,500 $3,850 $3,000 $2,600 $2,050 $1,725 $1,500 $1,325 $1,100 $875

Add 30% for 20 ga. shotgun.

Add 30% for Takedown Model.

Add 25% for No. 5 barrel.

Add 10% for set trigger.

Add 30% for .405, .45, and .50 caliber.

* ***Model 1885 Schuetzen Rifle*** – high wall, 30 in. octagon barrel, double-set triggers, spur lever, aperture sight, Schuetzen style stock, adj. palm rest and buttplate.

N/A N/A $9,750 $7,000 $5,250 $4,350 $3,650 $3,200 $2,850 $2,500 $2,250 $1,875

Add 30% for Takedown frame.

Add 50% for case colored frame, if in 95%+ original condition.

Prices are for factory original guns only. Since this model had many shooting alterations performed by various aftermarket suppliers of its time, perhaps only 10% of remaining specimens are unaltered (or 100% factory).

* ***Model 1885 Deluxe Sporting Rifle*** – various cals., available in Low Wall, High Wall, or Schuetzen configuration, distinguishable by case colored receiver and fancy pistol grip checkered wood.

N/A N/A $7,000 $5,500 $4,550 $3,750 $3,300 $2,975 $2,650 $2,300 $1,850 $1,450

Add 50%-100% for Deluxe Schuetzen Model with fancy pistol grip checkered wood and case colored receiver, depending on original condition.

* ***Model 1885 High Wall Musket*** – usually found in .22 LR cal.

N/A N/A $1,500 $1,350 $1,150 $975 $850 $750 $650 $550 $475 $400

Add 100% for .45-70 Govt. or .45-90 cal.

* ***Model 1885 Low Wall Musket (Winder Musket)*** – low wall, 3rd model, .22 Short or LR (most common) cal., 28 in. barrel, standard trigger and lever, military style stock and sights, grooved forearm, one barrel band.

N/A N/A $1,550 $1,325 $1,125 $950 $800 $700 $600 $500 $400 $300

MODEL 1885 (RECENT MFG.) – please refer to the RIFLES: SINGLE SHOT, POST 1964 MFG. section for these listings.

100% 98% 95% 90% 80% 70% 60% 50% 40% 30% 20% 10%

MODEL 1900 SINGLE SHOT - .22 S and L cal., bolt action, 18 in. round barrel, blue metal, open sights, one-piece straight grip gumwood stock without fitted buttplate, takedown, not serial numbered. Approx. 105,000 mfg. between 1899-1902.

N/A N/A $1,100 $900 $675 $425 $300 $200 $165 $145 $125 $110

Add 100% for later models marked M1900 on barrel, and Win. stamped butt.

This model is usually encountered with flaked frames.

MODEL 1902 SINGLE SHOT - similar to 1900, bolt action, with minor improvements. Distinguishable by specially shaped extended trigger guard. Not serial numbered. Approx. 640,299 mfg. between 1902-1931.

N/A $650 $525 $400 $275 $200 $150 $100 $90 $80 $70 $60

Chambering included .22 cal. Extra Long cal. in 1914 (interchangeable with S&L).

THUMB TRIGGER MODEL 99 - similar to 1902, with button behind cocking piece used to fire with thumb instead of trigger, not serial numbered. Approx. 75,433 were mfg. between 1904-1923.

N/A $2,250 $2,000 $1,750 $1,500 $1,200 $1,000 $800 $700 $600 $400 $350

MODEL 1904 SINGLE SHOT - improved version of 1902, 21 in. round barrel, chambering included .22 Extra Long in 1914, not serial numbered. Approx. 302,859 mfg. between 1904-31.

N/A $525 $450 $375 $300 $200 $175 $160 $150 $125 $100 $90

* ***Model 1904-A Single Shot*** - introduced 1927 with new sear bar and chambered for .22 LR.

N/A $525 $450 $375 $300 $200 $175 $160 $150 $125 $100 $90

MODEL 47 - .22 S, L, or LR cal., single shot bolt action, 25 in. round barrel, unique bolt design, uncheckered walnut stock, 5 1/4 lbs., approx. 43,000 (not serial numbered) mfg. during 1948-54.

$525 $450 $325 $250 $200 $175 $150 $135 $125 $120 $115 $110

MODEL 52 - please refer to listings in the Rifles: Bolt Action section.

MODEL 55 - .22 cal. only, top loading single shot, bottom ejection, 22 in. round barrel, open sporting sights, not serial numbered. Over 45,000 mfg. between 1958-61.

$200 $175 $160 $130 $115 $100 $95 $85 $75 $70 $65 $60

MSR 100% 98% 95% 90% 80% 70% 60%

MODEL 58 SINGLE SHOT - similar to Models 1902 and 1904, .22 LR cal., 18 in. round barrel, open sights, takedown. Approx. 38,992 mfg. between 1928-31.

$1,100 $950 $800 $700 $550 $450 $350

MODEL 59 SINGLE SHOT - improved Model 58 with 23 in. round barrel and pistol grip stock with buttplate. Approx. 9,200 mfg. between 1930-31.

$1,325 $1,095 $950 $825 $600 $500 $350

This model was disc. due to lack of sales.

MSR	100%	98%	95%	90%	80%	70%	60%

MODEL 60 – .22 S, L, or LR cal., improved Model 59, 23 in. round barrel increased to 27 in. 1933. Approx. 160,754 mfg. between 1930-34.

	$465	$395	$335	$275	$195	$160	$125

Add 20% for 23 in. barrel.

MODEL 60A SPORTER – .22 S, L, or LR cal., sporter variation of Model 60, pistol grip walnut stock. Disc.

	$600	$495	$435	$375	$325	$250	$225

MODEL 60A TARGET – similar to Model 60 with Lyman 55W aperture rear sight, heavier target stock, and 27 in. round tapered barrel. Approx. 6,118 mfg. between 1932-39.

	$725	$625	$550	$475	$425	$350	$295

MODEL 67/67A – .22 S, L, LR or .22 WRF (introduced 1935) cal., 20 in. (Boys Rifle), 24 (miniature target boring), and 27 in. (sporting or smooth bore) round barrels, same basic action as the Model 60, not serial numbered. Approx. 383,000 mfg. between 1934-1963.

	$300	$250	$225	$175	$125	$100	$75
.22 WRF cal.	$685	$600	$500	$465	$375	$310	$240

Add 30% for Boys rifle.

Add 100%-150% for smooth bore, depending on condition.

MODEL 677 – same basic specifications as Model 67, except no iron sights or sight cuts in barrel, not serial numbered, supplied with Win. 5-A scope, .22 WRF is scarce. Approx. 2,240 mfg. between 1937-39.

	$2,525	$2,215	$1,850	$1,625	$1,295	$1,050	$805

MODEL 68 – .22 LR or .22 WRF cal., bolt action single shot, similar to Model 67, walnut stock, supplied with aperture sight (no rear sight), not serial numbered. Approx. 100,000 mfg. between 1934-46.

.22 LR cal.	$350	$295	$235	$200	$165	$135	$100
.22 WRF cal.	$1,325	$1,125	$950	$825	$650	$525	$400

MODEL 121 SINGLE SHOT RIFLE – .22 LR cal., bolt action, 20 3/4 in. barrel, open sights, plain pistol grip stock. Mfg. 1967-73.

	$115	$100	$85	$80	$65	$50	$40

MODEL 121Y SINGLE SHOT RIFLE – similar to 121, with shorter stock.

	$115	$100	$85	$80	$65	$50	$40

MODEL 121 DELUXE – similar to 121, with ramp front sight and sling swivels.

	$125	$110	$95	$85	$70	$55	$45

MODEL 310 SINGLE SHOT – .22 LR cal., bolt action, 22 in. barrel, open sights, checkered pistol grip stock, swivels. 13,544 mfg. 1972-1975.

	$240	$200	$175	$150	$125	$100	$85

WINGO "ICE PALACE" RIFLE – 5mm shot cartridge, 22 in. round barrel with vent. rib, modified lever action Martini type single shot, walnut Monte Carlo stock and forearm, marked "WINGO" on both sides of receiver, mfg. in England for Winchester "Ice Palace" shooting center,

MSR	100%	98%	95%	90%	80%	70%	60%

electrical cord extends from the magazine connecting to a target throwing device which threw black clay mini-pigeons, approx. 20 mfg.

	100%	98%	95%	90%	80%	70%	60%
	$2,750	$2,405	$2,065	$1,870	$1,515	$1,240	$965

Add approx. 33% if with electric cables, operating trap mechanism, and at least 50 rounds of 5mm ammo and mini-pigeons.

100%	98%	95%	90%	80%	70%	60%	50%	40%	30%	20%	10%

RIFLES: BOLT ACTION

On Models 52, 54, 56, 57, 58, 59, 60, 60A, 67, 677, 68, 69, 69A, 697, and 70 values in 50% or less original condition have been omitted since values in those conditions will approximate the 60% price. This reflects the fact that while these lower condition specimens are not as desirable to collectors, they are still sought after as shooters.

MODEL 1883 (HOTCHKISS REPEATER) - .45-70 Govt. cal., designed by Benjamin D. Hotchkiss, unique tube mag. located in buttstock attached to receiver, up-turn/pull-back bolt action, 26 in. round or octagon barrel standard on rifle. Over 84,000 mfg. between 1879-1889. Carbine extremely rare in Third Model (20 in. barrel).

Subtract 25% for carbine configuration (24 in. round barrel with one band), or musket (32 in. round barrel with cleaning rod and two barrel bands).

Add 25% for Deluxe Model with fancy pistol grip checkered wood.

* ***Model 1883 First Style*** - approx. 6,419 mfg. with magazine cut off and safety control incorporated into one unit.

100%	98%	95%	90%	80%	70%	60%	50%	40%	30%	20%	10%
N/A	N/A	$2,500	$2,150	$1,800	$1,500	$1,350	$1,200	$1,050	$900	$850	$800

* ***Model 1883 Second Style*** - approx. 16,102 mfg., magazine cut off on right receiver top, safety on left side.

100%	98%	95%	90%	80%	70%	60%	50%	40%	30%	20%	10%
N/A	N/A	$2,500	$2,150	$1,800	$1,500	$1,350	$1,200	$1,050	$900	$850	$800

* ***Model 1883 Third Style*** - most commonly encountered Hotchkiss, 2-piece stock, approx. 62,034 mfg. 1883-1899.

100%	98%	95%	90%	80%	70%	60%	50%	40%	30%	20%	10%
N/A	N/A	$2,150	$1,800	$1,500	$1,350	$1,200	$1,050	$900	$850	$750	$650

The Model 1883 Hotchkiss was the first bolt action designed for the U.S. military .45-70 Govt. cartridge. On the First and Second models, inspect wood directly below bolt and left frame side for cracks, breaks, or older repairs as it is frequently encountered on these early models with thin wrists.

LEE STRAIGHT PULL RIFLE - 6mm Lee (.236 U.S.N. cal.), 5 shot non-detachable box mag., 24 (Sporting Rifle) or 28 (Musket) in. barrel, folding leaf sight, blue metal, military style full stock, mfg. 1897-1902, Navy Issue Model is the Musket with "236 U.S.N." on barrels. Approx. 20,000 mfg. (including 15,000 Muskets for the U.S. Navy military contract) between 1895-1902 with parts clean up occurring in 1916.

* ***Lee Straight Pull Rifle U.S.N. Military Musket***

100%	98%	95%	90%	80%	70%	60%	50%	40%	30%	20%	10%
N/A	$2,750	$2,350	$2,000	$1,750	$1,500	$1,250	$1,100	$1,000	$875	$750	$625

100%	98%	95%	90%	80%	70%	60%	50%	40%	30%	20%	10%

* ***Lee Straight Pull Rifle Sporting*** – similar to Musket, with 24 in. barrel, sporter style stock. Approx. 1,700 mfg. 1897-1902.

N/A	$3,000	$2,650	$2,300	$2,000	$1,750	$1,500	$1,250	$1,050	$975	$875	$800

This design was originally patented by James Paris Lee and assigned to the Lee Arms Company. Winchester obtained manufacturing rights to produce this model for the U.S Navy military contract 1895-1902.

MODEL 43 – .218 Bee, .22 Hornet, .25-20 WCF, or .32-20 WCF cal., dubbed "Poor Man's Model 70," 24 in. round tapered barrel, box type mag. Approx. 62,617 mfg. between 1949-1957.

$800	$675	$575	$500	$425	$375	$325	$275	$225	$175	$150	$125

Add 100% for Deluxe Model with fancy checkered wood.

Add 150% for .32-20 WCF and .25-20 WCF cal.

Add 20% for .218 Bee cal.

Subtract 40% if non-factory drilled and tapped (early models).

MSR	100%	98%	95%	90%	80%	70%	60%

MODEL 52 TARGET – .22 S (rare) or LR cal., 5 shot mag., 28 in. standard or heavy barrel (1st cataloged 1933), target sights and target style stock, speedlock trigger feature was introduced in 1929. Approx. 125,233 Model 52s in all variations were mfg. between 1919-79.

	$825	$750	$650	$550	$500	$450	$400
altered w/aftermarket speedlock	$700	$625	$575	$525	$475	$425	$350

Barrel drilling and tapping for scope blocks was not standard until ser. no. 5200.

A few Model 52 Target models with stainless steel barrels have been encountered. Values range from $1,500-$2,100, depending on condition.

* ***Model 52A Target*** – similar to Model 52, except all "A" suffix Model 52s have a speedlock trigger. Values are similar to Model 52 Target with speedlock trigger. In terms of rarity, it seems the "E" suffix is probably the scarcest (also the most poorly mfg.), followed by the "A" suffix variation.

MODEL 52A HEAVY BARREL – similar to Standard Target, with heavy barrel.

	$1,050	$900	$775	$675	$550	$450	$400

MODEL 52-B TARGET – extensively redesigned action, improved stock design, offered with a variety of sights. Approx. mfg. 1940-47.

	$1,225	$1,100	$1,000	$900	$750	$650	$550

MODEL 52-B HEAVY BARREL – similar to 52-B, with heavy barrel, with adj. sling swivel as to position of front swivel, and single shot adapter became available.

	$1,325	$1,200	$1,100	$1,000	$900	$800	$700

MODEL 52-B BULL GUN – extra heavy weight barrel.

	$1,950	$1,750	$1,500	$1,150	$975	$850	$675

MSR	100%	98%	95%	90%	80%	70%	60%

MODEL 52 SPORTER (SPORTING RIFLE) - 24 in. round lightweight barrel with front sight cover, sporting type select walnut stock with cheekpiece, hard rubber pistol grip cap, black plastic tipped forearm, checkered steel buttplate, 5 shot mag. is standard, about 7 1/4 lbs. Mfg. 1934-1958. There is some controversy as to whether any of the Model 52 Sporters were drilled and tapped per factory worksmanship. Be cautious of "factory" drilled and tapped receivers on all model 52s, as there are many "gunsmith" Sporters that have been made with turned down, shortened target barrels.

* ***Model 52 Sporter*** - advertised approx. 1936.

$4,500 $3,750 $2,750 $2,250 $1,650 $1,400 $1,100

* ***Model 52A Sporter*** - introduced approx. 1937, receiver and locking lug were strengthened.

$6,000 $5,500 $5,000 $4,000 $3,000 $2,000 $1,500

* ***Model 52B Sporter*** - introduced approx. 1940.

$4,500 $3,600 $2,750 $2,250 $1,650 $1,400 $1,100

* ***Model 52B (1993 Re-issue) Sporter*** - .22 LR cal., patterned after the original Model 52B and includes steel buttplate, 24 in. barrel w/o sights, Micro Motion trigger with adjustment screw on bottom plate, high-polish blue, 5 shot mag., checkered 52B style stock with ebony forend tip, 7 lbs. Mfg. by Miroku in Japan 1993-2002.

$1,100 $1,000 $900 $800 $600 $500 $450

Last MSR was $662.

* ***Model 52C Sporter*** - introduced 1947 with adj. Micro Motion trigger, approx. 500-1,000 mfg., 2 screws in trigger guard.

$5,500 $4,350 $3,950 $2,950 $2,250 $1,650 $1,400

A few Model 52 Sporters & Targets were mfg. with stainless steel barrels (17,XXX-27,XXX serial range) - these guns will command a premium over values shown. Stainless steel barrels were also offered by Winchester as after market parts.

MODEL 52-C STANDARD TARGET - "Micro Motion" trigger and "Marksman" stock, single shot adaptor, 5 or 10 shot mag. was avail., standard barrel, otherwise similar to 52-B. Mfg. 1947-61.

$1,300 $1,200 $1,100 $1,000 $800 $600 $500

MODEL 52-C HEAVY TARGET - similar to Standard Target, with heavy barrel.

$1,350 $1,250 $1,100 $1,000 $800 $700 $650

MODEL 52-C BULL TARGET - extra heavy (bull) barrel model of Heavy Target 52-C. Mfg. approx. 1947-1961.

$2,150 $1,750 $1,450 $1,325 $1,200 $1,050 $900

MODEL 52-D TARGET - improved version of 52-C with free-floating standard or heavy barrel and adj. bedding device, all 52-Ds were single shot. Fewer than 750 rifles were shipped.

$1,300 $1,150 $1,000 $900 $800 $700 $600

MSR	100%	98%	95%	90%	80%	70%	60%

MODEL 52-D INTERNATIONAL MATCH - similar to 52-D, with free rifle stock, accessory rail. Mfg. 1969-1975.

	$1,650	$1,400	$1,125	$925	$775	$650	$525

Previous Model 52s had ser. no. suffixes - either A, B, C, or D" After approx. 1975, rifles started appearing with an "E" serial prefix. Both Model 52 International and Prone could have factory stocks that were not Winchester mfg.

MODEL 52-D PRONE - similar to International Match, with prone style stock. Mfg. 1960-75.

	$1,525	$1,350	$1,150	$900	$750	$600	$550

MODEL 52-E TARGET - similar to Model 52-D Target, approx. 652 mfg. 1975-1980.

	$1,925	$1,650	$1,350	$1,075	$895	$765	$650

MODEL 52-E INTERNATIONAL PRONE - similar to 52-D, with lighter colored wood stock, removable roll over cheekpiece. Approx. 37 mfg. 1975-1980.

	$1,525	$1,350	$1,150	$900	$750	$600	$550

MODEL 52-E INTERNATIONAL MATCH - heavy match barrel, lower accessory rail, uncheckered light colored walnut thumbhole stock with adj. buttplate and beavertail forend, no sights, scattered in ser. no. range E-123,000 - E125,000. Approx. 44 mfg. 1975-1980.

	$2,150	$1,750	$1,450	$1,325	$1,200	$1,050	$900

MODEL 54 HIGH POWER SPORTER - .270 Win., 7x57mm, 7.65x57mm Mauser (rare), .30-30 Win., .30-06, 9x57mm Mauser (rare) cal., 5 shot mag., 24 in. barrel, open sights, checkered pistol grip stock. Mfg. 1925-30. Approx. 50,145 Model 54s were mfg. in all variations between 1925-36.

	$1,500	$1,250	$1,000	$850	$725	$600	$500

Rare cals. will add premiums to the values listed. This model was also mfg. with a stainless steel barrel during the late 1920s-early '30s with premiums also being asked.

MODEL 54 CARBINE - introduced 1927, similar to Rifle, with 20 in. barrel, plain stock.

	$1,650	$1,300	$1,075	$925	$800	$650	$500

MODEL 54 IMPROVED SPORTER - .22 Hornet, .220 Swift, .250-3000, .257 Robts., .270, 7x57mm, or .30-06 cal., 5 shot mag., 24 or 26 in. barrel, one piece firing pin, checkered pistol grip stock. Mfg. 1930-36.

	$1,495	$1,275	$1,050	$925	$800	$700	$600

Rare cals. will add premiums to the values listed.

MODEL 54 CARBINE IMPROVED - similar to Rifle, with 20 in. barrel.

	$1,925	$1,625	$1,325	$1,050	$875	$750	$650

MODEL 54 SUPER GRADE - introduced 1934, similar to Sporter, with better wood and black forend tip and pistol grip cap.

	$3,300	$2,825	$2,350	$1,800	$1,525	$1,375	$1,200

Rare calibers will command considerable premiums (i.e. this variation in 7x57mm cal. will sell for $2,500 in mint condition).

MSR	100%	98%	95%	90%	80%	70%	60%

MODEL 54 SPORTING SNIPER'S RIFLE – .30-06 cal., similar to Sporter, with 26 in. heavy barrel, Lyman #48 W receiver sight. Mfg. 1929-1935.

	$2,625	$1,975	$1,600	$1,350	$1,150	$1,000	$900

MODEL 54 NATIONAL MATCH – introduced 1935, similar to Standard, with Lyman sights and Marksman stock.

	$1,950	$1,750	$1,500	$1,150	$975	$850	$675

MODEL 56 SPORTER – .22 S or LR cal., 5 or 10 shot box mag., 22 in. round barrel, open sights, plain pistol grip stock. Approx. 8,297 mfg. between 1926-29.

	$1,650	$1,350	$1,100	$1,000	$850	$725	$600

Approx. 1,000 mfg. in .22 Short cal.

MODEL 57 TARGET – .22 S (disc. 1930) or LR cal., 22 in. barrel with barrel band, open sights, stock cutaway for aperture sight on left side, drilled and tapped receiver, heavy target uncheckered pistol grip walnut stock, 5 (standard) or 10 shot mag., left side push-button mag. release, checkered steel buttplate approx. 5 lbs. Approx. 18,600 were mfg. between 1927-1936.

	$925	$800	$675	$550	$475	$425	$375

MODEL 57 SPORTING SNIPER'S MATCH – .30-06 cal., 26 in. extra heavy barrel (1 1/4 at breech and 7/8 at the muzzle), Lyman #48 W receiver sight, Marksman stock, approx. 12 lbs., rare. Introduced late 1935.

	N/A	$4,750	$4,250	$3,850	$3,450	$2,950	$2,500

MODEL 69 & 69A – .22 S, L, or LR cal., 5 or 10 shot repeater, 25 in. barrel, aperture or open rear sight, not serial numbered. Approx. 355,000 mfg. between 1935-63.

	$425	$365	$300	$235	$150	$100	$85

Add 40% for Target Model.

Add 20% for grooved receiver (Model 69A only).

Add 5% for chrome plated bolt handle and trigger guard.

The Model 69 was cocked by the closing motion of the bolt and had a non-swept back bolt handle, whereas the 69A was cocked by the opening motion of the bolt and had a swept back bolt handle. Number 97B rear aperture sight and 80A hooded front target sights and standard open sights were offered on both the Model 69 and 69A.

MODEL 72/72A – .22 LR and Gallery Model (.22 short only), tube mag., bolt action, 25 in. round, tapered barrel, aperture or open rear sight, not serial numbered. Over 161,000 mfg. between 1938-59.

	$450	$375	$300	$250	$115	$100	$85

Add 30% for Target Model.

Add 100% for Gallery Model (mfg. 1939-1942) - rare.

Add 20% for grooved receiver (Model 72A only).

Add 5% for chrome plated bolt handle and trigger guard.

The Model 72 and 72A both cocked on opening. The Model 72A has a swept back bolt handle and some minor internal mechanical improvements. Same open sight options as Models 69/69A.

MSR	100%	98%	95%	90%	80%	70%	60%

MODEL 75 TARGET – .22 LR cal., 5 or 10 shot mag., 28 in. barrel, target sights, slight variation used by Government in WWII. Approx. 88,715 Model 75 Target and Model 75 Sporter rifles were mfg. between 1938-1958.

	$850	$725	$600	$525	$450	$375	$325

Add 25% for Olympic sights.

Add 20% for original Winchester leather sling.

MODEL 75 SPORTER – similar to Model 75, except 24 in. tapered barrel, detachable mag., non-target sights and select checkered walnut.

	$1,500	$1,300	$1,000	$725	$650	$600	$500

Add 20%-25% for "grooved" receiver allowing "tip-off" scope mounts.

MODEL 131 – .22 S, L, and LR cal., 7 shot mag.

	$225	$200	$175	$150	$125	$95	$75

MODEL 141 – .22 S, L, and LR cal., butt loading tube mag.

	$225	$200	$175	$150	$125	$95	$75

MODEL 320 RIFLE – .22 LR cal., similar to Single Shot Model 310, with 5 shot mag. Mfg. 1972-74.

	$325	$325	$300	$265	$235	$185	$150

MODEL 325 RIFLE – .22 WMR cal., otherwise similar to Model 320, limited mfg. 1972-74.

	$375	$350	$325	$300	$250	$200	$100

MODEL 670 RIFLE – another economy version of the Model 70, .225 Win., .243 Win., .270 Win, .308 Win., or .30-06 cal., 22 in. barrel, open sights, no hinged floorplate, pistol grip stock. Mfg. 1967-73.

	$325	$275	$235	$195	$175	$165	$140

MODEL 670 CARBINE – similar to 670, with 19 in. barrel, not available in .308 Win. Mfg. 1967-70.

	$325	$275	$235	$195	$175	$165	$140

MODEL 670 MAGNUM – similar to 670, with reinforced stock, .264 Mag., 7mm Mag., or .300 Win. Mag. cal. Mfg. 1967-70.

	$365	$295	$265	$225	$205	$195	$165

MODEL 697 – .22 WRF cal., same general specifications as the Model 69, except no iron sights or sight cuts in barrel and no ramp or sight cover. Telescope bases attached to barrel were standard.

	$2,500	$2,200	$2,000	$1,500	$1,300	$1,100	$1,000

MODEL 770 – .22-250 Rem., .222 Rem., .243 Win., .270 Win., .30-06, or .308 Win. cal., 22 in. barrel, open sights, no floorplate or forend tip. Mfg. 1969-71.

	$375	$335	$300	$275	$250	$225	$200

MODEL 770 MAGNUM – similar to Model 770, .264 Mag., 7mm Mag., or .300 Win. Mag. cal., recoil pad. Mfg. 1969-71.

	$395	$350	$315	$285	$260	$240	$220

MSR	100%	98%	95%	90%	80%	70%	60%

MODEL 777 – .30-06 cal., bolt action, 4 shot mag., mfg. by Nikko in Japan during 1979-80 for sale to Winchester subsidiaries in Australia, Germany, Italy, and Scandinavia, only 3 were shipped to the U.S., checkered Monte Carlo stock with Wundhammer swell grip, lightweight barrel, engraved action, "Winchester" is cast on the left side of the receiver near the top, approx. 1,000 mfg. with 250 in .30-06 cal. - 750 mfg. in different cal. and sold elsewhere, 8 1/2 lbs.

MSR	100%	98%	95%	90%	80%	70%	60%
	$1,850	$1,675	$1,500	$1,350	$1,200	$1,100	$1,000

WILDCAT – .22 LR cal., 21 in. regular or heavy (Target/Varmint model) barrel with (Sporter) or w/o (Target/Varmint) sights, detachable 5 or 10 shot mag., checkered hardwood stock and forend (Target or Sporter configuration), sling swivels, fold down rear sight, includes one 5 and three 10 shot mags., two-stage trigger, two-position safety on trigger guard, 4 1/2 or 5 1/2 (Target/Varmint) lbs. Importation from Russia 2007-2009.

MSR	100%	98%	95%	90%	80%	70%	60%
	$215	$185	$150	$130	$110	$90	$80

Last MSR was $259.

Add $50 for Wildcat Target/Varmint variation with heavy barrel and beavertail forend (no sights).

This model with 21 in. Sporter barrel was featured as a SHOT Show Special during 2006.

100%	98%	95%	90%	80%	70%	60%	50%	40%	30%	20%	10%

RIFLES: SEMI-AUTO

MODEL 1903 – .22 Win. Auto rimfire cal., 10 shot tube mag., 20 in. round barrel, open sights, straight grip stock cut out for partial magazine filling. Approx. 126,000 mfg. between 1903-1932.

100%	98%	95%	90%	80%	70%	60%	50%	40%	30%	20%	10%
N/A	$1,595	$1,375	$1,050	$900	$775	$650	$550	$475	$400	$325	$250

Add 100% for deluxe checkered model.

First U.S. semi-auto rifle designed for a special .22 cal. rimfire cartridge. Regular .22 cal. rimfire will not function or chamber properly in this model. Early models up to around ser. no. 1,800 were mfg. w/o a safety. Safety became standard around ser. no. 5,400. Watch for fake boxes.

MODEL 1905 – .32 Win. or .35 Win. cal., 5 or 10 shot box mag., 22 in. round barrel, open sights, straight or plain pistol grip stock. Approx. 29,113 mfg. between 1905-20.

100%	98%	95%	90%	80%	70%	60%	50%	40%	30%	20%	10%
N/A	$725	$650	$575	$525	$465	$400	$365	$330	$300	$275	$250

MODEL 1907 – .351 Win. cal., 5 or 10 shot box mag., 20 in. round barrel, open sights, plain pistol grip stock, an improved version of the Model 1905. Approx. 58,490 mfg. between 1907-57.

100%	98%	95%	90%	80%	70%	60%	50%	40%	30%	20%	10%
N/A	$675	$595	$525	$450	$375	$325	$295	$265	$230	$195	$175

MODEL 1910 – .401 Win. cal., 4 shot box mag., 20 in. barrel, open sight, plain pistol grip stock. Mfg. 20,786 between 1910-36.

100%	98%	95%	90%	80%	70%	60%	50%	40%	30%	20%	10%
N/A	$850	$750	$625	$550	$500	$450	$400	$365	$330	$300	$275

Add 50% for Fancy Sporting Rifle (special checkered walnut).

100%	98%	95%	90%	80%	70%	60%	50%	40%	30%	20%	10%

MODEL 55 – please refer to listing in Rifles: Single Shot.

MODEL 63 – .22 LR cal., styling similar to Model 1903, takedown, 10 shot tube mag., 20 (disc. 1936) or 23 in. barrel, open sights, plain pistol grip stock. Approx. 174,692 mfg. between 1933-1958.

100%	98%	95%	90%	80%	70%	60%	50%	40%	30%	20%	10%
$1,395	$1,200	$1,000	$850	$750	$675	$550	$425	$350	$300	$265	$235

Add 100%-150% for 20 in. barrel (carbine) depending on condition.

The Model 63 was introduced to take advantage of the new .22 LR cartridge, which the older Model 1903 couldn't chamber.

Watch for fake boxes and hanging tags on this model, especially with rifles in over 95%+ original condition.

* ***Model 63 w/Grooved Receiver*** – with grooved receiver.

100%	98%	95%	90%	80%	70%	60%	50%	40%	30%	20%	10%
$2,000	$1,800	$1,600	$1,400	$1,000	$800	$700	$600	$500	$400	$300	$250

MSR	100%	98%	95%	90%	80%	70%	60%

MODEL 63 GRADE I - RECENT PRODUCTION – .22 LR cal., similar to original Model 63, 10 shot mag., 23 in. barrel, checkered walnut stock and forearm, blue finish with engraved receiver, 6 1/4 lbs. Mfg. 1997-98.

MSR	100%	98%	95%	90%	80%	70%	60%
	$675	$600	$550	$500	$430	$375	$315

Last MSR was $678.

* ***Model 63 High Grade - Recent Mfg.*** – .22 LR cal., similar to original Model 63, 10 shot mag., deluxe checkered walnut stock and forearm, blue finish with engraved gold animals and accents on receiver, 6 1/4 lbs. 1,000 mfg. 1997 only.

MSR	100%	98%	95%	90%	80%	70%	60%
	$1,050	$875	$750	N/A	N/A	N/A	N/A

Last MSR was $1,083.

MODEL 74 – .22 S or LR (introduced in 1940) cal., tubular mag. in stock, pop-out bolt assembly. Approx. 406,574 mfg. between 1939-1955. Distinguishable by squared-off rear receiver.

MSR	100%	98%	95%	90%	80%	70%	60%
	$395	$325	$250	$200	$165	$140	$90

Add 25% for .22 Short cal. (mfg. 1939-1952).

Add 25% for pre-WWII mfg.

MODEL 77 – .22 LR cal., detachable box mag. or tubular mag. under barrel. Over 217,000 mfg. between 1955-62.

MSR	100%	98%	95%	90%	80%	70%	60%
	$325	$275	$225	$180	$140	$120	$80

Add $50 for tube mag.

MODEL 100 RIFLE – .243 Win., .284 Win., or .308 Win. cal., 4 shot detachable mag., 22 in. round barrel with open sights, gas operated, basket weave checkering impressed on stock, pistol grip cap. Over 262,000 mfg. 1961-73 with some production occurring in Japan.

MSR	100%	98%	95%	90%	80%	70%	60%
	$800	$700	$600	$500	$325	$275	$250

The pre-1964 .284 Win. cal. with cut checkering was made for less than one year (WFF, ser. range 72,XXX with no letter suffix or prefix).

MSR	100%	98%	95%	90%	80%	70%	60%

* *Model 100 Rifle Pre-1964 Mfg.*

	$725	$625	$550	$495	$425	$350	$295

Add $100 for .243 Win. cal.
Add $350 for .284 Win. cal.

MODEL 100 CARBINE – similar to rifle, with 19 in. barrel, plain pistol grip stock, barrel band. Mfg. 1967-1973.

	$795	$675	$550	$475	$400	$325	$295

Add $100 for .243 Win. cal.
Add $400 for .284 Win. cal.

MODEL 190 RIFLE – .22 S, L, or LR cal., 15 shot LR tube mag., alloy receiver, uncheckered walnut finished hardwood stock, 20 1/2 (Carbine Model) or 24 (Rifle Model) in. barrel, approx. 2,150,000 (including the Model 290 listed also) during 1967-1980.

	$175	$150	$125	$100	$85	$75	$65

MODEL 290 DELUXE RIFLE – similar to 190, with select Monte Carlo stock. Mfg. 1965-1973.

	$225	$200	$175	$150	$115	$100	$90

MODEL 490 RIFLE – .22 LR cal., 5 shot mag., 22 in. barrel, folding sight, checkered one piece stock. Mfg. 1975-1980.

	$295	$250	$225	$185	$155	$145	$130

SUPER X RIFLE GRADE I (SXR) – .30-06, .270 WSM, .300 WSM, or .300 Win. Mag. cal., gas operated action with multi-lug rotating bolt locking system, blued alloy receiver, 22 (.30-06 cal.) or 24 in. blue barrel w/o sights, hinged floorplate with 3 or 4 shot detachable box mag., enlarged trigger guard with cross bolt safety, walnut stock and raked forearm featuring unique circle pattern checkering on stock and forearm for grip, removable trigger assembly, approx. 7 1/4 lbs. Mfg. 2006-2009.

	$850	$750	$625	$500	$450	$375	$325

Last MSR was $949.

Add $30 for Mag. cals.

SUPER X RIFLE GRADE II (SXR) – similar to Super X Grade I, except also available in .325 WSM cal., deluxe wood ergonomic stock with adj. LOP and recoil reduction system, with or w/o TruGlo fiber optic sight system, 7 1/2 lbs. Mfg. 2007 only.

	$750	$675	$575	$500	$425	$375	$325

Last MSR was $864.

Add $28 for Mag. cals.
Add $68 for adj. LPA Sights with TruGlo fiber optic elements (.300 Win. Mag. or .325 WSM cal. only).

MODEL SX-AB – .308 Win. cal., 20 in. heavy barrel w/o sights, fully adj. stock with textured pistol grip and forearm, includes three interchangeable cheekpieces, 10 shot detachable mag., Picatinny bottom rail on forearm, 100% Mossy Oak Brush camo coverage, 10 lbs. Approx. 2,000 mfg. during 2009 only.

	$1,250	$1,075	$950	$825	$700	$600	$550

Last MSR was $1,379.

100%	98%	95%	90%	80%	70%	60%	50%	40%	30%	20%	10%

RIFLES: SLIDE ACTION, DISC.

MODEL 1890 – .22 S, L, LR, or WRF rimfire, cals. are non-interchangeable (don't shoot a .22 S in a gun chambered for .22 L) and the barrel is marked for single cal. only, visible hammer, solid-frame (first 15,000) or takedown, 24 in. octagonal barrel, case hardened receivers until 1901, model nomenclature changed to Model 90 circa 1919 at approx. ser. no. range 640,000. Approx. 849,000 mfg. between 1890-1932.

* ***Model 1890 First Model Solid Frame*** – color case hardened receiver, mfg. 1890-1892.

100%	98%	95%	90%	80%	70%	60%	50%	40%	30%	20%	10%
N/A	$17,000	$15,000	$12,000	$8,500	$6,500	$5,000	$4,750	$4,000	$3,500	$2,750	$2,250

Add 20% for .22 L or WRF cal.

* ***Model 1890 Second Model Takedown*** – color case hardened or blue receiver, takedown feature was added in 1892 after over 15,000 solid frames had been made, approx. ser. no. range 15,500-326,000. Mfg. 1892-1907.

» ***Model 1890 Second Model Takedown w/Case Colored Receiver***

100%	98%	95%	90%	80%	70%	60%	50%	40%	30%	20%	10%
N/A	$8,000	$7,250	$6,500	$6,000	$5,000	$4,275	$3,750	$3,200	$2,500	$2,000	$1,500

» ***Model 1890 Second Model Takedown w/Blue Finish***

100%	98%	95%	90%	80%	70%	60%	50%	40%	30%	20%	10%
N/A	$3,200	$2,750	$2,500	$2,000	$1,425	$1,100	$900	$750	$575	$500	$450

* ***Model 1890 Third Model Takedown w/Blue Finish*** – most commonly encountered Model 1890, post-1901 manufacture.

100%	98%	95%	90%	80%	70%	60%	50%	40%	30%	20%	10%
N/A	$3,000	$2,000	$1,250	$825	$650	$550	$450	$385	$335	$300	$250

Add 50% for .22 LR cal. (mfg circa 1919-1932, starting at ser. no. approx. 610,000).

.22 LR cal. accounted for approx. 10% of the total production on this model.

Deluxe model will bring premiums over values listed. There were also a limited amount of guns mfg. with stainless steel barrels which will add to values of post-1901 mfg.

The Model 1890 was Winchester's first slide action repeating rifle. It replaced the Model 1873 .22 cal. It was an excellent and inexpensive .22 rifle that rapidly became the universal firearm used in shooting galleries. Even though production reached approx. 849,000 units, most guns were heavily used and specimens existing today in 98%+ condition are rare. Check carefully for rebarreling (notice proof marks on barrel).

MODEL 1906 – .22 S, L, or LR, 20 in. round barrel, tube mag., visible hammer, open sights, straight stock with shotgun buttplate. Approx. 848,000 mfg. between 1906-1932.

100%	98%	95%	90%	80%	70%	60%	50%	40%	30%	20%	10%
N/A	N/A	$2,500	$1,750	$900	$550	$450	$350	$275	$250	$200	$175

Add 20% for non-grooved forearm.

Add 20% for .22 S cal. only.

This model is seldom encountered in over 90% original condition - original mint specimens can top $2,000.

Model nomenclature was changed to the Model 06 circa 1918.

100%	98%	95%	90%	80%	70%	60%	50%	40%	30%	20%	10%

* ***Model 1906 Expert*** – similar to Model 1906, except has a pistol grip stock and different shaped slide handle, finish choices included blue, nickel trimmed receiver, guard, and bolt, or full nickel trimmed, .22 S cal. only until approx. 70,000, mfg. 1917-1925.

N/A N/A $3,000 $2,500 $1,500 $900 $750 $600 $475 $350 $275 $225

MODEL 61 HAMMERLESS – .22 S, L, LR, WRF or Mag. cal., 24 in. round or octagon barrel (disc. 1947), with rifling or smooth bore (either small bore or Routledge), tube mag., open sights, plain grip stock. Approx. 350,000 mfg. between 1932-1963.

$1,400 $1,300 $1,100 $1,000 $800 $600 $500 $375 $325 $275 $225 $200

Add up to 150% for single cal. barrel marking (S or LR, Short is very rare).

Add $400 for pre-war mfg. w/small forearm.

Add 10% for grooved receiver.

Add 10% for pre-WWII rust blue metal finish.

Mint original pre-war Model 61s in the proper picture box are selling in the $3,800-$4,500 range. Post-war boxed Model 61s (Kraft box) are selling in the $2,800-$3,200 range. Smooth bore small diameter shot variations are selling in the $3,000-$4,000 range, while the Routledge shot variation with .410 diameter bore are selling in the $8,500-$10,000 range.

Pre-war manufacture has small forearm. "WRF" marked round barrel is rare - front of receiver must be marked "W.R.F."

Watch for fake boxes and hanging tags on this model, especially with rifles in over 95%+ original condition.

* ***Model 61 WRF*** – .22 WRF cal. only, front of the receiver, bottom side, must be stamped "WRF", octagon barrel mfg. 1932-1946, and round barrel mfg. 1947-1950.

$3,150 $2,825 $2,575 $2,100 $1,750 $1,250 $1,000 $750 $575 $475 $400 $250

Add 20% for round barrel.

Mint original pre-war WRF Model 61s in the proper picture box are selling in the $3,750-$4,000 range. Post-war boxed WRF Model 61s (Kraft box) are selling in the $3,800-$4,500 range.

* ***Model 61 Octagon .22 LR*** – .22 LR cal., octagon barrel variation of the Model 61. Disc. approx. 1947.

$4,000 $3,500 $3,000 $2,600 $2,100 $1,750 $1,425 $1,100 $900 $750 $575 $500

* ***Model 61 Octagon .22 WRF*** – .22 WRF cal., octagon barrel variation of the Model 61. Disc. approx. 1947.

$3,900 $3,600 $3,175 $2,750 $2,200 $1,850 $1,525 $1,250 $1,000 $750 $500 $400

* ***Model 61 Magnum*** – similar to Standard 61, but chambered for .22 WMR, three variations include two barrel marking differences and the third has an additional letter "A" stamped on the bottom of the trigger guard assembly, indicating a factory update. Mfg. 1959-1961.

$2,525 $2,300 $2,000 $1,575 $1,325 $1,050 $875 $750 $600 $500 $450 $375

Add $600-$1,000 for rare "WMRF" barrel marking.

Mint original rifles in the proper Kraft box are currently selling for approx. in the $3,500-$4,000 range.

100%	98%	95%	90%	80%	70%	60%	50%	40%	30%	20%	10%

* ***Model 61 Octagon .22 Short*** – .22 Short cal., octagon barrel variation of the Model 61. Disc. approx. 1947.

$4,250	$3,950	$3,625	$3,225	$2,750	$2,200	$1,850	$1,525	$1,250	$1,000	$750	$500

* ***Model 61 Smoothbore*** – .22 cal. shot cartridge only, 24 in. round smoothbore barrel, three variations include the Routledge bore with 3/8 in. muzzle bore diameter and matted frame top (approx. 75 mfg. in the 45,000-47,000 ser. range), second variation is referred to as the Winchester Counter Bore (bore is slightly larger than a .22 cartridge), third variation is the Straight Smoothbore with bore diameter the same as the .22 cartridge.

$4,150	$3,750	$3,300	$2,825	$2,200	$1,850	$1,525	$1,250	$1,000	$750	$500	$400

Add 100% for Routledge bore.

Mint original boxed guns are currently selling for $4,500-$6,000 for the Winchester Counter Bore and Straight Smoothbore, and $8,000-$10,000 for the Routledge Bore.

MODEL 62/62A VISIBLE HAMMER – modern version of 1890, will shoot calibers interchangeably, 23 in. round tapered or octagon barrel. Over 409,000 mfg. between 1932-1958.

$1,550	$1,000	$700	$475	$375	$300	$250	$200	$185	$170	$155	$130

Add 50% for Gallery model (Gallery style loading port).

Add 30% for pre-WWII mfg.

Pre-war Model is 62, distinguishable by small forearm. The Model 62-A was introduced 1940 at approx. serial number 99,200 with minor changes. Model 62A single cal. barrel markings do not add premiums. .22 Short only models without the Winchester roll die receiver marking are more scarce than the so-called "Gallery Rifle" - mint specimens without the roll die marking are approx. $2,000. Also watch for fake roll die markings. Gallery variations of these models will also command sizable premium. Watch for fake boxes and hanging tags on this model, especially with rifles in over 95%+ original condition.

MSR	100%	98%	95%	90%	80%	70%	60%

MODEL 270 – .22 LR cal., tube mag., 20 1/2 in. barrel, checkered walnut pistol grip stock. Mfg. 1963-73.

	$175	$150	$135	$120	$100	$80	$70

* ***Model 270 Plastic Forearm Variation***

	$150	$135	$120	$100	$80	$70	$60

* ***Model 270 Deluxe*** – similar to 270, with select wood, Monte Carlo stock. Mfg. 1965-73.

	$250	$200	$150	$110	$80	$70	$60

MODEL 275 – similar to 270, in .22 WMR cal.

	$200	$175	$150	$135	$100	$80	$70

* ***Model 275 Deluxe*** – similar to 270 Deluxe, in .22 WMR cal.

	$350	$295	$250	$200	$150	$125	$90

MSR	100%	98%	95%	90%	80%	70%	60%

RIFLES: LEVER ACTION - POST 1964 PRODUCTION

MODEL 64 1972-1974 MODEL – .30-30 Win. cal., lever action, 5 shot, 2/3 tube mag., 24 in. barrel, open sight, plain pistol grip stock. Mfg. 1972-74.

	$450	$400	$350	$300	$250	$200	$150

MODEL 71 STANDARD – .348 Win. cal., 24 in. round tapered barrel with buckhorn rear and hooded ramp front sight, top tang safety, 4 shot half mag., uncheckered walnut stock with steel buttplate and forearm, approx. 8 lbs. Mfg. by Miroku 2012 only.

	$1,275	$1,125	$900	$800	$700	$600	$500

Last MSR was $1,470.

MODEL 71 DELUXE – .348 Win. cal., similar to Model 71 Standard, except has deluxe checkered walnut stock and forearm. Mfg. 2012 only.

	$1,475	$1,275	$1,075	$950	$825	$700	$575

Last MSR was $1,660.

MODEL 88 RIFLE (1955-1963 MFG.) – Please see listing under Rifles: Lever Action - 1860-1964.

MODEL 88 RIFLE (1964-1973 MFG.) – .243 Win., .284 Win., or .308 Win. cal., 1964 model with impressed basket weave checkering, no barrel band, 22 in. barrel. Mfg. 1964-1973.

.308 Win. cal.	$1,100	$800	$550	$425	$365	$300	$250
.243 Win. cal.	$1,450	$1,000	$650	$575	$495	$450	$350
.284 Win. cal.	$2,150	$1,800	$1,550	$1,200	$1,000	$750	$600

MODEL 88 CARBINE – introduced 1968, no checkering, one-piece stock, barrel band, 19 in. barrel. Mfg. 1968-1973.

.308 Win. cal. (1968-1973)	$1,625	$1,350	$975	$775	$575	$475	$425
.243 Win. cal.	$2,100	$1,650	$1,400	$1,125	$975	$825	$650
.284 Win. cal.	$3,250	$2,750	$2,325	$2,050	$1,600	$1,300	$1,000

MODEL 150 – .22 LR, 20 1/2 in. barrel, tube mag., hammerless, uncheckered hardwood stock and forearm, sling swivels, approx. 47,400 mfg. 1967-74.

	$135	$115	$95	$70	$60	$50	$40

MODEL 250 – .22 LR, 20 1/2 in. barrel, tube mag., hammerless, checkered pistol grip stock. Mfg. 1963-73.

	$195	$165	$125	$110	$95	$70	$60

* ***Model 250 Deluxe*** – similar to Model 250, with select wood and sling swivels. Mfg. 1965-71.

	$275	$215	$170	$115	$95	$70	$60

MODEL 255 – .22 WMR, otherwise similar to Model 250. Mfg. 1964-70.

	$250	$225	$175	$150	$135	$110	$85

* ***Model 255 Deluxe*** – .22 WMR cal., with select wood and swivels. Mfg. 1965-73.

	$335	$275	$225	$165	$150	$135	$100

MSR	100%	98%	95%	90%	80%	70%	60%

MODEL 1866 150TH COMMEMORATIVE – .44-40 WCF cal., 24 in. octagon barrel with gold ring on muzzle, barrel marked "Winchester Repeating Arms 1866-2016", blade front and ladder-type carbine rear sight, Grade 5/6 satin oil finished uncheckered straight grip walnut stock and forearm, extensively engraved brass receiver with Winchester horse and rider on right side and WRA scroll trademark on left, engraved brass crescent buttplate and forearm cap, 7 1/2 lbs. New 2016.

MSR $3,330	$3,000	$2,650	$2,300	$2,100	$1,900	$1,700	$1,500

MODEL 1873 150TH COMMEMORATIVE – .44-40 WCF cal., 24 in. octagon barrel marked "The American Legend 1866-2016", gold band on muzzle, 13 shot mag., Marbles gold bead front sight, buckhorn rear, and upper tang mounted aperture sights, silver Nitride finished receiver with Winchester 150th Anniversary logo and the WRA scroll trademark, Grade 5/6 checkered walnut straight grip stock and forearm, crescent buttplate and forearm cap are engraved, 7 1/2 lbs. New 2016.

MSR $3,330	$3,000	$2,650	$2,300	$2,100	$1,900	$1,700	$1,500

MODEL 1873 SHORT RIFLE – .357 Mag./.38 Spl., .44-40 Win. (new 2014) or .45 Colt (new 2014) cal., 10 or 11 shot full mag., 20 in. round barrel with semi-buckhorn rear sight and Marbles gold bead front sight, straight grip satin oil finished walnut stock and forearm, crescent buttplate, blue or color case hardened (new 2014) finish, firing pin/striker block safety, rear tang is drilled and tapped, brass carrier block, 7 1/4 lbs. New 2013.

MSR $1,300	$1,150	$995	$850	$725	$625	$525	$425

Add $280 for color case hardened finish (new 2014).

MODEL 1873 SPORTER RIFLE – .357 Mag./.38 Spl. or .44-40 WCF cal., 24 in. octagon barrel with full mag., 13 or 14 shot mag., Marble Arms front sight and semi-buckhorn rear sight, satin finished uncheckered stock and forearm, upper rear tang is drilled and tapped, case colored receiver, lever, crescent buttplate, and forearm cap, 7 1/2 lbs. New 2015.

MSR $1,740	$1,575	$1,375	$1,175	$975	$850	$725	$600

MODEL 1873 SPORTER PISTOL GRIP – .357 Mag./.38 Spl., .45 LC, or .44-40 WCF cal., 24 in. octagon barrel with full mag., 13 or 14 shot mag., Marble Arms front sight and semi-buckhorn rear sight, pistol grip satin finished uncheckered stock and forearm, upper rear tang is drilled and tapped, blue or case colored receiver, lever, crescent buttplate, and forearm cap, 7 1/2 lbs. New 2016.

MSR $1,470	$1,295	$1,075	$900	$825	$700	$575	$475

Add $270 for case colored receiver.

MODEL 1886 DELUXE RIFLE – .45-70 Govt. cal., 24 in. octagon barrel with bead front and buckhorn rear sight, 8 shot mag., color case hardened receiver, lever, crescent buttplate, grip cap, lower tang, and forearm cap, blued barrel and mag. tube, Grade 3/4 satin finished checkered pistol grip stock and forearm, 8 3/8 lbs. New 2016.

MSR $1,740	$1,575	$1,375	$1,175	$975	$850	$725	$600

MSR	100%	98%	95%	90%	80%	70%	60%

MODEL 1886 GRADE I – .45-70 Govt. cal., 26 in. octagon barrel. Mfg. 1997-1998.

	$1,075	$950	$875	$750	$650	$600	$500

Last MSR was $996.

This model was originally manufactured in Japan w/o a top tang safety. However, once these guns were imported, the BATF decided not to approve the configuration unless the guns were shipped back to Japan for a top tang safety update.

* ***Model 1886 High Grade*** – .45-70 Govt. cal., features gold-line receiver engraving with multiple gold animals, polished blue, deluxe checkered walnut stock and forearm with metal cap, 1,000 mfg. 1997 only.

	$1,750	$1,400	$1,075	N/A	N/A	N/A	N/A

Last MSR was $1,588.

MODEL 1886 TAKEDOWN – .45-70 Govt. cal., features original takedown action design, uncheckered semi-pistol grip walnut stock with crescent buttplate, 26 in. octagon barrel with buckhorn rear sight, forend has ebony cap, 9 1/4 lbs. Mfg. 1999 only.

	$1,300	$1,125	$950	$775	$700	$600	$500

Last MSR was $1,140.

MODEL 1886 EXTRA LIGHT GRADE I – .45-70 Govt. cal., 22 in. round tapered barrel, shotgun buttplate, half magazine, high polish receiver and barrel bluing, open sights, uncheckered walnut stock and forearm, 7 1/4 lbs. 3,500 mfg. 2000-2001, and 2010-2012.

	$1,250	$975	$800	$725	$650	$575	$495

Last MSR was $1,270.

* ***Model 1886 Extra Light High Grade*** – similar to Model 1886 Extra Light Grade I, except features engraved elk and whitetail deer and game scenes on blue receiver, extra fancy checkered walnut stock and forearm, 7 1/4 lbs. 1,000 mfg. 2000-2001.

	$1,650	$1,200	$1,000	N/A	N/A	N/A	N/A

Last MSR was $1,440.

MODEL 1886 SHORT RIFLE – .45-70 Govt. cal., 24 in. round barrel with full length mag. tube, adj. buckhorn rear sight and gold bead Marble's front sight, 8 shot mag., blued metal finish, uncheckered satin finished walnut stock and forearm, crescent steel buttplate, approx. 8 3/8 lbs. New 2011.

MSR $1,340	$1,175	$925	$825	$700	$600	$500	$425

MODEL 1892 GRADE I – .357 Mag. (new 1998), .44-40 WCF (new 1998), or .45 LC cal., similar to original Model 1892 Winchester, 24 in. round barrel, top tang mounted manual hammer stop, blue finish with etched receiver engraving, gold trigger, satin finished walnut straight grip stock and forend with metal cap, 6 1/4 lbs. Mfg. 1997-99.

	$785	$635	$485	$400	$350	$295	$250

Last MSR was $744.

MSR	100%	98%	95%	90%	80%	70%	60%

* *Model 1892 Grade I Short Rifle* - .44 Mag. cal., 20 in. round barrel with full mag., uncheckered staight grip walnut stock with crescent buttplate, buckhorn rear sight, high polish blue finish only, 6 lbs. Mfg. 1999-2000.

	$815	$675	$535	$435	$375	$325	$275

Last MSR was $752.

* *Model 1892 Grade I Short Rifle (2009-2012 Mfg.)* - .44 Rem. Mag. or .357 Mag. cal., 20 in. round gloss blue barrel, steel receiver, tube mag., oil finished Grade I straight grip walnut stock with crescent buttplate, short forearm with steel cap, Marble's gold bead front sight, buckhorn style rear sight, tang safety, 6 lbs., 8 oz. Mfg. 2009-2012.

	$995	$850	$725	$625	$500	$400	$300

Last MSR was $1,069.

* *Model 1892 Trapper* - .44-40 WCF, .44 Rem. Mag., .357 Mag., or .45 LC cal., 16 in. round gloss blue barrel, high polish blue steel receiver, tube mag., oil finished Grade I straight grip walnut stock with plastic shotgun style buttplate, Marble's gold bead front sight, buckhorn style rear sight, tang safety, 5 lbs. 14 oz. Mfg. mid-2011-2012.

	$995	$850	$725	$625	$500	$400	$300

Last MSR was $1,069.

* *Model 1892 Trapper Takedown* - .44-40 WCF, .44 Rem. Mag., .357 Mag., or .45 LC cal., 16 in. octagon gloss blue barrel, takedown action, high polish blue steel receiver, tube mag., oil finished Grade I pistol grip checkered walnut stock with polished crescent buttplate, rifle forearm, Marble's gold bead front sight, buckhorn style rear sight, tang safety, 6 lbs. 4 oz. Mfg. mid-2011-2012.

	$1,500	$1,275	$1,050	$900	$775	$650	$525

Last MSR was $1,549.

This model was originally featured as a 2010 SHOT Show Special.

* *Model 1892 Case Hardened Sporter* - .44-40 WCF, .44 Rem. Mag., .357 Mag., or .45 LC cal., 24 in. octagon gloss blue barrel, case colored steel receiver, tube mag., oil finished Grade I straight grip uncheckered walnut stock with case colored crescent buttplate, rifle forearm, with case colored forearm cap, Marble's gold bead front sight, buckhorn style rear sight, tang safety, 7 lbs., 4 oz. Mfg. mid-2011-2012.

	$1,250	$975	$800	$725	$650	$575	$495

Last MSR was $1,269.

* *Model 1892 High Grade* - .45 LC cal., features gold accents and receiver game scene, 1,000 mfg. 1997 only.

	$1,375	$1,125	$825	N/A	N/A	N/A	N/A

Last MSR was $1,285.

MODEL 1892 CARBINE - .357 Mag., .44 Rem. Mag., .44-40 Win., or .45 LC cal., top tang safety, 20 in. round button rifled barrel with barrel band and full length mag., rebounding hammer, blade front and semi-buckhorn rear

MSR	100%	98%	95%	90%	80%	70%	60%

sight, satin finish, uncheckered straight grip walnut stock and forearm, steel contoured carbine strap buttplate, loop lever, 10 shot mag., saddle ring, approx. 6 lbs. Mfg. by Miroku in Japan. Mfg. 2011-2013.

	$1,075	$950	$875	$750	$650	$600	$500

Last MSR was $1,160.

* *Model 1892 Large Loop Carbine* - .357 Mag. (disc. 2015), .44 Rem. Mag., .44-40 Win., or .45 LC cal., similar to Model 1892 Carbine, except has large loop lever and carbine ladder rear sight (disc. 2012) or semi-buckhorn rear sights with Marble Arms front sight (new 2014), 6 lbs. Mfg. 2011-2012, re-introduced 2014.

MSR $1,260	$1,075	$925	$800	$675	$550	$425	$300

MODEL 1892 SHORT RIFLE - .357 Mag. (disc. 2015), .44 Rem. Mag., .or .45 LC cal., 20 in. round barrel with full length mag. tube, 10 shot mag., semi-buckhorn rear sight with Marble Arms gold bead front, steel loading gate, walnut straight grip stock with satin finish, classic rifle-style forearm with blued steel cap and crescent buttplate, 6 lbs. New 2014.

MSR $1,070	$950	$850	$750	$650	$575	$500	$425

MODEL 1892 JOHN WAYNE HIGH GRADE - .44-40 WCF cal., 18 1/2 in. barrel, 9 shot, silver nickel nitride receiver with engraved John Wayne portrait, initials, and flowing banner with "Courage, Strength, Grit" on right side, two portraits and banner with "John Wayne American 1907-2007" on left side, blue loading gate and action screws, ladder style adj. rear sight, saddle ring, blue hammer and trigger, large loop lever, uncheckered walnut stock, limited mfg. of 4,000, first 1,000 offered as match set with Custom Grade. Disc. 2009.

	$2,050	$1,625	$1,400	N/A	N/A	N/A	N/A

Last MSR was $1,999.

MODEL 1892 JOHN WAYNE CUSTOM GRADE - .44-40 WCF cal., 18 1/2 in. barrel with gold signature, 9 shot, blue receiver with engraved John Wayne portrait, initials, and flowing banner with "Courage, Strength, Grit" on right side, two portraits and banner with "John Wayne American 1907-2007" on left side, blue loading gate and action screws, ladder style adj. rear sight, saddle ring, blue hammer and trigger, large loop lever, checkered Grade 5/6 satin walnut stock and forearm, limited mfg. of 1,000. Disc. 2009.

	$3,575	$3,000	$2,450	N/A	N/A	N/A	N/A

Last MSR was $3,499.

MODEL 1895 GRADE I - .270 Win. (disc. 1999), .30-06 (mfg. 1998-1999, reintroduced 2010), .30-40 Krag (new 2010), or .405 Win. (mfg. 2000-2004, reintroduced 2010) cal., similar to original Model 1895 Winchester, checkered straight grip stock and Schnabel forearm, 24 in. round barrel, with buckhorn rear sight, 4 shot mag., top tang safety, blue finish, 8 lbs. Mfg. 1997-2004, and limited production 2010.

	$1,150	$975	$825	$700	$575	$525	$475

Last MSR was $1,179.

MSR	100%	98%	95%	90%	80%	70%	60%

MODEL 1895 LIMITED EDITION - .30-06, similar to original Model 1895 Winchester, blue receiver, 24 in. round barrel, 4 shot mag. (box mag.), uncheckered woodstock and forearm, rear buckhorn sight, 2 piece cocking lever, 8 lbs. 4,000 mfg. 1995-97.

	$1,050	$750	$575	N/A	N/A	N/A	N/A

Last MSR was $853.

* ***Model 1895 Limited Edition High Grade*** - .30-06 (mfg. 1995-99) or .405 Win. (mfg. 2000-2002) cal., same general specifications as the Model 1895 Limited Edition, features older No. 3 engraving pattern with double scenes, gold borders with multiple gold inlays, deluxe checkered walnut stock and forearm. 4,000 mfg. 1995-2002.

	$1,925	$1,400	$1,150	N/A	N/A	N/A	N/A

Last MSR was $1,532.

Add 20% for .405 Win. cal.

MODEL 1895 THEODORE ROOSEVELT 150TH ANNIVERSARY CUSTOM GRADE - .405 Win. cal., high polish blue receiver engraved with North American big game scenes, extensive gold plating, gold "Theodore Roosevelt" signature on receiver, top of barrel is matted, deluxe high grade walnut stock, includes commemorative brochure. 500 mfg. in sets with High Grade matching serial numbers 2008.

	$3,000	$2,500	$1,950	$1,525	$1,200	$995	$795

Last MSR was $3,299.

This model was featured as a 2008 SHOT Show Special.

MODEL 1895 THEODORE ROOSEVELT 150TH ANNIVERSARY HIGH GRADE - .405 Win. cal., nitride finished receiver engraved with North American big game scenes, gold accents, gold "Theodore Roosevelt" signature on receiver, top of barrel is matted, deluxe high grade walnut stock, includes commemorative brochure. 1,000 mfg. 2008.

	$1,650	$1,375	$1,100	$900	$775	$650	$525

Last MSR was $1,599.

This model was featured as a 2008 SHOT Show Special.

MODEL 1895 THEODORE ROOSEVELT SAFARI HIGH GRADE - .405 Win. cal., 4 shot mag., 24 in. blue barrel, checkered Grade II/III walnut stock and forearm, silver nitride receiver with deep engraving, gold African big game inlays and embellishments, matte blue finish, TR "Safari Centennial 1909-2009" medallion on stock, gold signature on trigger guard, buckhorn rear sight, Marbles front sight, drilled and tapped, special matching ser. nos., includes full color box sleeve, special edition hang tag, owner's manual, and hardcover copy of Roosevelt's book, *African Game Trails,* and deluxe double gun case, 8 lbs. Ltd. mfg. of 1,500, the first 1,000 sold as a set with the Custom Grade, remaining 500 sold individually. Mfg. 2009.

	$1,725	$1,450	$1,175	N/A	N/A	N/A	N/A

Last MSR was $1,749.

MSR	100%	98%	95%	90%	80%	70%	60%

MODEL 1895 THEODORE ROOSEVELT SAFARI CUSTOM GRADE TWO GUN SET - .405 Win. cal., 4 shot mag., 24 in. blue barrel, checkered Grade III/IV walnut stock and forearm, blue receiver with deep engraving, gold African big game inlays and embellishments, matte blue finish, TR "Safari Centennial 1909-2009" medallion on stock, jeweled hammer, special matching ser. nos., patterned after Roosevelt's 1895 rifle featured in Cody Firearms Museum, includes full color box sleeve, special edition hang tag, owner's manual, and hardcover copy of Roosevelt's book, *African Game Trails,* and deluxe double gun case, 8 lbs. Ltd. mfg. of 1,000 two gun sets, sold only with Model 1895 Safari High Grade. Mfg. 2009.

$3,650	$3,150	$2,550	N/A	N/A	N/A	N/A

Last MSR was $3,649.

RIFLES: LEVER ACTION - MODEL 94, 1964-2006 MFG.

Due to engineering changes in 1992, all Model 94s and variations (not including the 9422 models) had a crossbolt safety in the upper rear of the receiver which prevents the hammer from contacting the firing pin.

100th Anniversary Model 1894s (mfg. 1994) are marked "1894-1994" on the receiver. During 2003, Winchester discontinued the crossbolt receiver safety, and introduced the new top tang safety.

U.S. Repeating Arms closed its New Haven, CT manufacturing facility on March 31, 2006, and an auction was held on Sept. 27-28, 2006, selling the production equipment and related assets.

AE suffix on the following models indicates angle eject.

Winchester made a major change in Model 94 production when it went to an investment cast receiver during 1964. The Model 94s listed below w/crossbolt safety (1992-2006 mfg.) are not as desirable as those models w/o the crossbolt safety manufactured pre-1992, unless a rare variation, configuration and/or caliber is involved.

MODEL 94 STANDARD MODEL - .30-30 Win., .32 Win. Spl. (disc. 1973, reintroduced 1992), 7-30 Waters (new 1989), .44 Mag. (mfg. circa late 1960s-1970s), .44 Spl. (mfg. 1984), .444 Marlin (mfg. 1984), or .45 LC (mfg. 1984) cal., lever action, 6 or 7 (24 in. barrel only) shot tube mag., 20 or 24 (mfg. 1987-88 only) in. round barrel, open sights, straight walnut stock, two barrel bands on forearm, Angle Eject became standard 1984, 6 1/2 lbs. Mfg. 1964-1997.

$500	$400	$350	$300	$200	$175	$150

Last MSR was $363.

Add 25% for 7-30 Waters cal.

MODEL 94 TRADITIONAL (DELUXE WALNUT) - .30-30 Win., .44 Mag. (new 1999), or .480 Ruger Big Bore (mfg. 2002-2003) cal., similar to Standard Rifle, except has plain (new 1998, not available in .44 Mag. cal.) or checkered walnut stock and forearm, 6 (.30-30 Win. cal.) 10 (.480 Ruger cal.), or 11 (.44 Mag. cal.) shot mag., 6 1/4 lbs. Mfg. 1988-2004.

$600	$500	$400	$300	$225	$200	$175

Last MSR was $436.

MSR	100%	98%	95%	90%	80%	70%	60%

Add $34 for Traditional-CW Model (w/checkered stock and forearm).

Add $57 for .44 Mag. cal. (Traditional-CW Model with checkered stock, mfg. 1999-2004).

Add for .480 Ruger Big Bore cal. (mfg. 2002-2003) - $43 (Traditional) or $105 (Traditional-CW).

Add $55 for 1.5 - 4.5X scope with low mounts (disc.).

MODEL 94 LEGACY ROUND – .30-30 Win., .357 Mag. (new 1997), .44 Mag. (new 1997), or .45 LC (new 1997) cal., 7 (.30-30 Win. cal. only) or 12 shot mag., pistol grip checkered walnut stock and forearm, 20 (disc. 1999) or 24 (new 1997) in. round barrel, 6 3/4 lbs. Mfg. 1995-2006.

	$600	$435	$375	$285	$225	$200	$175

Last MSR was $497.

Subtract $15 for 20 in. barrel.

* ***Model 94 Legacy Round 26 In.*** – .30-30 Win. or .38-55 Win. cal., 7 shot mag., adj. Marble's rear tang sight, similar to Model 94 Legacy Round, except features blue or color case hardened receiver and 26 in. round barrel, 7 lbs. Mfg. 2004-2006.

	$795	$625	$450	$350	$300	$250	$200

Last MSR was $783.

Add 15% for case colored receiver.

Add a slight premium for .38-55 WCF cal.

MODEL 94 LEGACY OCTAGON – .30-30 Win. or .38-55 Win. cal., 7 shot mag., adj. Marble's rear tang sight, crescent buttplate, blue or color case hardened receiver and 26 in. octagon barrel, 7 1/4 lbs. Mfg. 2004-2006.

	$825	$650	$475	$375	$325	$300	$275

Last MSR was $882.

Add 20% for case colored receiver.

Add a slight premium for .38-55 WCF cal.

MODEL 94 RANGER – .30-30 Win. cal. only, 20 in. barrel, uncheckered hardwood stock and forearm, 6 shot mag., 6 1/4 lbs. Mfg. 1985-2006.

	$435	$350	$285	$225	$200	$175	$150

Last MSR was $386.

Add approx. 15% for 4x32 scope with see-through mounts (disc. 1999).

* ***Model 94 Ranger Compact*** – .30-30 Win. or .357 Mag. cal., 16 in. barrel, uncheckered hardwood stock with 12 1/2 LOP with recoil pad, post-style front sight, 5 (.30-30 Win. cal.) or 9 shot mag., 5 7/8 lbs. Mfg. 1998-2004.

	$575	$450	$300	$200	$175	$150	$125

Last MSR was $402.

MODEL 94 TRAILS END – .357 Mag., .44-40 WCF (mfg. 1998-99), .44 Mag., or .45 LC cal., similar to standard rifle, except has 11 shot tube mag., 20 in. barrel, choice of standard or large loop lever (disc. 1998), crossbolt safety, 6 1/2 lbs. Mfg. 1997-2006.

	$775	$625	$475	$300	$225	$175	$150

Last MSR was $480.

Add approx. $20 for large loop lever (disc. 1998).

MSR	100%	98%	95%	90%	80%	70%	60%

* ***Model 94 Trails End Takedown*** – similar to Model 94 Trails End, except has takedown action. Limited mfg. 2006.

	$825	$650	$475	$375	$325	$300	$275

Last MSR was $559.

* ***Model 94 Trails End Octagon*** – similar to Model 94 Trails End, except has octagon barrel, choice of blue or case colored receiver finish, 6 3/4 lbs. Mfg. 2004-2006.

	$895	$750	$600	$425	$300	$250	$200

Last MSR was $757.

Add 15% for case colored receiver.

MODEL 94 TRAILS END HUNTER ROUND – .25-35 Win., .30-30 Win., or .38-55 Win. cal., 20 in. round barrel, 6 shot mag., uncheckered walnut stock and forearm, shotgun buttplate, 6 1/2 lbs. Mfg. 2005-2006.

	$750	$595	$475	$325	$250	$175	$150

Last MSR was $480.

Add a premium for .25-35 WCF or .38-55 WCF cal.

* ***Model 94 Trails End Hunter Round Takedown*** – similar to Model 94 Trails End Hunter Round, except has takedown action. Limited mfg. 2006.

	$850	$650	$500	$350	$275	$225	$200

Last MSR was $559.

* ***Model 94 Trails End Hunter Octagon*** – similar to Model 94 Trails End Hunter, except has blued (new 2006) or case colored receiver and octagon barrel, crescent buttplate. Mfg. 2005-2006.

	$875	$750	$575	$425	$325	$275	$250

Last MSR was $757.

Add 15% for case colored receiver.

Add a premium for .25-35 WCF or .38-55 WCF cal.

MODEL 94 SHORT HUNTER TAKEDOWN – .30-30 Win., .44 Mag., or .450 Marlin cal., takedown action, 18 in. barrel, 6 or 10 (.44 Mag. only) shot mag., uncheckered walnut stock, XS ghost ring sight, 6 lbs. Limited mfg. 2006.

	$850	$650	$500	$350	$275	$225	$200

Last MSR was $587.

MODEL 94 PACK RIFLE – .30-30 Win. or .44 Mag. cal., 18 in. barrel, 4 or 5 shot 3/4 mag., over-dimension walnut stock and forearm cap w/o checkering, removable hood sight, 6 1/4 lbs. Mfg. 2000-2001.

	$495	$400	$325	$250	$200	$175	$140

Last MSR was $496.

MODEL 94 TIMBER CARBINE – .444 Marlin (disc. 2001) or .450 Marlin (new 2004) cal., 18 in. ported barrel with 4 (.450 Marlin cal. only) or 5 (disc. 2001) shot 2/3 mag., top tang safety, checkered semi-pistol grip stock and forearm, blue finish only, adj. XS ghost ring rear sight (new 2004), hooded front sight (disc. 2001) or ramp style front sight, 6 lbs. Mfg. 1999-2001, reintroduced 2004-2006.

	$995	$875	$750	$625	$500	$375	$225

Last MSR was $623.

MSR	100%	98%	95%	90%	80%	70%	60%

* ***Model 94 Timber Carbine Scout*** – .30-30 Win. or .44 Mag. cal., similar to Model 94 Timber Carbine, 18 in. non-ported barrel with rail base, 4 (.30-30 Win.) or 8 (.44 Mag.) shot mag., XS ghost ring sights, uncheckered walnut stock and forearm, 6 lbs. Mfg. 2005-2006.

	$795	$625	$450	$350	$300	$250	$200

Last MSR was $623.

* ***Model 94 Timber Carbine Scout Takedown*** – similar to Model 94 Timber Scout, except has takedown action and Pachmayr recoil pad. Limited mfg. 2006.

	$895	$750	$600	$425	$300	$250	$200

Last MSR was $699.

MODEL 94 WIN-TUFF RIFLE – .30-30 Win. cal., similar to Model 94 Rifle, except has laminated hardwood stock and forearm with checkering. Drilled and tapped for scope mounts. Mfg. 1987-disc.

	$375	$300	$250	$200	$180	$160	$140

Last MSR was $404.

MODEL 94 BLACK SHADOW – .30-30 Win. or .44 Mag./.44 Spl. cal., 20 or 24 (.30- 30 Win. cal. only) in. barrel, 4 or 5 shot mag., non-glare finish, black composite synthetic stock with recoil pad and Fuller forearm, approx. 6 1/4 lbs. Mfg. 1998-2000.

	$575	$450	$325	$225	$175	$150	$135

Last MSR was $381.

* ***Model 94 Black Shadow Big Bore*** – .444 Marlin cal., 20 in. barrel only, otherwise similar to Model 94 Black Shadow, 6 1/2 lbs. Mfg. 1998-2000.

	$550	$425	$325	$250	$200	$150	$135

Last MSR was $394.

MODEL 94 TRAPPER – .30-30 Win., .357 Mag. (mfg. beginning 1992), .44 Mag./.44 Spl. (new 1985), or .45 LC (new 1985) cal., 16 in. barrel, side ejection, walnut stock, 5 (.30-30 Win. cal.) or 9 shot tube mag., blue finish, dovetailed front sight, 6 lbs. Mfg. 1980-2006.

	$750	$595	$475	$325	$250	$175	$150

Last MSR was $470.

* ***Model 94 Trapper Compact*** – .357 Mag. cal., similar to Model 94 Trapper, except has 12 1/2 in. LOP stock. Limited mfg. 2006.

	$850	$650	$500	$350	$275	$225	$200

Last MSR was $486.

MODEL 94 BIG BORE – .307 Win. (disc. 1998), .356 Win. (disc. 1998), or .375 Win. (disc. 1987), or .444 Marlin (new 1998) cal., angled ejection port provides scope mounting, checkered walnut Monte Carlo stock with recoil pad, 20 in. barrel, 6 shot mag., sling swivels, 6 1/2 lbs. New 1983.

	$850	$650	$500	$350	$275	$225	$200

Last MSR was $465.

Add 25% for .356 Win. or .375 Win. cal.

Also mfg. in a top eject (pre-USRA). This model had an "XTR" suffix until 1989.

MSR	100%	98%	95%	90%	80%	70%	60%

MODEL 94 HERITAGE CUSTOM 1 OF 100 - .38-55 WCF cal., special edition for the NSSF Heritage Fund, features Winchester's historic No. 2 pattern hand engraved with 24Kt. gold inlays and individually signed by the engraver, deluxe spade checkered straight grip stock and forearm with metal cap, 1/2 round, 1/2 octagon 26 in. barrel, 6 3/4 lbs. Mfg. by the custom shop 2002-2003.

	$5,225	$3,750	$2,250	N/A	N/A	N/A	N/A

Last MSR was $5,200.

MODEL 94 HERITAGE HIGH GRADE 1 OF 1000 - .38-55 WCF cal., special edition for the NSSF Heritage Fund, features Winchester's historic No. 3 engraving pattern with 24Kt. gold inlays, deluxe checkered straight grip stock and forearm with metal cap, 1/2 round, 1/2 octagon 26 in. barrel, signed by engraver with factory letter, ser. no. prefix HER, 6 3/4 lbs. Mfg. 2002 only. While 1,000 rifles were scheduled to be manufactured, only 255 were mfg.

	$2,400	$1,875	$1,700	N/A	N/A	N/A	N/A

Last MSR was $1,883.

MODEL 94 CUSTOM LIMITED EDITION - .44-40 WCF (mfg. 2000 only) or .38-55 WCF (new 2001) cal., case colored receiver and 24 in. octagon match (.44-40 WCF cal. only) or 1/2 round, 1/2 octagon (.38-55 WCF cal. only) barrel with satin bluing, full (.44-40 WCF only) or 3/4 mag. tube, spade checkered straight grip walnut stock and forearm with metal cap, 7 1/4 (.38-55 WCF cal.) or 7 3/4 lbs. Only 75 mfg. in .44-40 WCF cal. 2000-2002.

	$2,600	$2,025	$1,800	N/A	N/A	N/A	N/A

Last MSR was $2,393.

MODEL 94 NEW GENERATION CUSTOM - .30-30 Win. cal., fancy pistol grip stock and long forearm with spade checkering, high lustre bluing with custom scroll engraving and hand engraved gold moose on right side of frame and gold doe/buck on left, new tang safety, 20 in. barrel. Limited mfg. 2003-2004.

	$3,000	$2,425	$1,975	N/A	N/A	N/A	N/A

Last MSR was $2,995.

MODEL 94 LIMITED EDITION CENTENNIAL - .30-30 Win. cal., crossbolt safety, manufactured to commemorate the 100th anniversary of the Model 94 in 1994.

* ***Model 94 Limited Edition Centennial Grade I*** - features No. 9 style Winchester engraving pattern (rolled) on both sides of receiver, 26 in. half-round half-octagonal barrel, pistol grip stock and forearm with cut checkering, half mag., open sights, crescent buttplate, 12,000 mfg. 1994.

	$1,075	$850	$675	N/A	N/A	N/A	N/A

Last MSR was $811.

* ***Model 94 Limited Edition Centennial High Grade*** - features No. 6 style Winchester engraving pattern (rolled) on both sides of receiver with gold outlines and 2 gold animals (mountain sheep and deer), Lyman

MSR	100%	98%	95%	90%	80%	70%	60%

No. 2 tang mounted rear sight, F-style checkering and carving, deluxe walnut, 26 in. half-round half-octagonal barrel, half-mag., crescent buttplate, 3,000 mfg. 1994.

	$2,150	$1,675	$1,250	N/A	N/A	N/A	N/A

Last MSR was $1,272.

* ***Model 94 Limited Edition Centennial Custom High Grade*** - .30 WCF cal., features No. 5 style Winchester engraving pattern (hand-executed) on both sides of greyed receiver, etched by Baron Technology, gold outline panel scenes featuring caribou and pronghorns, Lyman No. 2 upper tang sight, F-style checkering and carving, 26 in. half-round half-octagonal barrel, half-mag., crescent buttplate, 94 mfg. in 1994.

	$5,995	$4,850	$3,950	N/A	N/A	N/A	N/A

Last MSR was $4,684.

MODEL 94 XTR - .30-30 Win. or 7-30 Waters (new 1985) cal., 20 or 24 (7-30 Waters only) in. barrel, checkered select walnut, hooded front sight (except 7-30 Waters which has dovetailed front blade), 6 1/2 lbs. Disc. 1988.

	$695	$585	$450	$335	$250	$175	$150

Last MSR was $285.

Add $100 for 7-30 Waters cal. rifle.

The XTR nomenclature was disc. 1988.

* ***Model 94 XTR Deluxe*** - .30-30 Win. cal. only, deluxe American walnut stock and lengthened forearm with fancy checkering, 20 in. barrel with deluxe script, rubber buttpad. Mfg. 1987-88 only.

	$725	$615	$475	$335	$250	$175	$150

Last MSR was $426.

MODEL 94 .44 MAG. S.R.C. - .44 Mag. cal., top eject, 20 in. barrel, SRC. Mfg. 1967-1972.

	$650	$515	$325	$235	$175	$150	$135

MODEL 94 CLASSIC SERIES - .30-30 Win. cal., 20 or 26 in. octagon barrel. Approx. 47,000 mfg. 1967-1970.

	$625	$465	$295	$225	$175	$150	$135

MODEL 94 ANTIQUE CARBINE - similar to Standard, with case hardened scroll engraved receiver, gold-plated saddle ring. Mfg. 1964-1983.

	$600	$500	$400	$300	$225	$200	$175

MODEL 94 CARBINE - .30-30 Win. cal., uncheckered walnut stock and hooded front sight, w/o saddle ring. Manufactured circa 1976.

	$600	$500	$400	$300	$225	$200	$175

MODEL 94 WRANGLER - .32 Win. Special, top ejection, saddle ring, 16 in. barrel, oversized loop lever, western scene roll engraved on receiver, "Wrangler" logo on barrel, 5 shot mag. Only 7,947 mfg. 1983-1984.

	$625	$465	$295	$225	$175	$150	$135

MSR	100%	98%	95%	90%	80%	70%	60%

MODEL 94 WRANGLER IA - .30-30 Win. cal., top ejection, 18 in. barrel, small loop lever, western scene roll engraved on receiver, "Wrangler IA" logo on barrel. Limited mfg. 1983 only.

	$695	$585	$450	$335	$250	$175	$150

MODEL 94 WRANGLER II - .32 Win. Spl. (disc. 1984) or .38-55 WCF cal., angle ejection, 16 in. barrel, saddle ring, oversized loop-shaped lever, western scene roll-engraved receiver, 5 shot mag., uncheckered stock and forearm, "Wrangler II" logo on barrel, 6 1/8 lbs. Made 1983-85 only.

	$625	$465	$295	$225	$175	$150	$135

Last MSR was $275.

MODEL 94 WRANGLER LARGE LOOP - .30-30 Win., .44 Mag., or .45 LC (new 1999) cal., 16 in. barrel, has large loop lever, uncheckered walnut stock and forearm, blue finish, open sights, 6 lbs. Mfg. 1992-99.

	$465	$385	$295	$215	$175	$150	$140

Last MSR was $400.

MODEL 94 DU - .30-30 Win. cal., approx. 2,800 rifles were mfg. in the U.S. during 1986. Serial numbered DU-860001-DU-8628000.

	$1,075	$850	$675	$550	$425	$325	$250

MODEL 94 DU GOLD - .30-30 Win. cal., gold plated receiver, 300 mfg. 1986. Serial numbered DU-863000-DU-863299.

	$1,500	$1,325	$1,050	$800	$675	$550	$450

MODEL 9417 TRADITIONAL - .17 HMR cal., 11 shot mag., 20 1/2 in. barrel, checkered straight grip stock and forearm, full mag., 6 lbs. Limited mfg. 2003-2004.

	$1,050	$950	$825	$600	$500	$400	$300

Last MSR was $515.

MODEL 9417 LEGACY - .17 HMR cal., 11 shot mag., 22 1/2 in. barrel, checkered pistol grip grip stock and longer forearm, 6 lbs. Limited mfg. 2003-2004.

	$1,150	$1,025	$850	$600	$500	$400	$300

Last MSR was $551.

MODEL 9422 XTR TRADITIONAL (STANDARD WALNUT) - .22 LR or .22 WMR cal., takedown, 20 1/2 in. round barrel, 15 shot (LR) or 11 shot (Mag. cal.) mag., grooved forged steel receiver, uncheckered (early mfg.) or checkered straight grip, uncheckered or checkered high gloss (disc.) or satin weather resistant finish (new 1988) walnut stock and forearm, regular or large loop (mfg. 1998-99) lever, sights, 6 lbs. Mfg. 1972-2004.

	$825	$650	$475	$375	$325	$300	$275

Last MSR was $479.

Add 25% for early pre-XTR mfg. with uncheckered straight grip stock.

Add 25% for large loop lever (disc. 1999).

Add approx. 15% for .22 WMR cal.

This model had an "XTR" suffix until 1989. Earlier mfg., including pre-XTR and early XTR rifles, had no checkering.

MSR	100%	98%	95%	90%	80%	70%	60%

MODEL 9422 XTR CLASSIC – same general specifications as Model 9422 XTR Standard, except has 22 1/2 in. barrel and non-checkered, satin finished, pistol grip walnut stock and extended forearm, stock also has fluted comb with crescent steel buttplate, curved finger lever, 6 1/2 lbs. Mfg. 1985-1987.

	$995	$875	$775	$695	$600	$475	$325

Last MSR was $301.

MODEL 9422 LEGACY – .22 LR or .22 WMR (new 1999) cal., 22 1/2 in. barrel with deluxe checkered semi-pistol grip stock, 11 (.22 WMR) or 15 shot non-full length mag., 6 lbs. Mfg. 1998-2004.

	$995	$875	$775	$695	$600	$475	$325

Last MSR was $512.

Add 15% for .22 WMR cal.

MODEL 9422 SPECIAL EDITION TRADITIONAL TRIBUTE – .22 LR or .22 WMR cal., 20 1/2 in. round barrel, features a Winchester horse and rider engraved on right side of receiver, and Model 9422 Tribute banner on left, checkered straight grip walnut stock and forearm, 6 lbs. While 9,422 were scheduled to be mfg. 2005-2006, this production total was not achieved.

	$950	$795	$625	$425	$300	$250	$200

Last MSR was $516.

Add 10% for .22 WMR cal.

MODEL 9422 SPECIAL EDITION LEGACY TRIBUTE – .22 LR or .22 WMR cal., similar to Model 9422 Special Edition Traditional, except has 22 1/2 in. barrel and pistol grip stock with crescent recoil pad, although 9,422 were scheduled to be mfg. 2005-2006, production total was not achieved.

	$1,225	$1,125	$895	$600	$500	$400	$300

Last MSR was $551.

Add 10% for .22 WMR cal.

MODEL 9422 HIGH GRADE TRADITIONAL TRIBUTE – .22 LR or .22 WMR cal., 20 1/2 in. round barrel, features silver banner with Model 9422 Tribute on left receiver side and horse and rider on right side, etched engraving on blued receiver, checkered straight grip walnut stock and forearm, 6 lbs. Although 9,422 were scheduled to be mfg. 2005-2006, production total was not achieved.

	$1,650	$1,400	$1,075	$850	$675	$550	$450

Last MSR was $1,050.

Add 10% for .22 WMR cal.

MODEL 9422 HIGH GRADE LEGACY TRIBUTE – .22 LR or .22 WMR cal., similar to High Grade Traditional Tribute, except has 22 1/2 in. barrel and crescent recoil pad, pistol grip stock, 6 lbs. Although 9,422 were scheduled to be mfg. 2005-2006, production total was not achieved.

	$1,750	$1,450	$1,150	$850	$675	$550	$450

Last MSR was $1,085.

Add 5% for .22 WMR cal.

MSR	100%	98%	95%	90%	80%	70%	60%

MODEL 9422 CUSTOM TRIBUTE – .22 LR cal., 20 1/2 in. barrel, engraved silver plated receiver with gold inlaid Model 9422 Tribute banner on left side of receiver and gold horse and rider on right, engine turned bolt and extractor, gold plated trigger, select walnut with fleur-de-lis checkering on straight grip stock and forearm, 6 lbs. 222 mfg. by the Custom Shop 2005.

	$3,400	$2,575	$1,850	N/A	N/A	N/A	N/A

Last MSR was $2,313.

MODEL 9422 TRAPPER – .22 S, L, LR, or .22 WMR (new 1998), 16 1/2 in. barrel, checkered walnut stock and forearm, 11 (.22 LR), 8 (.22 WMR), 15 (.22 S), or 12 (.22 L) shot tube mag., 5 3/4 lbs. Mfg. 1996-2001.

	$1,150	$925	$825	$600	$500	$400	$300

Last MSR was $437.

Add $150 for .22 WMR cal.

500 Trapper special edition models were made for W.A.C.A. with engraving and silver and gold wash. Current estimated value is $1,300 for NIB condition. C.D.N.N. Sports Inc. in Abilene, TX ordered 1,002 Trapper models (501 in .22 WMR and 501 in .22 S, L, LR cal.) with case colored receivers and special serial numbers. Current estimated value is $1,200 for NIB condition.

Some barrel markings on this model may not have the "S" for .22 Short cal.

MODEL 9422 WIN-CAM – .22 WMR cal. only, similar to 9422 XTR Standard, except has checkered greenish laminated hardwood stock and forearm. Mfg. 1987-1997.

	$895	$750	$600	$425	$300	$250	$200

Last MSR was $424.

MODEL 9422 WINTUFF – .22 LR or .22 WMR cal., 20 1/2 in. barrel, checkered laminated brown hardwood stock and forearm, 6 1/4 lbs. Mfg. 1988-1999.

	$750	$595	$475	$325	$250	$175	$150

Last MSR was $423.

Add 10% for .22 WMR cal.

MODEL 9422 HIGH-GRADE – .22 LR cal., features engraved receiver with raccoon and coonhound, deluxe checkered walnut stock and forearm. Mfg. 1995-96 only.

	$950	$795	$625	$425	$300	$250	$200

Last MSR was $489.

MODEL 9422 HIGH GRADE SERIES II – .22 LR cal., 20 1/2 in. barrel, high grade walnut stock and forearm with cut checkering, engraved receiver includes dog and squirrels, 6 lbs. Mfg. 1998-99.

	$975	$815	$635	$425	$300	$250	$200

Last MSR was $504.

MSR	100%	98%	95%	90%	80%	70%	60%

MODEL 9422 25TH ANNIVERSARY GRADE I - .22 LR cal., deluxe checkered walnut stock and forearm, engraved receiver with Winchester Horse and Rider, 2,500 mfg. 1997 only, inventory remained through 1999.

	$1,125	$895	$800	$600	$500	$400	$300

Last MSR was $606.

MODEL 9422 25TH ANNIVERSARY HIGH GRADE - .22 LR cal., extra deluxe checkered walnut stock and forearm, high gloss blue and engraved receiver with Winchester Horse and Rider, featuring silver borders and lever accents, 250 mfg. 1997 only.

	$2,000	$1,550	$1,050	N/A	N/A	N/A	N/A

Last MSR was $1,348.

RIFLES: LEVER ACTION - MODELS 94 AND 1894, 2010-CURRENT

The following models in this category are manufactured in Miroku, Japan beginning 2010.

MODEL 1894 OLIVER WINCHESTER 200TH ANNIVERSARY CUSTOM GRADE - .30-30 Win. cal., 24 in. half-round, half-octagon barrel, top tang safety, buckhorn rear sight, Marble's front sight, checkered Grade IV/V walnut stock with high gloss finish, 8 shot mag., blue receiver with deep scroll engraving, left side has Winchester Repeating Arms crest, right side has "Two Hundred Years, Oliver F. Winchester" and "1810-2010" in gold, Oliver F. Winchester signature in gold on top of bolt, approx. 8 lbs. 500 mfg. in sets with High Grade during 2010 only.

	$2,250	$1,850	$1,475	N/A	N/A	N/A	N/A

Last MSR was $1,959.

MODEL 1894 OLIVER WINCHESTER 200TH ANNIVERSARY HIGH GRADE - .30-30 Win. cal., 24 in. half-round, half-octagon barrel, top tang safety, buckhorn rear sight, Marble's front sight, checkered Grade II/III walnut stock with high gloss finish, 8 shot mag., silver nitride receiver with delicate scroll engraving, left side has Winchester Repeating Arms crest, and right has "Two Hundred Years, Oliver F. Winchester" and "1810-2010" in gold, Oliver F. Winchester signature in gold on top of bolt, approx. 8 lbs. 500 mfg. in sets with Custom Grade during 2010 only, remaining quantities were sold individually.

	$1,595	$1,175	$975	N/A	N/A	N/A	N/A

Last MSR was $1,469.

MODEL 94 CARBINE - .30-30 Win. or .38-55 Win. cal., 7 shot tube mag., 20 in. barrel with barrel band, semi-buckhorn rear sight and Marbles blade front sight, uncheckered satin finished plain walnut stock and forearm, blue metal finish, top tang safety, drilled and tapped, 6 1/2 lbs. New 2013.

MSR $1,200	$1,050	$925	$825	$700	$600	$500	$400

MSR	100%	98%	95%	90%	80%	70%	60%

MODEL 94 SHORT RIFLE - .30-30 Win., .38-55 Win. (new 2012), or .450 Marlin (new 2015) cal., top tang safety, similar to Model 94 Sporter, except has 20 in. round barrel and uncheckered satin finished walnut stock and forearm, 7 shot mag., black synthetic buttplate, approx. 6 3/4 lbs. New 2011.

MSR $1,230	$1,075	$950	$825	$700	$600	$500	$400

MODEL 94 SPORTER - .30-30 Win. or .38-55 Win. cal., 24 in. half-round, half-octagon barrel, 8 shot full length mag., all steel construction, includes knurled hammer spur, rebounding hammer, Marble's front sight and semi-buckhorn rear sight, checkered satin finished walnut stock and forearm with crescent buttplate, top tang safety, articulated cartridge stop, blue finish, satin finished stock, approx. 7 1/2 lbs. New 2011.

MSR $1,400	$1,275	$1,075	$950	$825	$675	$550	$425

MODEL 94 TRAILS END TAKEDOWN - .30-30 Win., .38-55 Win. (new 2014) or .450 Marlin cal., top tang safety, 20 in. ported round barrel with Marble's front sight and semi buckhorn rear sight, satin finished plain walnut stock and forearm, .450 Marlin cal. has Pachmayr decelerator recoil pad, 6 shot mag., approx. 6-3/4 lbs. New 2012.

MSR $1,460	$1,275	$1,025	$900	$775	$650	$525	$400

MODEL 94 150TH COMMEMORATIVE - .30-30 Win. cal., 24 in. octagon barrel marked "The American Legend 1866-2016", gold band on muzzle, 8 shot mag., gold bead front and buckhorn rear sight, silver Nitride finished receiver with Winchester 150th Anniversary logo and the WRA scroll trademark, Grade 5/6 checkered walnut straight grip stock and forearm, crescent buttplate and forearm cap are engraved, 7 1/2 lbs. New 2016.

MSR $2,670	$2,400	$2,100	$1,900	$1,700	$1,500	$1,350	$1,200

RIFLES: BOLT ACTION - PRE-1964 MODEL 70

The Pre-'64 Model 70 Bolt Action Rifle (advertised by Winchester throughout much of its production history as "The Rifleman's Rifle") was produced from 1936 through 1963. Collectors recognize three major manufacturing periods: "Pre-War" (1936-1941); "Transition" (1946-1948); and "Latter" (1949-1963). There were only eighteen (18) original chamberings, these are: .22 Hornet, .220 Swift, .243 Win.(standard cal.), .250 Savage (.250-3000), .257 Roberts, .264 Win. Mag.(standard cal.), .270 Win.(standard cal.), 7x57mm Mauser, .300 Savage (standard cal.), .300 H&H, .300 Win. Mag., .30-06 (standard cal., .30 Govt. '06 Springfield - approx. 80% of total mfg. by cal.), .308 Win. (standard in Featherweight Style only), .338 Win. Mag.(standard cal.), .35 Rem.(standard cal.), .358 Win. (in Featherweight Style only), .375 H&H, and .458 Win. Mag. (in Super Grade AFRICAN Style only). It is important to note that every caliber was not available during each manufacturing period. Any other caliber encountered (including 7.65mm Argentine and 9x57mm Mauser) may be regarded as either special ordered or non-original. Magazine capacities are as follows: "Standard Calibers" (including .22 Hornet) five (5) rounds; "H&H Magnums" (.300 & .375) four (4) rounds; and "Winchester Short Magnums" (.264, .300, .338, .458) three (3) rounds. The rifle was produced in a myriad of styles and variations - most of which are covered individually. Unfortunately, a veritable "cottage industry" has developed involving the alteration, "upgrading," and/or outright faking of these guns. Be careful when contemplating a purchase of any rare Model 70 (and get a receipt describing the purchase accurately).

MODEL 70 PRE-WWII PRODUCTION STANDARD GRADE - 12 standard cals., 5 shot mag., 4 shot mag. on Magnums, 24, 25, or 26 in. barrel, open sights, checkered walnut pistol grip stock, approx. ser. range is 1-41,750. Mfg. 1937-1941.

MSR	100%	98%	95%	90%	80%	70%	60%
Standard Cals. (see listings above)	$2,275	$1,975	$1,725	$1,150	$875	$725	$525
.22 Hornet	$3,350	$3,000	$2,550	$1,925	$1,525	$1,200	$950
.220 Swift	$2,600	$2,325	$1,925	$1,150	$975	$800	$650
.257 Roberts	$4,000	$3,500	$2,925	$1,825	$1,450	$1,050	$775
.270 Win.	$2,400	$2,225	$1,925	$1,250	$975	$800	$650
.300 H&H	$3,500	$3,100	$2,525	$1,850	$1,425	$1,100	$825
.375 H&H	$4,650	$3,900	$3,450	$2,450	$1,975	$1,600	$1,200
7x57mm Mauser	$6,000	$5,400	$4,500	$3,800	$3,100	$2,625	$2,100
.250-3000 Savage	$5,600	$5,100	$4,650	$3,900	$3,200	$2,625	$2,100

Add approx. 100% for Super Grades in common cals.

Values listed assume original, unaltered specimens - modifications/ alterations to either the metal or wood surfaces can reduce prices by large amounts. All pre-war Model 70s have only 2 holes drilled in the front of the receiver (none in the back). An extra set of "holes" can decrease value as much as 50%. Some pre-WWII Model 70s have a "D" suffix indicating a doubled up serial number - this variation will command a premium because of its rarity. The Model 70 is one gun for which caliber ranks before condition in terms of desirability. Specimens encountered in under 60% condition will not decrease in price substantially since almost any shooter is worth $500-$600.

There are more fakes than legitimate specimens in cals. 7x57mm and .250-3000 Savage!

Rare cals. such as the .300 Savage, .35 Rem., 7.65mm, and 9x57mm Mauser are seldom encountered, and their scarcity precludes accurate price evaluation. Cals. 7.65mm and 9x57mm Mauser were special order only and were made up from leftover Model 54 barrels. Also, the original factory box, papers, and hanging tag will add 25%-30% to the values listed. Believe it or not, there are getting to be a lot of fake Model 70 boxes that have been intentionally aged. Carefully screen NIB (watch the hanging tag also) specimens in this model for possible expert refinishing.

MODEL 70 CARBINE (MFG. 1936-1946) – available in most cals. during its period, 20 in. barrel, short rifle variation of the Pre-'64 Model 70 (Winchester never officially used the "Carbine" terminology). If original, front sight base will be an integral part of the barrel. All carbines were disc. shortly after WWII. Beware of fakes.

Add 50%-75% for carbine variations mfg. 1936-1946 with 20 in. barrel in .22 Hornet

MSR	100%	98%	95%	90%	80%	70%	60%

(watch for fakes with cut off barrels, rechambered "K" models, and examine the front sight carefully), .250-3000 Savage, .257 Roberts, .270 Win., 7mm, or .30-06 (most common) cal.

MODEL 70 TRANSITION (MFG. 1946-1948) – several of the post-war Model 70s mfg. between 1946-48 exhibit the pre-war receiver characteristics and have a transition safety. This variation is more rare than normal models, ser. no. range is 60,000-100,000.

Add 10%-20% above values for post-Transitional models.

On this Transitional Model, the receiver bridge may or may not be factory drilled.

MODEL 70 STANDARD GRADE (1946-1963 PRODUCTION) - 18 standard cals. including .22 Hornet, .220 Swift, .243 Win., .250 Savage (.250-3000), .257 Roberts, .264 Win. Mag., .270 Win., 7x57mm Mauser, .300 Savage, .300 H&H, .300 Win. Mag., .30-06, .308 Win., .338 Win. Mag., .35 Rem., .358 Win., and .375 H&H, 5 shot mag., 4 shot mag. on Magnums, 24, 25, or 26 in. barrel, open sights, checkered walnut pistol grip stock, ser. range is 52,549-581,471. Mfg. 1946-1963.

	100%	98%	95%	90%	80%	70%	60%
Standard cals. (those cals. not listed below)	$1,450	$1,200	$1,100	$900	$650	$550	$500
.22 Hornet	$3,750	$3,350	$2,700	$2,350	$1,625	$1,225	$1,050
.220 Swift	$2,450	$1,975	$1,800	$1,125	$825	$625	$550
.243 Win.	$2,100	$1,875	$1,475	$1,050	$900	$775	$700
.257 Roberts	$3,250	$2,500	$2,075	$1,650	$1,150	$800	$625
.264 Mag. (Westerner)	$2,200	$1,900	$1,750	$1,125	$850	$650	$550
.270 Win.	$1,850	$1,625	$1,375	$1,100	$825	$625	$525
.300 H&H	$2,650	$2,300	$1,775	$1,175	$975	$750	$625
.300 Win. Mag.	$3,850	$3,400	$2,900	$2,375	$1,800	$1,325	$1,050
.338 Win. Mag.	$3,350	$2,700	$2,400	$1,650	$1,250	$1,000	$825
.375 H&H	$4,000	$3,500	$3,150	$2,375	$2,150	$1,850	$1,500

Add 10% for .300 H&H or .375 H&H if rear receiver is not drilled and tapped.

Add 30% for stainless steel barrel in .300 H&H or .270 Win. cal.

Values listed assume original, unaltered specimens - modifications/ alterations to either the metal or wood surfaces can reduce prices by large amounts. Most post-war Model 70s are drilled on top of the receiver (2 holes in front and 2 holes in back) to accept scope mounts (except early .300 and .375 H&H cals.). Pre-1962 mfg. Model 70s are desirable since Winchester implemented manufacturing techniques that lowered the quality beginning in 1964.

Rare cals. such as the .250-3000, .300 Savage, .308 Win. (extremely rare, so watch for fakes), .35 Rem., and 7x57mm Mauser are seldomly seen or sold. Premiums depend on the rarity of the caliber and original condition.

Believe it or not, there are getting to be a lot of fake Model 70 boxes that have been intentionally aged. Carefully screen NIB (watch the hanging tag also) specimens in this model.

MSR	100%	98%	95%	90%	80%	70%	60%

MODEL 70 SUPER GRADE - similar to Standard Model, except has deluxe wood, black pistol grip cap and forend tip, all Super Grades have a raised cheekpiece with deluxe wraparound checkering, and Super Grade marked floorplate. Disc. 1960.

.375 H&H	$7,000	$6,150	$5,250	$4,600	$4,000	$3,500	$3,000

A general rule for Super Grades is that if you add 100% to the standard grade in similar cals., values should be rather close. For .375 H&H cal., values are listed.

Later Model 70 Super Grades have jeweled action components and rust blued barrels.

MODEL 70 SUPER GRADE AFRICAN - .458 Win. Mag. cal. only, front swivel base relocated and attached to bottom of barrel, nearly all possess one or two visible stock crossbolts (usually covered with Bakelite). Most have all action components (bolt body, extractor, extractor ring and magazine follower) jeweled (i.e., engine turned), rust blued barrel. 1,226 mfg. 1956-63.

	$8,000	$7,500	$7,000	$6,500	$5,500	$4,500	$4,000

While other Super Grades were disc. approx. 1960, the "AFRICAN" continued in that style until the end of all production. Normal attrition and collectors owning more than one contribute to extreme rarity. Retains considerable "shooter" value in lesser external conditions. Watch for cracked and/or repaired stocks.

MODEL 70 FEATHERWEIGHT - lightened version of Standard, .243 Win., .264 Win. Mag. (Westerner, mfg. 1962-1963), .270 Win., .308 Win., .30-06, or .358 Win. cal., 22 (standard) or 26 (Westerner only) in. barrel, aluminum trigger guard and floor plate, plastic (introduced circa 1958) or aluminum buttplate, ser. range is 206,626-581,471. Mfg. 1952-1963.

.243 Win.	$1,700	$1,475	$1,200	$950	$775	$650	$575
.264 Mag. (Westerner)	$2,600	$2,200	$1,875	$1,550	$1,250	$1,000	$850
.270 Win.	$1,625	$1,450	$1,275	$1,050	$900	$775	$650
.30-06	$1,700	$1,475	$1,200	$950	$775	$650	$575
.308 Win.	$1,700	$1,475	$1,200	$950	$775	$650	$575
.358 Win. Alum. butt only	$4,350	$3,750	$2,950	$2,450	$1,950	$1,600	$1,250

Add 10-20% for .30-06, .308 Win., .243 Win., or .270 Win. cal. models with aluminum buttplate, depending on condition.

The .358 Win. cal. is rare because Winchester had problems with this cal. Many of them were exchanged for other calibers, and the result is that original guns are rare in this cal. The .264 Mag. Westerner was only mfg. with a Win. recoil pad.

MODEL 70 SUPER GRADE FEATHERWEIGHT - .243 Win., .270 Win., .30-06, or .308 Win. cal. only, because of inconsistencies of Super Grade action component jeweling (i.e., engine turning), a simple stock and hinged floorplate change can create an "instant" Super Grade Featherweight (check stock carefully for wood filling near area of Standard Super Grade rear sight "boss" in barrel channel), all Super

MSR	100%	98%	95%	90%	80%	70%	60%

Grade Featherweights have a raised cheekpiece with wraparound "fish tail" checkering, all have rust blued barrels, less than 1,000 mfg.

	$7,000	$6,500	$6,000	$5,000	$4,000	$3,000	$2,500

This is perhaps the rarest variation of the Pre-'64 Model 70 - beware of fakes.

MODEL 70 NATIONAL MATCH – similar to Standard, with target stock and scope bases, .30-06 only. Disc. 1960.

	$3,500	$3,150	$2,600	$2,200	$2,000	$1,700	$1,500

MODEL 70 TARGET – similar to Model 70 Standard, in .243 Win. or .30-06 cal. (mfg. 1955-1963), earlier pre-'51 Target guns were available in virtually any cal. (i.e., .22 Hornet, .220 Swift, etc.), 24 in. medium weight barrel and target stock. Disc. 1963.

Add 50%-75% over standard values if condition is over 90%. 60% condition will be priced the same.

MODEL 70 BULL GUN – similar to Standard Model 70, with 28 in. heavy barrel, .300 H&H or .30-06 cal. only, .30-06 cal is much rarer.

.300 H&H cal.	$4,500	$4,000	$3,750	$3,500	$3,000	$2,500	$2,250
.30-06	$4,950	$4,250	$3,875	$3,600	$3,100	$2,800	$2,400

MODEL 70 VARMINT – similar to Standard Model 70, in .220 Swift or .243 Win. cal., 26 in. heavy barrel, scope bases, varmint style stock. Mfg. 1956-63.

	$2,300	$1,925	$1,625	$1,325	$1,050	$800	$700

Add 40% for .220 Swift cal. Add 10% for steel buttplate.

Less than 900 were mfg. in .220 Swift cal. Stainless steel barrels are also encountered in this model with 3 different types of finishes.

MODEL 70 ALASKAN – similar to Standard Model 70, in .300 Win. Mag. (mfg. 1963 only with 25 in. barrel - known as Alaskan), .338 Win. Mag., or .375 H&H cal., 24 (Westerner Alaskan) or 25 in. barrel, recoil pad. Mfg. 1960-63.

.375 H&H	$3,750	$3,200	$2,650	$2,100	$1,500	$1,300	$1,200
.300 or .338 Win. Mag.	$3,850	$3,400	$2,900	$2,375	$1,800	$1,325	$1,050

RIFLES: BOLT ACTION - MODEL 70, 1964-2006 MFG.

Beginning 1994, Winchester began using the Classic nomenclature to indicate those models featuring a pre-1964 style action with controlled round feeding.

U.S. Repeating Arms closed its New Haven, CT manufacturing facility on March 31, 2006, and an auction was held on Sept. 27-28, 2006, selling the production equipment and related assets.

WSM cals. will bring an approx. 10% premium, and WSSM cals. will bring an approx. 15% premiums on most of the following models, if in 95%+ condition.

MODEL 70 STANDARD – .22-250 Rem., .222 Rem., .225 Win. (mfg. 1964-1972), .243 Win., .25-06 Rem., .270 Win., .308 Win., or .30-06 cal., 5 shot, 22 or 24 in. heavy barrel, open sights, Monte Carlo stock with sling swivels. Mfg. 1964-1980.

	$650	$525	$425	$350	$300	$250	$200
.225 Win. cal.	$1,325	$1,000	$825	$700	$600	$500	$400

MSR	100%	98%	95%	90%	80%	70%	60%

MODEL 70 WESTERNER – .22-250 Rem. (new 1983), .223 Rem. (new 1983), .243 Win., .270 Win., .30-06, .300 Win. Mag., or 7mm Rem. Mag. cal., 22 or 24 (Mag. cals. only) in. barrel, checkered satin finished straight comb stock with recoil pad, folding rear sight in middle of barrel, polished blue barrel with satin finished receiver, no forend tip or sling swivels. Mfg. 1982-1985.

	$750	$600	$500	$425	$375	$325	$275

MODEL 70 MAGNUM – .264 Win. Mag., 7mm Rem. Mag., .300 H&H Mag., .300 Win. Mag., .338 Win. Mag., .375 H&H, or .458 Win. Mag. cal., 24 in. barrel.

	$750	$600	$500	$425	$375	$325	$275

Add 25%-35% for .375 H&H or .458 Win. Mag. (African Model) cal.

MODEL 70 SUPER GRADE – various cals., deluxe wood with ebony forend cap, Super Grade appears on the floor plate. Disc.

	$950	$800	$675	$550	$475	$450	$425

MODEL 70 DELUXE – .243 Win., .270 Win., .30-06, or .300 Win. Mag. cal., 22 in. barrel, open sight, hand-checkered, black forend tip. Mfg. 1964-71.

	$775	$625	$525	$425	$375	$275	$225

The Model 70 Deluxe was redesignated the Standard Model 70 in 1972.

MODEL 70 TARGET RIFLE 1964-1971 – .308 Win. or .30-06 cal., 24 in. heavy barrel, no sights, target bases, heavy target style stock with hand stop. Disc. 1971.

	$850	$725	$650	$550	$425	$400	$325

MODEL 70 INTERNATIONAL ARMY MATCH 1971 – .308 Win. cal., 5 shot, 24 in. heavy barrel, no sights, adj. trigger, ISU stock with forearm, accessory rail, adj. butt. Disc. 1971.

	$1075	$950	$850	$725	$600	$525	$450

MODEL 70 MANNLICHER 1969-1971 – .243 Win., .270 Win., .30-06, or .308 Win. cal., 19 in. barrel, open sight, full-length Monte Carlo stock with steel forend cap. Disc. 1971.

	$1,050	$900	$800	$700	$575	$500	$425

MODEL 70A – economy version of 1972 type Model 70, same cals., no hinged floorplate or forend tip. Mfg. 1972-78.

	$495	$400	$350	$275	$240	$200	$165

MODEL 70A MAGNUM – similar to Model 70A, except in Mag. cals. but not .375 H&H or .458. Mfg. 1972-78.

	$550	$450	$375	$300	$250	$210	$170

MODEL 70 FEATHERWEIGHT – .22-250 Rem., .223 Rem., .243 Win., .25-06 Rem. (disc. 1993), .257 Roberts (disc.), .270 Win., .280 Rem., 6.5x55mm Swedish (new 1991), 7x57mm Mauser (disc.), .30-06, .308 Win., 7mm-08 Rem. (new 1992), 7mm Rem. Mag. (mfg. 1991-92 only), or .300 Win. Mag. (mfg. 1991-92 only) cal., bolt action, both short and medium action, 5 shot mag., 22 in. barrel (24 in. with .300 Win. Mag.), checkered walnut stock, with or w/o sights, approx. 6 1/2 lbs. Mfg. 1981-94.

	$750	$650	$500	$400	$325	$275	$250

Last MSR was $562.

MSR	100%	98%	95%	90%	80%	70%	60%

In 1981, during U.S.R.A. takeover transition, guns were distinguishable by the U.S.R.A. trademark on the recoil pad. Some collectors will pay a premium for Win. marked pads. Cals. .257 Robts. and 7x57mm Mauser were disc. 1985.

This model had an "XTR" suffix until 1989.

MODEL 70 CLASSIC FEATHERWEIGHT - .22-250 Rem. (new 1994), .223 Rem. (mfg. 1994 only), .243 Win. (new 1994), .270 Win., .280 Rem. (disc. 2000), .30-06, .308 Win. (new 1994), 6mm Rem. (limited mfg. circa 1995), 6.5x55mm Swedish (new 1997), or 7mm-08 Rem. (new 1994) cal., 22 in. barrel, 5 shot mag., blue action, features claw-controlled round feeding action bedded into standard grade walnut stock, jewelled bolt, knurled bolt handle, includes rings and bases, approx. 7 lbs. Mfg. 1992-2006.

	$750	$650	$500	$400	$325	$275	$250

Last MSR was $762.

* ***Model 70 Classic Featherweight WSM*** - .270 WSM (new 2002), .300 WSM, .325 WSM (new 2005) or 7mm WSM (new 2002) cal., controlled round feeding, 24 in. round barrel, 3 shot internal mag., approx. 7 1/4 lbs. Mfg. 2001-2006.

	$825	$725	$550	$450	$350	$300	$260

Last MSR was $792.

Add $39 for left-hand action (new late 2003, not available in .325 WSM cal.).

* ***Model 70 Classic Featherweight Super Short WSSM*** - similar to Model 70 Classic Featherweight, except available in .223 WSSM, .243 WSSM, and .25 WSSM (new 2004) cals., 22 in. barrel, 3 shot mag., 6 lbs. Mfg. 2003-2006.

	$825	$725	$550	$450	$350	$300	$260

Last MSR was $814.

* ***Model 70 Classic Featherweight BOSS*** - similar to Model 70 Classic Featherweight, except has 22 in. barrel with BOSS. Mfg. 1996 only.

	$800	$700	$525	$425	$325	$275	$250

Last MSR was $735.

* ***Model 70 Classic Featherweight Stainless (Recent Mfg.)*** - .223 WSSM, .243 WSSM, .25 WSSM, .270 WSM, .300 WSM, .325 WSM, or 7mm WSM cal., 22 or 24 in. stainless barrel and action, no sights, three position safety, controlled round feed, Pachmayr Decelerator pad on WSM models, 3 shot mag., cut checkering with Schnabel forend, 6-7 1/4 lbs. Mfg. 2005-2006.

	$850	$775	$575	$450	$350	$300	$260

Last MSR was $806.

* ***Model 70 Classic Featherweight Stainless*** - .22-250 Rem., .243 Win., .270 Win., .30-06, .308 Win., .300 Win. Mag. (disc. 1998), or 7mm Rem. Mag. cal., 22 or 24 (Mag. cals. only) in. stainless barrel, checkered walnut stock, 3 or 5 shot mag., approx. 7-7 1/2 lbs. Mfg. 1997-99.

	$750	$650	$500	$400	$325	$275	$250

Last MSR was $746.

MSR	100%	98%	95%	90%	80%	70%	60%

* *Model 70 Classic Featherweight All-Terrain* - .270 Win., .30-06, .300 Win. Mag., or 7mm Rem. Mag. cal., 22 or 24 in. matte finish stainless steel barrel/receiver, black fiberglass/graphite stock with checkering, with (1996-1997 only) or without BOSS, 3 or 5 shot mag., 7 1/4 lbs. Mfg. 1996-98.

	$750	$650	$500	$400	$325	$275	$250

Last MSR was $672.

Add 20% for BOSS (disc. 1997).

* *Model 70 Classic Featherweight Win-Tuff Rifle* - .22-250 Rem., .223 Rem., .243 Win., .270 Win., .30-06, or .308 Win. cal., features brown laminated checkered stock with Schnabel forend, includes base and rings, pistol grip cap, 7 lbs. Mfg. 1988-90. Reintroduced 1992-93.

	$575	$500	$450	$375	$325	$275	$250

Last MSR was $572.

* *Model 70 Classic Featherweight Special* - .243 Win. cal., features custom fitted stock, hand-honed action, barrel, and bolt/follower, custom shop proof stamp, select American walnut with rounded pistol grips, no sights. Only 50 mfg.

	$875	$695	$650	$500	$425	$380	$340

This model is distinguishable by the Super Grade floorplate marking.

MODEL 70 XTR EUROPEAN FEATHERWEIGHT - 6.5x55 Swedish Mauser cal., 22 in. barrel, 5 shot mag., rifle sights, 6 3/4 lbs. Made 1986 only.

	$550	$475	$400	$350	$305	$280	$260

Last MSR was $460.

MODEL 70 LIGHTWEIGHT RIFLE - .22-250 Rem. (disc. 1992), .223 Rem., .243 Win., .270 Win., .280 Rem. (mfg. 1988-92), .30-06, or .308 Win. cal., 22 in. barrel, checkered walnut stock, no sights, 6 1/2 lbs. Mfg. 1987-1995.

	$600	$500	$450	$350	$300	$250	$225

Last MSR was $513.

* *Model 70 Lightweight Rifle Win-Tuff* - .22-250 Rem. (mfg. 1988-89), .223 Rem. (new 1989), .243 Win. (new 1988), .270 Win. .30-06 or .308 Win. (new 1989) cal., similar to Model 70 Lightweight Rifle, except has laminated brown hardwood stock with checkering. Mfg. 1987-92.

	$550	$475	$400	$350	$275	$235	$190

Last MSR was $471.

* *Model 70 Lightweight Rifle Win-Cam* - .270 Win. or .30-06 cal., greenish laminated hardwood stock with checkering, 22 in. barrel. Mfg. 1987-disc.

	$550	$475	$400	$350	$275	$235	$190

Last MSR was $471.

This model was previously designated Featherweight before 1989.

MSR	100%	98%	95%	90%	80%	70%	60%

MODEL 70 CARBINE/LIGHTWEIGHT CARBINE – .22-250 Rem., .222 Rem. (scarce), .223 Rem., .243 Win., .250 Savage (new 1986), .308 Win., .270 Win., or .30-06 cal., bolt action, 5 shot mag., both short and medium action, 20 in. barrel, checkered walnut stock, no sights, approx. 6 lbs. Mfg. 1984-87.

	$600	$500	$450	$375	$300	$250	$225

Last MSR was $395.

Add $15 for open sights.

MODEL 70 SPORTER – .22-250 Rem. (mfg. 1989-1993), .223 Rem. (mfg. 1989-93), .243 Win. (mfg. 1989-93), .25-06 Rem. (mfg. 1985-87 and reintroduced 1990), .264 Win. Mag., .270 Win., .270 Wby. Mag. (new 1988), .30-06, .300 Win. Mag., .300 Wby. Mag. (new 1989), .300 H&H (mfg. 1989- 1992), .308 Win. (mfg. 1986-89), .338 Win. Mag., or 7mm Rem. Mag. cal., 24 in. barrel, 3 or 5 shot mag., custom Sporter styling, Monte Carlo cheek piece, detachable sling swivels, 7 3/4 lbs. Disc. 1994.

	$725	$600	$475	$375	$300	$275	$250

Last MSR was $556.

Add approx. 5% for iron sights (.270 Win., .30-06, .300 Win. Mag., or 7mm Rem. Mag. only).

This model had an "XTR" suffix until 1989.

* ***Model 70 Sporter Win-Tuff*** – .270 Win., .30-06, 7mm Rem. Mag., .300 Win. Mag., .300 Wby. Mag., or .338 Win. Mag. cal., similar to Model 70 Sporter, except has checkered brown laminate stock with sling swivels, solid recoil pad, 24 in. barrel, approx. 7 3/4 lbs. Mfg. 1992 only.

	$600	$500	$450	$375	$300	$250	$225

Last MSR was $572.

MODEL 70 CLASSIC SPORTER III (LT) – .25-06 Rem., .264 Win. Mag. (disc. 2000), .270 Win., .270 Wby. Mag. (disc. 1998), .270 WSM (new 2004), .30-06, .300 Win. Mag., .300 WSM (new 2004), .300 Wby. Mag. (disc. 2000), .325 WSM (new 2005), .338 Win. Mag., 7mm STW (mfg. 1997-2002), 7mm WSM (new 2004), or 7mm Rem. Mag. (disc. 2005) cal., similar to Model 70 Sporter, except features controlled round feeding, 3 (Mag. cals. only) or 5 shot internal mag., 24 or 26 in. barrel, checkered walnut stock, blue finish, stock was redesigned by David Miller in 1999 (denoted by "LT" Model suffix), approx. 7 3/4-8 lbs. Mfg. 1994-2006.

	$775	$675	$500	$400	$325	$275	$250

Last MSR was $742.

Add 10% for Mag. cals.

Add 10% for left-hand action (new 1997).

Add 10% for iron sights - disc. 1998 (available in .270 Win., .30-06, .300 Win. Mag., .338 Win. Mag., or 7mm Rem. Mag.).

This model's nomenclature was changed from Model 70 Classic Sporter LT to Model 70 Classic Sporter III during 2005. Sporter III improvements include a trimmer forend and stock, Pachmayr Decelerator pad, and a more open pistol grip.

MSR	100%	98%	95%	90%	80%	70%	60%

* *Model 70 Classic Sporter Stainless* – .270 Win., .30-06, .300 Win. Mag., .338 Win. Mag., or 7mm Rem. Mag. cal., 24 or 26 in. barrel with (1997 only) or without BOSS, checkered walnut stock, controlled round feeding, 3 or 5 shot mag., right or left-hand action, approx. 7 3/4 lbs. Mfg. 1997-98.

	$850	$725	$550	$475	$375	$300	$275

Last MSR was $716.

Add 10% for BOSS. Add 5% for left-hand action.

* *Model 70 Classic Sporter BOSS* – .25-06 Rem. (disc. 1996), .270 Win., .30-06, .264 Win. Mag. (disc. 1996), 7mm STW (new 1997), 7mm Rem. Mag., .270 Wby. Mag. (mfg. 1996 only), .300 Win. Mag., .300 Wby Mag. (mfg. 1996 only), or .338 Win. Mag. cal., 24 or 26 in. barrel with BOSS, 3 or 5 shot mag., checkered walnut stock, approx. 7 3/4 lbs. Mfg. 1995-98.

	$850	$725	$525	$425	$350	$275	$250

Last MSR was $728.

Add approx. 10% for left-hand action (new 1997).

* *Model 70 Classic Sporter Laredo* – .300 Win Mag., 7mm STW (mfg. 1997-98), or 7mm Rem. Mag. cal., features claw extraction and controlled round feeding, 26 in. round or fluted (new 1998) barrel with (.300 Win. Mag. and 7mm Rem. Mag. disc. 1997) or without BOSS. Mfg. 1996-99.

	$950	$800	$625	$500	$400	$325	$290

Last MSR was $794.

Add approx. 20% for BOSS (disc. 1998).
Add approx. $130 for fluted barrel.

* *Model 70 Classic Sporter Safari Express* – .375 H&H, .416 Rem. Mag., or .458 Win. Mag. cal., features Express style rear sight with standing blade, redesigned stock with negative drop and Pachmayr decelerator recoil pad, trigger guard and floorplate are one assembly, 3 shot mag., controlled round feed, 24 in. barrel with barrel band swivel attachment, checkered walnut stock and forearm, 8 1/2 lbs. Mfg. 1999-2006.

	$1,550	$1,300	$925	$750	$600	$500	$450

Last MSR was $1,149.

* *Model 70 Classic Sporter Super Express Mag.* – .375 H&H, .416 Rem. Mag. (new 1994), or .458 Win. Mag. cal., 3 shot mag., claw extractor controlled round feeding (new 1993), open sights, 22 or 24 in. (.375 H&H or .416 Rem. Mag.) barrel, 8 1/2 lbs. Disc. 1998.

	$1,375	$1,200	$900	$725	$600	$500	$450

Last MSR was $865.

This model had an "XTR" suffix until 1989.

MODEL 70 CLASSIC LAMINATED WSM – .270 WSM, .300 WSM, .325 WSM (new 2005) or 7mm WSM cals., claw extractor controlled round feed, brown laminate stock, 24 in. barrel w/o sights, one inch deluxe recoil pad, blued receiver and barrel, 3 shot mag., 7 3/4 lbs. Mfg. 2003-2005.

	$775	$625	$500	$425	$350	$300	$275

Last MSR was $810.

MSR	100%	98%	95%	90%	80%	70%	60%

MODEL 70 DBM (DETACHABLE BOX MAGAZINE) – .22-250 Rem. (mfg. 1993 only), .223 Rem. (mfg. 1993 only), .243 Win. (new 1993), .270 Win., .30-06, .308 Win. (mfg. 1993 only), 7mm Rem. Mag., or .300 Win. Mag. cal., checkered walnut stock and forend, features 3 shot detachable box mag., 24 or 26 in. barrel with or without sights, includes bases and rings or iron sights (new 1993, optional) in .30-06, .300 Win. Mag., or 7mm Rem. Mag., 7 3/4 lbs. Mfg. 1992-94.

	100%	98%	95%	90%	80%	70%	60%
	$775	$625	$500	$425	$350	$300	$275

Last MSR was $598.

Add $35 for iron sights.

MODEL 70 CLASSIC DBM – .22-250 Rem., .243 Win., .270 Win., .284 Win., .30-06, .308 Win., .300 Win. Mag., or 7mm Rem. Mag. cal., similar to Model 70 DBM, except has controlled round feeding, 24 or 26 in. barrel. Mfg. 1994 only.

	100%	98%	95%	90%	80%	70%	60%
Most cals.	$775	$625	$500	$425	$350	$300	$275
.284 Win. (less than 200 mfg.)	$1,050	$925	$750	$625	$500	$400	$325

Last MSR was $619.

Add $50 for iron sights (.270 Win., .30-06, .300 Win. Mag., or 7mm Rem. Mag.).

* ***Model 70 Classic DBM-S*** – .270 Win., .30-06, .300 Win. Mag., or 7mm Rem. Mag. cal., similar to Model 70 DBM, except has black synthetic stock, this model became a Classic series in 1994 (featuring controlled round feeding). Mfg. 1993-94.

	100%	98%	95%	90%	80%	70%	60%
	$775	$625	$500	$425	$350	$300	$275

Last MSR was $619.

MODEL 70 STAINLESS – .270 Win., .30-06, 7mm Rem. Mag., .300 Win. Mag., or .338 Win. Mag. cal., matte finished stainless steel receiver, barrel, and bolt, black synthetic composite stock, 22 (.270 Win. or .30-06 only, disc. 1992) or 24 in. barrel, approx. 6 3/4 lbs. Mfg. 1992-94.

	100%	98%	95%	90%	80%	70%	60%
	$725	$575	$500	$425	$350	$300	$250

Last MSR was $616.

MODEL 70 CLASSIC STAINLESS – .22-250 Rem. (disc. 1999), .223 Rem. (disc. 1994), .243 Win. (disc. 1998), .270 Win., .270 WSM (mfg. 2002), .30-06, .308 Win. (disc. 1998), .270 Wby. Mag. (mfg. 1997 only), .300 Win. Mag., .300 Wby. Mag. (disc. 2000), .300 Rem. Ultra Mag. (disc. 2002), .300 WSM (mfg. 2001-2003), .338 Win. Mag., .375 H&H, 7mm STW (mfg. 2001-2002), 7mm WSM (mfg. 2002), or 7mm Rem. Mag. (disc. 2003, reintroduced 2004) cal., features controlled round feeding, 22 (disc. 2001), 24, or 26 in. barrel, black synthetic composite stock, 3, 5, or 6 shot mag., without sights except for .375 H&H cal., 6 3/4-7 1/2 lbs. Mfg. 1994-2005.

	100%	98%	95%	90%	80%	70%	60%
	$850	$725	$550	$425	$325	$275	$225

Last MSR was $817.

Add $30 for Mag. cals., or $125 for .375 H&H cal.

MSR	100%	98%	95%	90%	80%	70%	60%

* ***Model 70 Classic Stainless BOSS*** – .22-250 Rem. (disc. 1996), .243 Win. (disc. 1996), .270 Win., .30-06, .308 Win. (disc. 1996), .270 Wby. Mag. (mfg. 1997 only), .300 Win. Mag., .300 Wby. Mag. (mfg. 1996-97), .338 Win. Mag., or 7mm Rem. Mag. cal., 22, 24, or 26 in. barrel with BOSS, black synthetic stock, 6 3/4-7 1/2 lbs. Mfg. 1995-98.

	$875	$750	$575	$450	$350	$300	$250

Last MSR was $788.

MODEL 70 CLASSIC LAMINATED STAINLESS – .270 Win., .30-06, .300 Win. Mag., .338 Win. Mag., or 7mm Rem. Mag. cal., 24 or 26 (Mag. cals. only) in. barrel without sights, checkered grey/black laminate stock with sporter style dimensions, stainless action and barrel, 3 or 5 shot mag., approx. 8 lbs. Mfg. 1998-99.

	$875	$750	$575	$450	$350	$300	$250

Last MSR was $753.

* ***Model 70 Classic Laminated Stainless Camo*** – similiar to Model 70 Classic Stainless, except has Mossy Oak Treestand finish composite stock, not available in .338 Win. Mag. cal. approx. 7 1/4 lbs. Mfg. 1998 only.

	$800	$700	$550	$450	$350	$300	$250

Last MSR was $745.

MODEL 70 COYOTE STAINLESS LAMINATED – various standard, WSSM, or WSM cals., push feed (non-WSM/WSSM cals.) or controlled round feed (WSM/WSSM cals. only) action, 24 in. medium heavy stainless steel sporter barrel, uncheckered brown or grey (new 2006) laminate stock with reverse taper on forend, 3 (WSM cals. only), 5, or 6 (.223 Rem. or .204 Ruger only) shot mag., 8 3/4 lbs. Mfg. 2000-2006.

	$750	$650	$475	$375	$325	$275	$250

Last MSR was $689.

Add 10% for WSM cals.
Add 15% for WSSM cals.

MODEL 70 COYOTE LAMINATED BLUE – .223 Rem., .270 WSM, .300 WSM, .325 WSM, 7mm WSM, .223 WSSM, .243 WSSM, or .25 WSSM cal., similar to Model 70 Coyote Laminated Stainless, except has blued barrel/receiver finish. Mfg. 2005 only.

	$800	$700	$550	$425	$350	$300	$260

Last MSR was $689.

Add 10% for WSM cals.
Add 15% for WSSM cals.

MODEL 70 COYOTE OUTBACK STAINLESS LAMINATED – various standard, Mag., or WSM cals., grey laminate stock with three oval holes in buttstock and four in forend, matte finished stainless receiver and 24 in. fluted barrel w/o sights, 3-6 shot mag., controlled round push feeding, approx. 7 3/4 lbs. Limited mfg. 2006.

	$1,325	$1,100	$875	$700	$575	$425	$350

Last MSR was $1,016.

Add 10% for WSM and standard Mag. cals.

MSR	100%	98%	95%	90%	80%	70%	60%

MODEL 70 COYOTE LITE – similar cals. as Model 70 Coyote Laminated Blue, except also available in .22-250 Rem., .243 Win., and .308 Win. (new 2006) cal., features 24 in. blued steel (WSSM cals. only) or stainless steel fluted barrel/action, controlled round feed action, floorplate, carbon fiber/fiberglass composite Bell & Carlson stock with vented forend, Pachmayr Decelerator pad, 7 1/2 lbs. Mfg. 2005-2006.

	$900	$775	$575	$450	$375	$325	$275

Last MSR was $889.

Add 10% for WSM cals.

MODEL 70 CLASSIC SM (SYNTHETIC MATTE) – .22-250 Rem. (mfg. 1993 only), .223 Rem. (mfg. 1993 only), .243 Win. (mfg. 1993 only), .270 Win., .30-06, .308 Win. (mfg. 1993 only), 7mm Rem. Mag., .300 Win. Mag., .338 Win. Mag., or .375 H&H (new 1993) cal., features black composite stock with checkering and sling swivels, 22 (.22-250 Rem., .223 Rem., .243 Win., or .308 Win. - mfg. 1993 only), 24, or 26 in. barrel with matte metal finish, 3 or 5 shot, approx. 7 1/2 lbs. Mfg. 1992-96.

	$750	$650	$525	$425	$350	$300	$275

Last MSR was $620.

Add 10% for Mag. cals.

Until 1993, this model was called the Model 70 SSM. In 1994, this model became the Model 70 Classic SM featuring controlled round feeding.

MODEL 70 CLASSIC SM BOSS – .270 Win., .30-06, 7mm Rem. Mag., .300 Win. Mag., or .338 Win. Mag. cal., 24 or 26 in. barrel with BOSS, 3 or 5 shot, approx. 7 1/4 lbs. Mfg. 1995-96 only.

	$850	$675	$550	$425	$350	$300	$275

Last MSR was $735.

MODEL 70 CLASSIC COMPACT – .243 Win., .308 Win. (disc. 2003), or 7mm-08 Rem. cal., features 12 1/2 in. LOP, 20 in. barrel and shallow profile, pre-'64 type action, 4 shot mag., checkered walnut stock and forearm, blue action and barrel, 6-6 1/2 lbs. Mfg. 1998-2006.

	$850	$675	$525	$375	$300	$275	$250

Last MSR was $762.

MODEL 70 VARMINT – same general specifications as standard Sporter, .22-250 Rem., .223 Rem., .225 Win., .243 Win., or .308 Win. cal., 26 in. cold hammer forged heavy barrel, counter-sunk muzzle, no sights, 5 shot mag., target scope bases, 7 3/4 lbs. Mfg. 1964-1993.

	$700	$550	$475	$400	$350	$300	$250

Last MSR was $720.

Add 50% for .225 Win. cal.

This model had an "XTR" suffix 1978-89.

* ***Model 70 Varmint Heavy (HBV)*** – .220 Swift (mfg. 1994-98), .22-250 Rem., .222 Rem. (mfg. 1997-98), .223 Rem., .243 Win., or .308 Win. cal., push-feed action, 26 in. heavy stainless fluted (new 1997) or plain barrel (countersunk muzzle) without sights, black synthetic beavertail H-S Precision stock with aluminum bedding block, 10 3/4 lbs. Mfg. 1993-1999.

	$825	$650	$525	$450	$400	$350	$300

Last MSR was $795.

Add approx. $125 for fluted barrel.

MSR	100%	98%	95%	90%	80%	70%	60%

MODEL 70 SHB (SYNTHETIC HEAVY BARREL) - .308 Win. cal., features checkered black composite stock, 26 in. barrel with matte metal finish, jeweled bolt, 9 lbs. Mfg. 1992 only.

	$675	$550	$475	$400	$350	$300	$250

Last MSR was $563.

MODEL 70 WINLIGHT - .25-06 Rem., .270 Win., .280 Rem. (new 1987), .30-06, 7mm Rem. Mag., .300 Win. Mag., .300 Wby. Mag., or .338 Win. Mag. cal., McMillan fiberglass stock, thermoplastic receiver bedding, blue metal parts, 22 or 24 (Mag. cals. only) in. barrel, 3 or 4 shot mag., no sights, approx. 6 1/2 lbs. Mfg. 1986-90.

	$825	$700	$650	$550	$500	$450	$400

Last MSR was $637.

MODEL 70 RANGER RIFLE - .22-250 Rem. (new 1999), .223 Rem. (new 1992), .243 Win. (new 1991), .270 Win., .30-06, or 7mm Rem. Mag. cal., push-feed action, 22 or 24 in. barrel, 3 (7mm Rem. Mag.), 5, or 6 shot mag., plain hardwood stock without checkering, open sights, approx. 7 lbs. Disc. 1999.

	$525	$425	$350	$300	$250	$200	$175

Last MSR was $503.

* ***Model 70 Ranger Rifle Compact (Ladies/Youth)*** - .22-250 Rem. (mfg. 1999 only), .223 Rem. (disc. 1989, reintroduced 1997, disc. 1998), .243 Win., .308 Win. (new 1991), or 7mm-08 Rem. (mfg. 1997-98, reintroduced 2000) cal., push-feed action, 20 (disc. 1992) or 22 (new 1993) in. barrel, 5 or 6 shot mag., shorter hardwood stock dimensions, open sights, 6 1/2 lbs. Disc. 2000.

	$550	$475	$350	$300	$250	$225	$200

Last MSR was $528.

MODEL 70 STEALTH - .22-250 Rem., .223 Rem., .308 Win. cal., push-feed action, 26 in. heavy barrel w/o sights, non-glare matte metal finish, Accu-Block black synthetic stock with full length aluminum bedding block, 5 or 6 shot mag., 10 3/4 lbs. Mfg. 1999-2003.

	$925	$775	$700	$600	$550	$500	$450

Last MSR was $800.

MODEL 70 STEALTH II - .22-250 Rem., .223 WSSM, .243 WSSM, .25 WSSM, or .308 Win. cal., push-feed action, 26 in. heavy barrel w/o sights, matte blue finish, redesigned black synthetic stock with aluminum pillar bedding, 3 or 5 shot mag., 10 lbs. Mfg. 2004-2006.

	$825	$675	$550	$425	$375	$325	$300

Last MSR was $886.

Add 10% for WSSM cals.

MSR	100%	98%	95%	90%	80%	70%	60%

MODEL 70 BLACK SHADOW - .270 Win., .30-06, .300 Win. Mag., or 7mm Rem. Mag cal., push-feed action, 3 (Mag. cals.) or 5 shot internal mag., 24 or 26 (Mag. cals.) in. barrel w/o sights, matte receiver and barrel finish, black composite stock with conventional floor plate mag., 7 1/4 lbs. Mfg. 1998-2003.

	$525	$375	$300	$275	$250	$225	$200

Last MSR was $523.

Add approx. 10% for Mag. cals.

MODEL 70 CLASSIC/CAMO ULTIMATE SHADOW - .223 WSSM (new 2004), .243 WSSM (new 2004), .25 WSSM (new 2004), .270 WSM, .300 WSM, .325 WSM (new 2005) or 7mm WSM cal., features controlled round feed, black or Dura-Touch armor coated Mossy Oak New Break-Up camo finished molded synthetic stock with rubber grip inserts and new recoil pad, matte black metal, 3 shot mag., 24 in. blued steel or stainless steel barrel, 6 3/4 lbs. Mfg. 2003-2005.

	$775	$650	$525	$450	$375	$335	$300

Last MSR was $817.

Add 10% for WSM cals. or 15% for WSSM cals.
Add 10% for stainless steel action.
Add approx. $100 Mossy Oak New Break-Up camo finish.

MODEL 70 SUPER SHADOW - various cals., similar to Classic Ultimate Shadow, except has oval dot textured gripping surfaces on pistol grip and forearm, blue finish, controlled round push feed action, available in either short or super short action, blind mag., 22 (.223 WSSM, .243 WSSM, or .25 WSSM cal.) or 24 in. barrel w/o sights, 6 (WSSM cals.) or 6 3/4 lbs. Mfg. 2003-2006.

	$525	$400	$300	$250	$200	$180	$165

Last MSR was $525.

Add 10% for WSM and Mag. cals. or 15% for WSSM cals.

MODEL 70 SHADOW ELITE STAINLESS - various standard, WSM, and Mag. cals., short or long action, lightweight black synthetic stock with rubberized overmolded gripping surfaces on pistol grip and forearm, and Dura-Touch Armor coating, WinSorb recoil pad, 24 or 26 in. stainless fluted barrel, no sights, except .375 H&H cal., controlled round feed action, 3 or 5 shot mag., 6 3/4 - 7 3/4 lbs. Limited mfg. 2006.

	$725	$575	$425	$325	$275	$235	$200

Last MSR was $739.

Add 10% for WSM and standard Mag. cals.
Add approx. $125 for .375 H&H cal.

* ***Model 70 Shadow Elite Stainless Camo*** - similar to Model 70 Shadow Elite Stainless, except available in Mossy Oak Break-Up camo. Limited mfg. 2006.

	$800	$600	$500	$400	$350	$300	$250

Last MSR was $808.

Add 10% for standard Mag. and WSM cals.
Add $200 for .375 H&H cal.

MSR	100%	98%	95%	90%	80%	70%	60%

MODEL 70 PRO SHADOW - various standard, WSM, and Mag. cals., short or long action, 22 or 24 in. blue barrel, black synthetic stock with Dura-Touch Armor coating and oval-dot gripping surfaces, controlled round push feed, 3 or 5 shot mag., 6 1/2 - 7 lbs. Limited mfg. 2006.

$700 $550 $475 $400 $350 $300 $250

Last MSR was $594.

Add 10% for standard Mag. and WSM cals.

* ***Model 70 Pro Shadow Stainless*** - similar to Model 70 Pro Shadow, except has stainless barrel/action. Limited mfg. 2006.

$750 $600 $525 $450 $400 $350 $300

Last MSR was $638.

Add 10% for standard Mag. and WSM cals.
Add $125 for .375 H&H cal.

MODEL 70 CLASSIC SUPER GRADE III - .25-06 Win. (new 2001), .270 Win. (mfg. 1991-2003), .270 WSM (new 2004), .30-06 (new 1991), 7mm STW (230 mfg. 1999 only), 7mm WSM (new 2004), 7mm Rem. Mag. (disc. 1998, reintroduced 2000-2003), .264 Win. Mag. (limited mfg. 2000 only), .300 WSM (new 2004), .300 Win. Mag. (disc. 2003, reintroduced 2005), .325 WSM (new 2005), or .338 Win. Mag. cal., 24 or 26 in. barrel, 3 (Mag. cals.) or 5 shot mag., jewelled bolt, stainless steel extractor for true claw controlled round feeding and ejecting, three-position safety, checkered satin finish walnut stock with wood cheekpiece, black forend tip, bases and rings included, approx. 7 3/4 - 8 lbs. Mfg. 1990-2006.

$1,495 $1,150 $1,000 $875 $725 $600 $500

Last MSR was $1,036.

Add 10% for WSM and Mag. cals.

This model was designated the Model 70 Super Grade until 1995. During 1999, this model was redesigned to include a new Express style rear sight with standing blade, negative stock drop, Pachmayr Decelerator pad, one-piece floor plate and full barrel band swivel attachment. This model was on its third generation of design improvements (now called the Super Grade III) with trimmer sporter style stock, steel stock crossbolt, and inlaid swivel studs.

* ***Model 70 Classic Super Grade III RMEF*** - .300 WSM or .325 WSM (new 2005) cal., similar to Model 70 Classic Super Grade, except is Rocky Mountain Elk Foundation special edition, includes Super Grade Stock with ebony forend and Pachmayr decelerator pad, special RMEF emblem on grip cap, 26 in. barrel, 8 lbs. Limited mfg. 2003-2006.

$1,695 $1,350 $1,125 $1,000 $875 $750 $550

Last MSR was $1,183.

This model was redesignated the Super Grade III RMEF in 2005.

* ***Model 70 Classic Super Grade III BOSS*** - similar to Model 70 Classic Super Grade, except has BOSS. Mfg. 1995-97.

$1,025 $825 $700 $550 $450 $350 $300

Last MSR was $956.

MSR	100%	98%	95%	90%	80%	70%	60%

MODEL 70 SUPER GRADE CENTENNIAL - .30-06 cal., deluxe checkered walnut stock, black forend cap, controlled round feed with engraved "1906-2006 - 100 Years of .30-06 Springfield" on bolt face, 24 in. blue steel barrel, 3 shot mag., polished engraved floorplate with special gold and nickel accents, 8 lbs. 306 mfg. 2005-2006.

	$1,550	$1,325	$1,200	N/A	N/A	N/A	N/A

Last MSR was $1,259.

MODEL 70 50TH ANNIVERSARY MODEL - .300 Win. Mag. cal., 24 in. barrel, deluxe walnut stock, engraving and special motifs on metal surfaces, serial numbered 50 ANV 1 - 50 ANV 500, 7 3/4 lbs. 500 mfg. 1987 only.

	$1,750	$1,500	$1,250	N/A	N/A	N/A	N/A

Last MSR was $939.

RIFLES: BOLT ACTION - POST 1964 MODEL 70 CUSTOM GRADES

MODEL 70 CUSTOM GRADE - various cals., old style Model 70 action, semi-fancy American walnut checkered stock, engine turned bolt and follower, hand honed internal parts. Mfg. 1988-89 only.

	$2,000	$1,600	$1,250	$1,000	$850	$700	$600

Last MSR was $1,172.

MODEL 70 XTR FEATHERWEIGHT ULTRA GRADE "1 OF 1,000" - .270 Win. cal., extensively engraved, finely checkered deluxe French walnut stock, with mahogany presentation case.

	$3,600	$2,850	$2,150	N/A	N/A	N/A	N/A

Last MSR was $5,000.

MODEL 70 CLASSIC CUSTOM GRADE - .264 Win. Mag. (new 1994), .270 Win., .30-06, 7mm Rem. Mag., .300 Win. Mag., .300 Wby. Mag. (new 1994) or .338 Win. Mag. cal., 24 or 26 in. barrel, similar to Model 70 Super Grade, but had to be special ordered through the Custom Gun Shop, and with many custom features including semi-fancy walnut with satin finish and hand-honed internal parts. Mfg. 1990-1994.

	$2,400	$2,000	$1,500	$1,200	$1,050	$800	$700

Last MSR was $1,757.

A Model 70 Collector Grade was also a variant of this model which was mfg. in the Custom Gun Shop - this model was priced on request only.

* ***Model 70 Classic Custom Grade Featherweight*** - .22-250 Rem. (new 1994), .223 Rem. (new 1994), .243 Win. (new 1994), .270 Win., .280 Rem., .30-06, .308 Win. (new 1994), 7mm-08 Rem. (new 1994) cal., 22 in. barrel, Featherweight features, controlled round feeding, higher grade wood. Mfg. 1992-1994.

	$2,000	$1,800	$1,400	$1,100	$1,000	$800	$700

Last MSR was $1,757.

* ***Model 70 Classic Custom Grade Sharpshooter I/II*** - .22-250 Rem. (new 1993), .223 Rem. (mfg. 1993-94), .30-06, .308 Win., or .300 Win. Mag. cal., specially designed McMillan A-2 (disc. 1995) or H-S Precision

MSR	100%	98%	95%	90%	80%	70%	60%

heavy target stock, Schneider (disc. 1995) or H-S Precision (new 1996) 24 (.308 Win. cal. only) or 26 in. stainless steel barrel, choice of blue or grey finish starting 1996. Mfg. 1992-1998.

	$1,950	$1,500	$1,050	$900	$850	$750	$675

Last MSR was $1,994.

Subtract $100 if without stainless barrel (pre-1995).

This model was designated the Sharpshooter II in 1996 (features H-S Precision stock and stainless steel barrel).

This model was also available in left-hand action beginning 1998 (.30-06 and .330 Win. Mag. cals. only).

* ***Model 70 Classic Custom Grade Sporting Sharpshooter I/II*** – .270 Win. (disc. 1994), 7mm STW, or .300 Win. Mag. cal., 1/2-minute of angle sporting version of the Custom Sharpshooter, custom shop only, Sharpshooter II became standard in 1996. Mfg. 1993-98.

	$1,875	$1,425	$1,000	$875	$825	$750	$675

Last MSR was $1,875.

This model was also available in left-hand action in 1998.

* ***Model 70 Classic Custom Grade Sporting Sharpshooter*** – .220 Swift cal., 26 in. Schneider barrel, controlled round feeding, available with either McMillan A-2 or Sporting synthetic (disc. 1994) stock. Mfg. 1994-95 only.

	$1,950	$1,525	$1,200	$975	$850	$750	$650

Last MSR was $1,814.

* ***Model 70 Classic Custom Grade Express*** – .300 Petersen (mfg. 1995 only), .375 H&H, .375 JRS (mfg. 1992-96), 7mm STW (mfg. 1993-94), .416 Rem. Mag., .458 Win. Mag., or .470 Capstick (disc. 1995) cal., 24 in. (22 in. on .458 Win. Mag.) barrel, claw controlled round feeding, deluxe walnut with satin finish and checkering, 3-leaf express (disc. 1995) or pre-64 style adj. rear sight (new 1996), high luster metal finish, bolt and follower are engine turned, available by special order through the custom gun shop only. Mfg. 1990-1998.

	$2,750	$2,200	$1,800	$1,500	$1,200	$1,050	$900

Last MSR was $2,512.

Subtract $200 for 7mm STW cal.

In 1994, the model nomenclature was changed from Model 70 Custom Grade Express, and in 1996 it was changed from Model 70 Classic Express.

MODEL 70 CUSTOM ULTIMATE CLASSIC – .25-06 Rem., 6.5x55mm Swedish (new 2001), .270 Win., .280 Rem. (mfg. 1996, reintroduced 1999), .30-06, 7mm STW (disc. 2006), .264 Win. Mag. (disc. 2006), .270 Wby. Mag. (disc. 1996), .35 Whelen (new 1998), 7mm Rem. Mag., 7mm Rem. Ultra Mag., .300 Win. Mag., .300 Wby. Mag., .300 H&H (mfg. 1996-99), .300 Rem. Ultra Mag. (new 2000), .338 Win. Mag., .338-06 (mfg. 1999-2001), .338 Rem. Ultra Mag. (new 2001), .340 Wby. Mag.

MSR	100%	98%	95%	90%	80%	70%	60%

(mfg. 1998), .375 H&H (1995 only), .416 Rem. Mag. (1995 only), or .458 Win. Mag. (1995 only) cal., controlled round feeding, engine turned bolt, checkered fancy walnut stock, choice of 22 (.458 Win. Mag. only), 24 or 26 in. tapered round full-fluted, 1/2 round, 1/2 octagonal, or full octagonal tapered stainless barrel, one inch black decelerator recoil pad, choice of blue or stainless barreled action, 3 or 5 shot mag., includes bases/rings except on some Mag. cals., approx. 7 3/4 lbs., except for large disc. cals., included hard case. Mfg. 1995-2006.

	$3,000	$2,750	$2,500	$2,200	$1,800	$1,500	$1,000

Last MSR was $3,060.

Add $100 for stainless steel barrel, $110 for fluted round barrel, or $235 for full or half octagon barrel.

Add approx. 15% for .375 H&H and larger Mag. cals (disc. 1995).

This model was previously designated the Model 70 Ultimate Classic until 2000, and was changed to the Model 70 Custom Ultimate Classic.

Left-hand action (new 1997) was available in all recent cals.

MODEL 70 CLASSIC CUSTOM SHORT ACTION - .243 Win. (disc. 2000, reintroduced 2002 only), .257 Roberts, .260 Rem. (disc. 2006), .270 WSM (new 2002), .284 Win. (new 2006), .308 Win., .358 Win., .300 WSM (new 2001), .325 WSM (new 2005), 7mm-08 Rem., 7mm WSM (new 2002), or .450 Marlin (mfg. 2001-2004) cal., 22 (disc. 2002) or 24 (new 2003) in. match grade tapered stainless or chrome moly barrel with cut rifling, controlled round feed, no sights, deluxe high gloss checkered walnut stock and forend, one inch black decelerator recoil pad, satin matte blue finished action and barrel, 3-5 shot mag., approx. 7 1/2 lbs. Mfg. 2000-2006.

	$2,650	$2,050	$1,650	$1,350	$1,125	$950	$800

Last MSR was $2,866.

Left-hand action was available on this model.

MODEL 70 CLASSIC CUSTOM FEATHERWEIGHT - .223 WSSM (mfg. 2004), .243 WSSM (mfg. 2004), .25 WSSM (mfg. 2004), .243 Win. (new 2006), .25-06 Rem. (new 2006), .270 Win., .280 Rem. (new 2004), .284 Win. (new 2006), .30-06, .308 Win. (new 2006), 6.5x55mm Swedish (new 2006), or 7mm-08 Rem. (mfg. 2003) cal., 5 shot mag., Featherweight stock with Schnabel forend, match grade 22 in. barrel w/o sights, matte blue or stainless action/barrel, 7 1/4 lbs. Mfg. 2003-2006.

	$2,650	$2,050	$1,650	$1,350	$1,125	$950	$800

Last MSR was $2,866.

MODEL 70 CLASSIC CUSTOM CARBON - .25-06 Rem., .270 WSM, .300 WSM, .338 Win. Mag., or 7mm WSM cal., satin stainless action, 24 or 26 in. carbon fiber barrel with Shilen stainless barrel liner, controlled round feed, reinforced black composite stock, 6 1/2 - 7 lbs. Mfg. 2003-2004.

	$3,050	$2,350	$1,825	$1,400	$1,150	$975	$825

Last MSR was $3,233.

MSR	100%	98%	95%	90%	80%	70%	60%

MODEL 70 CLASSIC CUSTOM EXTREME WEATHER - .25-06 Rem. (disc. 2001), .270 Win. (disc. 2000), .270 WSM (new 2004), .30-06, .300 Win. Mag., .300 Rem. Ultra Mag. (new 2001), .300 WSM (new 2004), .308 Win. (new 2004), .325 WSM (new 2005), .338 Win. Mag., 7mm WSM (new 2004), 7mm Rem. Mag., or .375 H&H (new 2001) cal., controlled round feed, matte finished stainless action and match grade 22 lightweight (.375 H&H only), 24, or 26 in. fluted stainless barrel w/o sights, black McMillan fiberglass stock with cheekpiece and 1 in. Pachmayr Decelerator pad, 3 or 5 shot mag., available in either right or left-hand action, approx. 7 1/2 lbs. Mfg. 2000-2005.

	$2,350	$1,900	$1,575	$1,375	$1,150	$950	$750

Last MSR was $2,576.

MODEL 70 CUSTOM EXTREME LIGHTWEIGHT WEATHER II - various standard, WSM, and Mag. cals., 22, 24, or 26 in. fluted Krieger barrel w/o sights, black lightweight McMillan Hunter's Edge fiberglass stock with Pachmayr Decelerator recoil pad, 3 or 5 shot mag., matte finished stainless steel action/barrel, 6 1/4 - 7 lbs. Limited mfg. 2006.

	$2,600	$2,025	$1,650	$1,400	$1,175	$975	$775

Last MSR was $2,800.

This model was also available with left-hand action, except in WSM cals.

MODEL 70 CUSTOM STAINLESS LAMINATE - .270 WSM, .300 WSM, .325 WSM, or 7mm WSM cal., choice of brown or black/grey featherweight stock with Pachmayr Decelerator recoil pad, controlled round feed, 24 in. stainless sporter barrel w/o sights, engine turned bolt, 8 lbs. Limited mfg. 2006.

	$2,150	$1,850	$1,450	$1,200	$1,050	$900	$725

Last MSR was $2,332.

MODEL 70 CLASSIC CUSTOM MANNLICHER - .260 Rem., .308 Win., or 7mm-08 Rem. cal., 19 in. barrel w/o sights (sights optional), 4 shot internal mag., full length checkered walnut stock, smooth tapered barrel and blue action, approx. 6 3/4 lbs. Mfg. 1999-2000.

	$2,475	$1,975	$1,550	$1,275	$1,000	$850	$750

Last MSR was $2,595.

This model was designated the Model 70 Custom Mannlicher until 2000.

MODEL 70 CUSTOM MAPLE - .270 Win., .284 Win., .30-06, or .308 Win. cal., 24 in. sporter barrel w/o sights, gloss finished checkered hand-made fiddleback curly maple stock with black forend cap, custom shop pistol grip cap, right or left-hand blue or stainless steel action, 7 3/4 lbs. Limited mfg. 2006.

	$4,100	$3,475	$3,025	$2,425	$1,950	$1,575	$1,325

Last MSR was $4,355.

MODEL 70 CUSTOM CONTINENTAL HUNTER - .270 Win., .284 Win., .30-06, or .308 Win. cal., 22 in. Krieger stainless or blue sporter barrel w/o sights, gloss finished Claro walnut stock with round pistol grip and

MSR	100%	98%	95%	90%	80%	70%	60%

Schnabel forend, Niedner style steel buttplate, controlled round feed, right or left-hand action, 4 or 5 shot mag., 6 3/4 lbs. Limited mfg. 2006.

	$4,900	$4,350	$3,850	$3,150	$2,625	$2,100	$1,625

Last MSR was $5,226.

MODEL 70 CLASSIC CUSTOM SAFARI EXPRESS - .340 Wby. Mag. (disc. 1999), .358 STA (disc. 2000), .375 H&H, .375 Rem. Ultra Mag. (new 2001), .404 Jeffery (mfg. 2004), .416 Rem. Mag., .416 Rigby (mfg. 2001), .458 Win. Mag., .458 Lott, or .470 Capstick (new 2002) cal., honed internal parts, engine turned bolt and follower, adj. Dietrich Apel Express rear and front sights, deluxe checkered walnut stock and forend, 22 (.458 Win. Mag. & .458 Lott) or 24 in. barrel with sling stud, 3 shot mag., approx. 9 1/4 lbs. Mfg. 1999-2006.

	$3,050	$2,375	$1,775	$1,375	$1,025	$875	$775

Last MSR was $3,252.

Add $490 for .416 Rigby cal. (mfg. 2001 only).

Beginning in 2000, this model was available in left-hand action in all cals. except .470 Capstick.

This model was designated the Model 70 Custom Safari Express until 2000.

MODEL 70 WSM CUSTOM NORTH AMERICAN BIG GAME SERIES - .270 WSM, .300 WSM, or 7mm WSM cal., controlled round feed, checkered XXX American walnut stock with Schnabel forend, Pachmayr Decelerator recoil pad, engraved receiver, trigger guard, and floorplate, high lustre bluing. Only 125 of each edition (Whitetail Deer - .270 WSM, Elk - .300 WSM, and Antelope - 7mm WSM) mfg. 2004-2005 with matching serial numbers.

	$2,875	$2,375	$1,775	$1,375	$1,025	$875	$775

Last MSR was $3,030.

This model was sold in sets only (all 3 calibers.)

MODEL 70 CLASSIC CUSTOM AFRICAN EXPRESS - .340 Wby. Mag. (disc. 1999), .358 STA (disc. 2000), .375 H&H, .416 Rem. Mag., .416 Rigby (mfg. 2001 only), .458 Win. Mag., .458 Lott, or .470 Capstick (mfg. 2001 only) cal., drop down floorplate, increasing mag. capacity to 4, checkered fancy English walnut stock with black Pachmayr Decelerator pad and ebony pistol grip and forend caps, adj. Dietrich Apel Express rear and front sights, 22 (.458 Win. Mag. only) or 24 in. barrel with sling stud, approx. 9 1/2 lbs. Mfg. 1999-2006.

	$4,575	$3,700	$3,150	$2,525	$1,975	$1,525	$1,325

Last MSR was $4,867.

Add $437 for .416 Rigby cal. (disc. 2001).

Beginning in 2000, this model was available in left-hand action in all cals. except .458.

This model was designated the Model 70 Custom African Express until 2000.

MSR	100%	98%	95%	90%	80%	70%	60%

MODEL 70 CLASSIC CUSTOM TAKE-DOWN – .300 Rem. Rem. Ultra Mag., .300 Win. Mag. (new 2002), .375 H&H, .416 Rem. Mag., or 7mm Rem. Mag. cal., all stainless construction with blue Teflon finish, takedown receiver/barrel assembly, brown synthetic stock and forearm, .75 MOA guaranteed for takedown action assembly/reassembly, 24 (.375 H&H or .416 Rem. Mag. cal. only) or 26 (fluted only) in. barrel, 3 shot internal mag., 8 1/2 - 9 lbs. Limited mfg. 2001-2006.

$3,475	$2,950	$2,550	$2,150	$1,800	$1,550	$1,250

While advertised beginning in 1998 with a MSR of $2,495, this model was finally produced during 2001. This model was only available from the Bass Pro Shops.

MODEL 70 ULTRA GRADE – .270 Win. cal., gold line engraved, includes wood display case, 500 mfg.

$3,000	$2,500	$2,000	$1,800	$1,500	$1,200	$1,000

Last MSR was $5,000.

MODEL 70 CUSTOM 100TH ANNIVERSARY .30-06 – 30-06 cal., 22 in. blue sporter barrel with "100th Anniversary Custom 1 of 100" engraved in gold, 5 shot mag., semi-fancy checkered American walnut stock with recoil pad, single steel crossbolt, controlled round feed action, gold and nickel engraved floor plate with WWI Allied soldiers and sport hunter with whitetail deer, 7 1/4 lbs. 100 mfg. 2006.

$2,500	$1,950	$1,650	N/A	N/A	N/A	N/A

Last MSR was $2,660.

MODEL 70 CUSTOM SPECIAL "70 YEARS OF THE MODEL 70" – .270 Win., .30-06, or .300 Win. Mag. cal., 24 or 26 (.300 Win. Mag. only) in. blue barrel with "One of Seventy" engraved in gold, semi-fancy checkered walnut stock with inletted sling swivel bases, controlled round feed action, each caliber has special engraved floor plate, 7 1/2 - 7 3/4 lbs. 70 of each caliber mfg. 2006.

$2,400	$1,900	$1,575	N/A	N/A	N/A	N/A

Last MSR was $2,547.

MODEL 70 COLLECTOR GRADE – various cals., this variation was a special order through the Winchester Custom Shop and values will vary per individual gun.

MODEL 70 CUSTOM BUILT – various cals., this variation was a special order through the Winchester Custom Shop and values will vary per individual gun.

MODEL 70 EXHIBITION GRADE – various cals., fancy checkered American walnut stock with hardwood forend tip. Mfg. 1988-89 only.

$2,050	$1,625	$1,075	N/A	N/A	N/A	N/A

Last MSR was $2,192.

RIFLES: BOLT ACTION - MODEL 70, 2007-CURRENT MFG.

In late 2007, Olin announced that its famous Winchester Model 70 would be reintroduced with a new M.O.A. trigger system, and manufactured by FN

MSR	100%	98%	95%	90%	80%	70%	60%

Manufacturing located in Columbia, SC. Winchester continues to introduce more variations of the new Model 70.

MODEL 70 ALASKAN – .30-06, .300 Win. Mag., .338 Win. Mag., or .375 H&H cal., 25 in. barrel with folding adj. rear sight and hooded gold bead front sight, satin finished Monte Carlo walnut stock and forearm with cut checkering, MOA trigger system, Pachmayr Decelerator recoil pad, Pre-64 style controlled round feed with claw extractor, 8-1/2 lbs. New 2012.

MSR $1,340	$1,150	$975	$750	$650	$550	$475	$425

Add $40 for .375 H&H Mag. cal.

This model in .375 H&H cal. was featured as a 2012 SHOT Show Special.

MODEL 70 COYOTE LIGHT – various cals. in standard short action, including WSM, 22 (disc. 2010) or 24 in. heavy stainless fluted free floating barrel, 3 or 5 shot mag., charcoal gray textured lightweight carbon fiber/fiberglass Bell & Carlson composite stock with diagonally vented forend, matte blue receiver, Pachmayr Decelerator recoil pad, 7 1/2 lbs. New 2009.

MSR $1,200	$1,025	$825	$700	$600	$500	$425	$395

Add $40 for Mag. cals.

MODEL 70 EXTREME WEATHER SS – various standard and Mag. cals., 3 or 5 shot mag., stainless steel action, 22, 24, or 26 in. free floating, stainless steel fluted barrel, charcoal gray textured Bell & Carlson synthetic stock with alloy skeletal bedding block and cheekpiece, M.O.A. trigger system, one-piece trigger guard and mag. frame, no sights, 7 - 7 1/4 lbs. New 2008.

MSR $1,270	$1,050	$795	$650	$550	$475	$425	$375

Add $30 for Mag. cals.

During the first year of manufacture (2008), this model featured an engraved custom one-piece floor plate marked "2008 Model 70 Limited Edition".

MODEL 70 FEATHERWEIGHT (DELUXE) – various short action, long action, and WSM cals., pre-64 style controlled round feeding, new M.O.A. trigger system adj. from 3-5 lbs., blade type ejector, 3 or 5 shot mag., 22 or 24 in. hammer forged blue barrel w/o sights, one-piece trigger guard and hinged mag. floor plate, high polish bluing, satin finished Grade II fleur-de-lis checkered walnut stock with Schnabel forend, jeweled bolt, knurled bolt handle, 3-position safety, Pachmayr Decelerator recoil pad, 6 1/2 - 7 lbs. New 2008.

MSR $940	$815	$695	$615	$525	$450	$375	$325

Add $40 for regular Mag. and WSM cals.

During the first year of manufacture (2008), this model featured an engraved custom one-piece floor plate marked "2008 Model 70 Limited Edition".

MSR	100%	98%	95%	90%	80%	70%	60%

* ***Model 70 Featherweight Compact*** – .22-250 Rem., .243 Win., .308 Win., or 7mm-08 Rem. cal., similar to Model 70 Featherweight except has 20 in. barrel and 13 in. LOP, approx. 6 1/2 lbs. New 2011.

MSR $940	$815	$695	$615	$525	$450	$375	$325

MODEL 70 JACK O'CONNOR TRIBUTE – .270 Win. cal., pre-64 action with controlled feed and ejection, 22 in. barrel, blue finish, jeweled bolt body and engraved handle, drilled and tapped, 5 shot mag., finely checkered French AA walnut stock and forearm with Shadowline cheekpiece, alloy floorplate with ram's head engraving, Pachmayr Decelerator pad, Jack O'Connor gold signature on trigger guard, engraved steel grip cap, three position safety, Hex guard screws, 7 lbs. 8 oz. Limited mfg. mid-2013-2014.

	$1,700	$1,495	$1,275	$1,150	$935	$765	$595

Last MSR was $2,000.

This model was featured as a 2012 SHOT Show Special with the following variations, free-floating barrel, ebony forearm tip, Jack O'Connor signature in nickel on trigger guard, included voucher to purchase an embroidered custom case from the Jack O'Connor Center.

* ***Model 70 Jack O'Connor Custom Tribute*** – .270 Win. cal., similar to Model 70 Jack O'Connor Tribute, except features French AAA walnut stock and forearm, 7 lbs. 8 oz. Limited mfg. mid-2013-2014.

	$2,300	$2,000	$1,725	$1,575	$1,275	$1,050	$800

Last MSR was $2,600.

This model was featured as a 2012 SHOT Show Special with the following variations: M.O.A. Trigger System, ebony forearm tip, Jack O'Connor signature in nickel on trigger guard, included voucher for free custom embroidered case that was redeemable through the Jack O'Connor Center.

MODEL 70 SAFARI EXPRESS – .375 H&H, .416 Rem. Mag., or .458 Win. Mag. cal., 24 in. blue barrel with hooded blade front sight, express rear barrel sight, 3 shot mag., pre-'64 type claw extractor, dual recoil lugs, reinforced crossbolts, checkered satin finished walnut stock with cheekpiece, one piece steel trigger guard, flush mount hinged magazine floor plate, barrel band front swivel base, Pachmayr Decelerator recoil pad, 9 lbs. New 2010.

MSR $1,500	$1,250	$950	$850	$750	$650	$575	$500

MODEL 70 SPORTER (DELUXE) – various cals., similar to Featherweight Deluxe, 3 or 5 shot mag., 24 or 26 (.300 Win. Mag. only) in. barrel w/o sights, satin finished Grade II walnut stock with cheekpiece and cut checkering, Pachmayr Decelerator recoil pad, high polish blued receiver/ barrel, 7 1/2 - 7 3/4 lbs. New 2008.

MSR $940	$815	$695	$615	$525	$450	$375	$325

Add $40 for Mag. cals.

During the first year of manufacture (2008), this model featured an engraved custom one-piece floor plate marked "2008 Model 70 Limited Edition".

MSR	100%	98%	95%	90%	80%	70%	60%

MODEL 70 SUPER GRADE - .270 Win. (new 2009), .30-06, .300 Win. Mag., 270 WSM (new 2009), .300 WSM (new 2009), .338 Win. Mag. (new 2010), or 7mm Rem. Mag. (new 2012) cal., similar to Model 70 Sporter Deluxe, except has fancy grade checkered walnut stock and forearm with cheekpiece and rosewood forend tip, no sights, one-piece steel trigger guard, and flush mounted hinged mag. floor plate marked "Super Grade", approx. 8 lbs. New 2008.

MSR $1,360	$1,175	$975	$750	$650	$550	$495	$450

Add $40 for Mag. cals.

During the first year of manufacture (2008), this model featured an engraved custom one-piece floor plate marked "2008 Model 70 Limited Edition".

MODEL 70 75TH ANNIVERSARY SUPER GRADE - .30-06 cal., 24 in. barrel w/o sights, features Grade IV/V fancy walnut stock with cut checkering and shadowline cheekpiece, floorplate features "75th Anniversary Model 70" with scroll engraving, right side of upper receiver has engraved banner "The Rifleman's Rifle", engraved steel grip cap, 8-1/4 lbs. Mfg. 2012 only.

	$1,775	$1,600	$1,400	$1,200	$1,000	$875	$750

Last MSR was $2,000.

MODEL 70 SUPER GRADE 150TH COMMEMORATIVE - .270 Win. cal., 28 in. round barrel with gold band at muzzle, "The American Legend 1866-2016" marked in gold on barrel, High Grade V/VI American black walnut stock with cut fleur-de-lis checkering and deluxe shadowline cheekpiece, Pachmayr Decelerator pad, black forend tip and recessed steel sling swivel studs, jeweled bolt, deep relief scroll engraving with gold embellishments on the highly polished blued receiver, barrel, trigger guard, floorplate, and grip cap including the Winchester 150th Anniversary logo and the WRA scroll trademark, steel trigger guard and one-piece bottom metal, three-position safety, 8 1/4 lbs. New 2016.

MSR $2,070	$1,850	$1,700	$1,550	$1,400	$1,250	$1,100	$1,000

MODEL 70 ULTIMATE SHADOW - various cals., 3 or 5 shot mag., 22, 24, or 26 in. blue barrel, black pistol grip composite stock with oval dot gripping surfaces, controlled round feed action, hinged mag. floor plate, external claw extractor, Winsorb recoil pad, no sights, M.O.A. trigger system, approx. 6 1/2 - 7 lbs. Mfg. 2009-2015.

	$675	$615	$540	$465	$415	$365	$335

Last MSR was $800.

Add $40 for Mag. cals.

* ***Model 70 Ultimate Shadow SS*** - various cals., similar to Model 70 Ultimate Shadow, except has matte stainless steel action and barrel, 6-3/4-7/14 lbs. Mfg. 2012-2015.

	$840	$725	$625	$550	$475	$395	$340

Last MSR was $990.

Add $40 for Mag. cals.

MSR	100%	98%	95%	90%	80%	70%	60%

MODEL 70 ULTIMATE SHADOW HUNTER – various standard and Mag. cals., Pre-64 style controlled round feed with claw extractor, 3 or 5 shot mag., 22, 24, or 26 in.Sporter free floating barrel, lightweight synthetic Mossy Oak Break-Up Infinity (disc. 2014), or Mossy Oak Break-Up Country (new 2015) camo finish, gray overmolded rubberized gripping surfaces, satin blued metal finish, three position safety, recessed target crown, M.O.A. trigger system, blade type ejector, Winsorb technology recoil pad, no sights, approx. 6 3/4 - 7 1/4 lbs. Mfg. 2013-2015.

	$750	$675	$595	$515	$465	$415	$365

Last MSR was $870.

Add $50 for Mag. cals.

* ***Model 70 Ultimate Shadow Hunter SS*** – various cals., similar to Model 70 Ultimate Shadow Hunter, except has matte stainless steel action and barrel, 6-3/4-7/14 lbs. Mfg. 2013-2015.

	$935	$825	$725	$625	$525	$450	$375

Last MSR was $1,100.

Add $40 for Mag. cals.

RIFLES: BOLT ACTION, MISC., 2015-CURRENT MFG.

In 2015, after 50 years, Winchester released its new XPR bolt action rifle.

XPR – .243 Win. (new 2016), .270 Win., .30-06, .300 Win. Mag., 7mm-08 Rem. (new 2016), .308 Win. (new 2016), .338 Win. Mag., .270 WSM (new 2016), .300 WSM (new 2016), .325 WSM (new 2016), or 7mm Rem. Mag. (new 2016) cal., free floating 22 (new 2016), 24 or 26 in. barrel w/o sights and recessed target crown, 3 shot detachable box mag., steel receiver, controlled round feed and claw extractor with blade-type ejector, M.O.A. trigger system with stainless steel components, black polymer stock with textured panels and Inflex technology recoil pad, 3 position safety on back of bolt, bolt unlock button and nickel Teflon coated bolt body, matte black finish, approx. 7 1/4 lbs. New 2015.

MSR $550	$475	$415	$375	$350	$325	$295	$275

XPR HUNTER – .243 Win., .270 Win., .30-06, .300 Win. Mag., 7mm-08 Rem., .308 Win., .338 Win. Mag., .270 WSM, .300 WSM, .325 WSM, or 7mm Rem. Mag. cal., free floating 22, 24, or 26 in. barrel w/o sights and recessed target crown, 3 shot detachable box mag., steel receiver, controlled round feed and claw extractor with blade-type ejector, M.O.A. trigger system with stainless steel components, 2 position thumb safety with cocking indicator, bolt unlock button and nickel Teflon coated bolt body, Mossy Oak Break-Up Country polymer stock with textured panels and Inflex technology recoil pad, 6 3/4-7 1/4 lbs. New 2016.

MSR $600	$525	$450	$395	$360	$330	$300	$275

COMBINATION GUNS

SHOTGUN/RIFLE COMBINATION - combination 12 ga. and .222 Rem., .223 Rem., .243 Win., .270 Win., .30-06, .308 Win., .300 Win. Mag., 5.6x57R, 6.5x55mm, 7x65R, 7x57 Mauser, or 9.3x74R cal. rifle,

MSR	100%	98%	95%	90%	80%	70%	60%

O/U, 25 in. barrels, top barrel is WinChoked, Grand European engraving and finish, 8 1/2 lbs. Mfg. 1983-85.

	$2,795	$2,475	$2,100	$1,875	$1,650	$1,550	$1,425

Last MSR was $2,550.

Add 50% for .300 Win. Mag. or 6.5x55mm cal.

This model was advertised in .222 Rem., .223 Rem., 6.5x55mm, or .300 Win. Mag. cal., but very few 6.5x55mm or .300 Win. Mag. cals. have been encountered to date.

RIFLES: O/U

DOUBLE XPRESS RIFLE - .30-06, .257 Roberts, .270 Win., 7x57M, 7x57R, 7x65R, or 9.3x74R cal., 23 1/2 in. O/U barrels, iron sights with claw scope mounts, ejectors, fully engraved satin finish receiver with game scene engraving, walnut specially hand checkered, sling swivels, 8 1/2 lbs. Mfg. 1984-85 only.

	$4,950	$4,500	$3,000	$2,500	$2,250	$2,000	$1,750

Last MSR was $2,995.

In 1984, Aero Marine located in Birmingham, AL special ordered 200 deluxe double rifles in 7x57mm Mauser cal. They featured better engraving and game scenes with bottom of receiver marked Jaeger. Of the 200, 100 were rifles with 90 being standard grade and 10 being deluxe. The other 100 were supplied with an extra set of O/U shotgun barrels. Sales were slow on these special guns and eventually they were liquidated to another wholesaler. Recently, prices are in the $3,500-$3,950 range for the rifle alone and $5,000-$5,500 for the Combo, depending on condition.

RIFLES: SINGLE SHOT, POST 1964 MFG.

MODEL 1885 LOW WALL GRADE I .22 LR CAL. - .22 LR cal., 24 1/2 in. half-round, half-octagon barrel with buckhorn rear sights, uncheckered straight grip walnut stock and forearm, crescent buttplate, blue finish only, 8 lbs. 2,400 mfg. late 1999-2001.

	$735	$625	$525	$450	$400	$350	$300

Last MSR was $828.

* ***Model 1885 Low Wall High Grade*** - similar to Model 1885 Low Wall Grade I, except features frame engraving, 24Kt. squirrel/cottontail scenes, fancy walnut stock and forearm with cut checkering. 1,100 mfg. late 1999-2001.

	$1,050	$875	$750	$650	$550	$450	$350

Last MSR was $1,180.

MODEL 1885 LOW WALL - .17 HMR (disc. 2006), .17 Mach 2 (new 2005), .22 Hornet, .223 Rem., .22-250 Rem., or .243 Win. cal., 24 in. octagon barrel, checkered straight grip or pistol grip walnut stock and Schnabel forearm, open sights, sling swivels, drilled and tapped, 8 lbs. Mfg. 2003-2006.

	$875	$700	$575	$500	$450	$400	$350

Last MSR was $1,069.

MSR	100%	98%	95%	90%	80%	70%	60%

MODEL 1885 HIGH WALL – .22-250 Rem. (new 2006), .223 Rem. (new 2006), .270 WSM, .300 WSM, .325 WSM (new 2006), or 7mm WSM cal., 28 in. full octagon barrel without sights, checkered walnut stock, Schnabel forearm, adj. trigger, Pachmayr Decelerator pad, blued receiver, 8 1/2 lbs. Mfg. 2005-2006.

	$1,000	$800	$675	$575	$500	$425	$375

Last MSR was $1,085.

MODEL 1885 BPCR – .45-70 Govt. cal., 30 in. half round, half octagon barrel, case colored receiver, lever, buttplate, and pistol grip cap, drilled and tapped, oil finished Grade III/IV walnut Creedmor style stock with Schnabel forearm, no sights, 10 lbs., 8 oz.

	$1,450	$1,275	$1,075	$925	$800	$700	$600

Last MSR was $1,779.

This model was featured as a 2009 SHOT Show Special.

MODEL 1885 HIGH WALL CENTENNIAL HUNTER – .30-06 cal., features gold embellished .30-06 seal on right side of engraved receiver, special barrel inscription, 28 in. octagon barrel, 8 1/2 lbs. Limited mfg. 2006.

	$1,525	$1,275	$975	N/A	N/A	N/A	N/A

Last MSR was $1,617.

MODEL 1885 HUNTER RIMFIRE – .17 HMR, .17 WSM, .22 LR, or .22 WMR cal., low wall action, 24 in. octagon barrel with button rifling, semi-buckhorn rear sight and Marbles gold bead front sight, checkered walnut stock and Schnabel forearm, Pachmayr rubber recoil pad, blued frame and barrel, approx. 7 1/2 lbs. Mfg. by Miroku. New 2014.

MSR $1,470	$1,325	$1,100	$975	$850	$725	$600	$500

100%	98%	95%	90%	80%	70%	60%	50%	40%	30%	20%	10%

SHOTGUNS: 1879-1963

BREECH LOADING SxS – 10 or 12 ga., imported from England for sales through the Winchester New York City office only, exposed hammers, available in 5 grades ranging from Class D - Class A and Match gun (lowest to highest). Higher grades were mfg. by W.C. Scott & Sons, C.G. Bonehill, W.C. McEntree, Richard Redmond, and H. & E. Hammond Gun Mfg.'s. Approx. 10,000 were imported between 1879-84.

Prices vary greatly due to condition and grade. Prices can range from $350 (poor condition Class D) to over $5,500 (95%+ condition specimen in Class A or Match gun).

This SxS model was the first shotgun bearing the Winchester name sold in the U.S. Identifiable by "Winchester Repeating Arms Co., New Haven, Connecticut, USA" marking on barrel rib top.

MODEL 1887 LEVER ACTION – 10 or 12 ga., 4 shot tube mag., 30 or 32 in. full choke fluid steel barrels, plain pistol grip stock, first Browning patent shotgun mfg. by Winchester, first lever action repeating shotgun mfg. domestically. Mfg. 1887-1901. Approx. 64,855 mfg.

N/A	$4,150	$3,600	$3,075	$2,650	$2,200	$1,875	$1,325	$1,100	$900	$775	$675

100%	98%	95%	90%	80%	70%	60%	50%	40%	30%	20%	10%

Standard frame finish on this model was color case hardening. Premiums exist for original bright case colored specimens. 10 ga. began production with serial number 22148. Also mfg. in Riot configuration (20 in. cylinder bore barrel). Gauges were chambered for 2 5/8 in. (12 ga.) and 2 7/8 in. (10 ga.). A very small amount was also made up in .70-150 cal. - add a significant premium.

* ***Model 1887 Lever Action Deluxe*** - damascus barrel, checkered stock, and other special order features.

N/A $8,250 $6,600 $5,500 $4,500 $3,100 $2,450 $1,975 $1,650 $1,325 $1,100 $900

MODEL 1893 SLIDE ACTION - 12 ga., 30 (standard) and 32 in. barrel, black powder only. First Winchester shotgun with sliding forearm action, first Browning slide action patent, disc. 1897 after run of some 34,050. Note: chambered for 2 5/8 shells only, damascus barrels were available at extra cost, as were fancy stocks.

N/A $1,150 $975 $850 $725 $625 $550 $500 $450 $400 $350 $300

This gun had limited sales because mechanical weaknesses developed when shooting smokeless powder. Winchester offered a brand new shotgun of the customer's choice when they returned their Model 1893.

MODEL 1897 SLIDE ACTION - 12 or 16 ga. (introduced 1900), improved Model 1893 action, 26-32 in. barrels, visible hammer, various chokes, takedown or solid frame, plain pistol grip stock. Over 1,024,700 mfg. between 1897-1957.

N/A $875 $675 $550 $500 $400 $300 $250 $225 $200 $175 $150

Add 50% for 16 ga.

Early 16 ga. Model 1897s were chambered for 2 9/16 in. shotshells, and are not as valuable because of the 2 3/4 in. shell length currently manufactured. This model was marked "Model 1897" on the slide action rails until circa 1912 (approx. ser. no. 500,000). After approx. ser. no. 500,000, the marking was moved to the barrel and changed to Model 97. The Model 1897 was the first Winchester shotgun chambered for 2 3/4 in. smokeless ammunition. This model was also manufactured with a damascus barrel for a short period of time, and is rare.

MODEL 1897 RIOT GUNS - see the "Trench/Riot Shotgun" category in the T section for more information and prices.

MODEL 1897 TRENCH GUNS - see the "Trench/Riot Shotgun" category in the T section for more information and prices.

This model changed its stock configuration after WWI.

MODEL 1897 TRAP - higher grade version of Standard, checkered stock, could have black diamond inlay in stock until 1919 (Black Diamond Trap), breech block marked "Trap" until approx. 1926. Mfg. 1897-1931.

N/A $2,750 $2,300 $1,995 $1,750 $1,450 $1,100 $825 $675 $500 $450 $400

* ***Model 1897 Trap Black Diamond Trap*** - distinguishable by diamond ebony inlays in stock pistol grip.

N/A $2,500 $2,200 $1,975 $1,750 $1,450 $1,100 $825 $675 $500 $450 $400

100%	98%	95%	90%	80%	70%	60%	50%	40%	30%	20%	10%

MODEL 1897 PIGEON – higher grade version of Standard 97, should have engraved pigeon behind hammer on frame, breech block marked "Pigeon", most exhibit black diamond stock inlays until 1919. Mfg. 1897-1939.

N/A	$12,750	$9,950	$8,550	$6,600	$4,950	$3,850	$3,300	$2,200	$1,650	$1,100	$900

MODEL 1901 – 10 ga. only, strengthened Model 1887 action to accept smokeless powder, lever action, standard barrel 32 in., blue barrel and frame, 5 shot mag., barrel address on upper tang. 13,500 mfg. between 1901-1920, starting with serial number 64,856.

N/A	$3,850	$3,500	$3,300	$2,750	$2,200	$1,975	$1,650	$1,375	$900	$775	$550

Add 50% for Deluxe Grade (checkered wood).

This shotgun was chambered for 2 7/8 in. smokeless powder ammunition.

MODEL 1911 SL AUTOLOADER – 12 ga., recoil operated, 26 or 28 in. barrel, various chokes, pistol grip laminated birch stock. Mfg. 1911-1921, with some production occuring between 1921-1928, 103,246 produced, action had design problems, nicknamed "Head Buster."

$925	$795	$650	$550	$500	$400	$325	$250	$200	$150	$140	$130

Values assume original wood without splitting, repair, or replacement. The Model 1911 was Winchester's first semi-auto shotgun. It did not prove to be satisfactory partly because the design had to avoid infringing the patents for Browning's famous A-5 model. Interestingly enough, this was a design which Winchester originally had helped Browning patent.

MSR	100%	98%	95%	90%	80%	70%	60%

MODEL 12 SLIDE ACTION – 12 (introduced 1914), 16 (introduced 1914), 20 (initial ga., mfg. 1912, 2 1/2 in. chamber mfg. until 1927), or 28 (introduced 1937) ga., 25 (20 ga. only, mfg. 1912-14), 26, 28, 30, or 32 in. standard, nickel, or stainless steel (scarce) barrel with or without rib (matted, solid, or VR), 2 9/16 (early 16 or 20 ga., until 1927, at ser. no. 464,565), 2 3/4 (became standard 1927) or 3 in. chamber, 6 shot, blue metal, various chokes, hammerless, plain pistol grip or straight walnut stock and forearm, marked Model 1912 from 1912-1919, approx. ser. no. 172,000. 14 in. LOP was original standard, then changed to 14 1/2 in. circa 1930. Mfg. 1912-1976.

	100%	98%	95%	90%	80%	70%	60%
12 ga. (28 or 30 in. FC bbl.)	$800	$650	$550	$450	$350	$320	$227
16 ga.	$950	$775	$650	$525	$400	$325	$300
20 ga.	$1,250	$1,000	$800	$700	$600	$525	$475
28 ga.	N/A	$5,175	$4,625	$4,200	$3,575	$2,950	$2,550

Subtract 50% if with non-factory Cutts compensator (has choke marked on barrel).

Add 50% for factory installed Cutts compensator (no choke marking on barrel).

Add 20% for 32 in. barrel.

Add 50% for original box with papers.

The following add-ons DO NOT apply to 28 ga. values.

Add 20%-40% for Win. solid rib, depending on original condition.

Add 50%-60% for Win. milled VR.

Add 25%-50% for "Deluxe Field Grade" with fancy checkered wood, depending on condition.
Add 10% for pre-WWII mfg.
Add 60% for each extra barrel(s).
Add 40%-50% for Win. special VR (offset barrel proofmark).

"Y" prefix appears on Model 12s built 1964-1980 - see listing under Post-64 Models. Publisher's Note: The "Y" was actually added in front of the already applied serial numbers to be shipped after the 1968 Gun Control Act took effect (1970). The "left over" pre "64" receivers were used up on custom orders until that law became effective, and then the "Y" was added.

Nickel steel barrel Model 12s (mfg. 1912-1931) have become very popular in recent years, and some collectors are actually specializing on nickel steel Model 12s only. Winchester proofed steel barrels were introduced in 1931.

Stainless steel barrel Model 12s were introduced during 1926 as a special order only, and discontinued in 1931 (65X,XXX serial range). Values typically range between $1,450 - $3,500, and are very rare in over 95% original condition, as the bluing easily wore off the stainless steel barrel since it was a "Japaned" finish, not regular bluing. Original gauge can be determined by removing the buttstock and observing the gauge marking on the stock screw boss.

"Donut" post Winchester VRs are more desirable than the rectangular post.

13-15 in. LOPs could be special ordered on Model 12s until 1964.

Special order features on field guns have captured much collector interest in recent years. Combinations of these features can add a considerable percentage to the base values listed. Rare special orders on rare variations are very desirable and prices can double and more if the combination is right. As is the case with most other collectible shotguns at this time, Model 12s with open choked barrels in shorter lengths are A LOT more desirable (and expensive) than a specimen with a 30 in. full choke barrel (most common). Values listed are for standard configuration (28 or 30 in. full choke barrel with no rib). For most Model 12s, values for condition factors less than 60% will approximate the 60% price, because of shooter demand. Premiums must be added for the rarer open choked barrels in shorter length on all gauges.

Recently, some non-original, re-stamped 28 ga. barrels have been added to 16 or 20 ga. frames "creating" a more desirable (and expensive) gun to unsuspecting buyers. Roll die markings are getting better and better so be very cautious when considering a non-Cutts 28 ga. (as in get a receipt specifying originality). 28 ga. ser. no. range is approx. 720,138 to 1,857,XXX. 28 ga. Model 12s were available with both 2 3/4 (common) or 2 7/8 (infrequent) in. chamber. The 28 ga. has a magazine tube which is crimped, swaged, and necked at the rear and is visible with barrel assembly off and slide pulled back, enabling mag tube to protrude slightly

MSR	100%	98%	95%	90%	80%	70%	60%

at the rear of receiver extension. Believe it or not, there are getting to be a lot of fake Model 12 boxes that have been intentionally aged. Carefully screen NIB (watch the hanging tag also) specimens in this model.

* ***Model 12 Special Information***

Editor's Note: The Model 12 Winchester was produced continuously from 1912-1980. Over 2,027,500 were produced both in standard and deluxe (Pigeon) grades. Pigeon grades were first listed in 1914 and disc. during the war (1941). Reintroduced in 1948, they were disc. permanently in 1964, after which the Super Pigeon Grade became available only on a custom-order basis from Winchester's Custom Gun Shop. These guns are worth 50%-300% premiums depending on gauge, barrel lengths, stock options, engraving patterns, etc.

With an attrition rate of approximately 33%, Model 12s with rare features produced 50 years ago will only be much rarer today (and expensive). 28 ga. guns were built between 1937 and 1960. Gauge rarity in increasing order is 12 ga. (approx. 360,000 mfg. 1925-1943), 16 ga. (approx. 190,000 mfg. 1925-1943), 20 ga. (approx. 71,000 mfg. 1925-1943), .410 bore (Model 42), and 28 ga. (approx. 2,600 mfg. 1925-1943). Serialization breakdown by year of manufacture is provided under the "Serialization" section of this book. When collecting Model 12s, ser. nos. on the underside of receiver (forward end), should match ser. no. on bottom rear of Mag. tube.

MODEL 12 FEATHERWEIGHT - similar to Standard, except with alloy guard and different takedown system. Mfg. 1959-62. "F" suffix after ser. no.

	$750	**$675**	**$575**	**$450**	**$375**	**$300**	**$250**

MODEL 12 RIOT GUNS - see the "Trench/Riot Shotgun" category in the T section for more information and prices.

MODEL 12 MILITARY TRENCH GUNS - see the "Trench/Riot Shotgun" category in the T section for more information and prices.

MODEL 12 HEAVY DUCK GUN - 12 ga., 3 in. chamber, 30 or 32 in. barrel, solid rubber recoil pad, 1/2 in. shorter pull than regular Model 12 (13 5/8 in LOP.). Mfg. 1935-1963.

	$1,350	**$1,175**	**$1,050**	**$925**	**$800**	**$600**	**$500**

Add 60% for solid rib.

Add 50% for 32 in. barrel.

* ***Model 12 Heavy Duck Gun Vent. Rib*** - factory Winchester or 2 different rib styles mfg. by Simmons, notice barrel proof marking - rare.

	$3,250	**$2,975**	**$2,600**	**$2,350**	**$1,850**	**$1,500**	**$1,400**

Add 25%-50% for "Deluxe Field Grade" with fancy checkered wood, depending on condition.

MSR	100%	98%	95%	90%	80%	70%	60%

MODEL 12 SKEET GUN - 12, 16, 20, or 28 ga., 26 in. barrel, skeet choke, checkered pistol grip stock, 14 in. LOP standard on pre-war guns. Mfg. 1933-1976.

	100%	98%	95%	90%	80%	70%	60%
12 ga.	$2,350	$1,825	$1,350	$1,150	$900	$750	$650
16 ga.	$3,350	$2,875	$2,400	$2,000	$1,750	$1,500	$1,250
20 ga.	$5,875	$4,500	$3,375	$2,875	$2,250	$1,800	$1,500
28 ga.	$9,750	$8,300	$7,200	$6,100	$5,000	$4,850	$3,500

Add 10% for solid rib.

Add 20% for Win. Special VR.

Add 50% for Win. milled VR.

Subtract 50% for non-Factory-Cutts compensator.

Add approx. 20%-25% for brown plastic Hydrocoil stock, 12 ga. only.

Add approx. 40%-50% for white plastic Hydrocoil stock (approx. 50 mfg, 12 ga. only).

Another variation of the Model 12 Skeet was called the "Lady and Junior Model", with a factory LOP of 13 in., supplied with an original Mershon recoil pad - the configuration could also be special order during later years.

MODEL 12 TRAP GUN – various gauges, full choke barrel, deluxe straight or pistol grip stock, solid recoil pad, 14 3/8 in. LOP standard on pre-war guns. Mfg. 1938-1964.

100%	98%	95%	90%	80%	70%	60%
$2,100	$1,600	$1,400	$1,200	$950	$800	$700

Add 20% for milled VR.

Add approx. 20% for brown plastic Hydrocoil stock.

Add approx. 50% for white plastic Hydrocoil stock (approx. 50 mfg).

While plain barreled variation is rare, it is not as desirable.

MODEL 12 SUPER FIELD GRADE – 12, 16, or 20 ga., 26, 28, or 30 in. matted rib barrel, deluxe walnut with checkered pistol grip stock and forearm, mfg. 1955-59.

100%	98%	95%	90%	80%	70%	60%
$2,250	$2,000	$1,800	$1,575	$1,350	$1,000	$850

Add 60% for 20 ga.

Add 50% for 16 ga.

MODEL 12 "BLACK DIAMOND" TRAP GRADE – various configurations, straight or pistol grip stock, features a small ebony diamond inlaid on each side of the pistol grip, 30 or 32 in. barrel with solid rib.

100%	98%	95%	90%	80%	70%	60%
$3,500	$3,250	$2,750	$2,500	$1,800	$1,650	$1,400

Add 50% for milled VR.

MODEL 12 TOURNAMENT GRADE – 12 ga. only, straight grip stock, small checkered forearm, usually stamped "Tourn" in wood on buttstock under buttplate. Mfg. 1914-1930.

100%	98%	95%	90%	80%	70%	60%
$3,250	$2,750	$2,500	$2,250	$1,800	$1,500	$1,300

MSR	100%	98%	95%	90%	80%	70%	60%

MODEL 12 PIGEON GRADE – finer and more deluxe version of Model 12, many variations. Mfg. 1914-41 and 1948-64, engine turned breech block and shell follower, usually with engraved pigeon on bottom rear of mag. tube.

	$4,000	$3,750	$3,100	$2,600	$2,100	$1,650	$1,400
28 ga.	N/A	$7,250	$6,500	$5,500	$4,750	$4,000	$3,600

Add 25% for VR.

Add 100% for 20 ga.

Beware of potential fakes (i.e., inspect the engraved pigeon carefully if engraved on gun, and also note the quality and finish of the extra grade wood).

MODEL 20 – .410 bore, single shot, hammer, boxlock, 26 in. full choke (a few guns have been observed with cylinder choking), 6 lbs. 23,616 mfg. between 1919-1924.

	$1,200	$950	$800	$650	$500	$350	$300

Add 50% to the value, if original.

While most Model 20s have 2 1/2 in. chambers, late parts cleanup guns could be chambered for 3 in. also. Very few of the Winchester Model 20's came with "deluxe" features.

* ***Model 20 Winchester Junior Trap Shooting Outfit*** – complete Shooting Outfit includes: Winchester Model 20, .410 bore sport gun, a Model 20 stock hang tag, six boxes of Winchester .410 shot shells, 100 midget-sized Winchester clay targets, a hand throwing trap, and three-section cleaning rod. The Outfit also includes an instructional manual, two informative brochures, a score sheet pad, Winchester gun grease, rust remover and gun oil. All of the Winchester Junior Trap Shooting Outfit components are packed in a sturdy carrying case (with lock and key) for transporting.

	$8,500	$8,000	$7,500	$7,000	$6,500	$6,000	$5,500

Prices for this model assume all accessories are included - if not, subtract substantially. Just the shotshell boxes and accessories from this outfit are worth $2,500+ in nice condition.

MODEL 21 – 12, 16, 20, 28 ga., or .410 bore, boxlock action, after years in the design stage, production began in 1929 with guns being shipped to the warehouse in 1930 and first offered in Winchester's 1931 price list. Regular production continued for thirty years, through 1959. Approx. 32,500 mfg. 1931-1988. Approx. 1,100 were mfg. by the Custom Shop (including Custom, Pigeon, and Grand American Grades) during 1960-1982. Factory records for these models (early mfg. is sketchy) are available by contacting the Cody Firearms Museum located in Cody, WY. The following retail prices are for a standard field gun with average wood, beavertail forearm, ejectors, and single selective trigger with no alterations.

12 ga.	$7,250	$6,450	$5,500	$4,950	$4,500	$4,000	$3,750
16 ga.	$9,000	$8,000	$7,000	$6,500	$6,000	$5,500	$5,000
20 ga.	$10,000	$8,750	$7,500	$7,000	$6,500	$6,000	$5,500

Add 15%-25% for VR depending on condition.
Add 15%-30% per extra barrel assembly, depending on original condition.
Add 25% for 3 in. chambers (Duck Gun, 12 ga. only).
Add 20% for "Deluxe" marked guns, depending on original condition.
Subtract approx. 20% for double triggers w/extractors.
Subtract 10% for double triggers with ejectors (normally encountered with splinter forearm).

The early guns were plain, standard 12 gauge models with double triggers and extractors. Later in 1931, 16 and 20 gauge chamberings became available, as did selective single trigger and automatic ejectors.

By the end of 1933 the Model 21 skeet gun had been introduced as well as Tournament, Trap, and Custom Built grades. By about this time options included fancier wood, beavertail or semi-beavertail forends, checkered butts (standard on skeet guns) or skeleton steel buttplates, recoil pads and almost any variation the customers might desire. Metal finishes on a Model 21 are unusual in that they have salt blue frames and rust blue barrels - this explains the difference in coloration between these metal surfaces.

The Tournament Grade was dropped in 1936 and the Trap Grade in 1940. A Standard Grade Trap Gun was added in 1941. The early Custom Built Grade was dropped in 1942 and the Deluxe Grade was added. This grade included as standard many of the previously available extra cost options.

Relatively few guns were produced in chamberings smaller than 20 gauge. 28 gauge first appeared in the 1936 catalog, although a few were probably produced before that. Winchester records are unclear as to the total but it is generally believed that fewer than 100 original factory guns were made. In addition, a number of original 20 gauge guns have been modified at the factory or elsewhere with factory 28 gauge barrels. These latter guns are just as valuable if the conversion was done at the Winchester Custom Gun Shop. Authenticity of the original guns should be established by factory letter.

.410 bore guns were first listed in 1955 but, again, some had been produced earlier, one having been built for John Olin in 1950. Throughout Winchester history all the rules seem to have had exceptions and nowhere is this more apparent than with respect to the Model 21 which, after all, has been pretty much a custom gun from the very beginning. Factory records and tallies among dealers indicate the existence of 40 to 50 original factory guns. As in the case of the 28 gauge, extra barrels were available and at least some of those have been added to original 20 gauge guns.

The 3 inch Magnum 12 gauge Duck gun (stamped "Duck" on floor plate) was offered in Winchester catalogs from 1940 through 1952. Selective single triggers and automatic ejectors were standard as were the solid red Winchester recoil pads and 30 in. or 32 in. barrels. Some cases of non-factory upgrading of 2 3/4 or 3 inch Magnum guns have been reported. If

MSR	100%	98%	95%	90%	80%	70%	60%

authenticity is important to the buyer, a factory letter should be requested available from the Cody Firearms Museum at $85 per gun. With respect to such letters, in cases where records may be missing or incomplete, the resultant letters may be less conclusive than desired. In some instances, consultation with, or a written appraisal from an authoritative collector arms dealer might be helpful. As can be seen, values are partly based on a certain interdependence between options. Higher grade guns, of course, will bring somewhat higher prices, although much of their increased value results from the many "options" being included as standard features.

Buyers or sellers with limited experience should always seek expert advice or appraisals in dealing with a Model 21. This is especially true with regard to higher grade guns and those with extra ornamentation.

Refinishing or Restoration: There is disagreement as to the effects of refinishing a Model 21. Many shooters and at least some collectors prefer a professionally refinished gun to a badly worn one. Higher grade guns restored by a master craftsman may approach factory original guns in value.

Six standard patterns of engraving and several stock checkering and carving styles evolved during the production years. Values added by these and other embellishments such as precious metal inlays are beyond the scope of this work.

* ***Model 21 Skeet Gun*** – available in Standard, Tournament, and Trap grades. Introduced 1933.

Add 10% to standard Model 21 values. Larger premiums exist for special order grades.

* ***Model 21 Trap Gun*** – introduced 1940, Trap Grade disc. same year.

Add 10-25% to standard Model 21 values (be wary of non-factory modifications, especially to the stock).

* ***Model 21 3 Inch Duck Gun*** – 12 ga. only, 30 or 32 in. barrels, introduced in 1940, must be so stamped (observe the 3 in. and Duck markings very carefully).

	$9,000	**$8,000**	**$7,000**	**$6,500**	**$6,000**	**$5,500**	**$5,000**

Add 10% for 32 in. barrels.

* ***Model 21 .410 Bore*** – retail prices for original guns may be expected to range between $37,500 and $50,000 for mechanically sound guns depending on quality of finish. Non-original guns with add-on factory barrels would probably be reduced by one-third.

* ***Model 21 28 Ga.*** – factory original guns will probably bring from $25,000 to $30,000 and, as with the .410 bore guns, 20 gauge guns modified to 28 gauge with factory barrels would be worth approx. the same if done at the factory.

MODEL 21: RECENT PRODUCTION – refer to listing under SHOTGUNS: RECENT PRODUCTION SxS.

MSR	100%	98%	95%	90%	80%	70%	60%

MODEL 24 SxS – 12, 16, or 20 ga., boxlock, hammerless, double triggers. Introduced 1940, disc. 1957 after approx. 116,280 mfg.

12 ga.	$825	$725	$625	$475	$350	$275	$225
16 ga.	$950	$775	$675	$525	$400	$325	$275
20 ga.	$1,000	$900	$800	$675	$550	$425	$350

MODEL 25 SLIDE ACTION – 12 ga. only, non-takedown version of the Model 12, 26 or 28 in. barrel. 87,937 mfg. between 1949-1954.

	$550	$475	$400	$350	$300	$250	$200

MODEL 36 SINGLE SHOT – 9mm Rimfire cal., long shot, short shot, and ball, 18 in. round barrel, single shot bolt action, guns were not serial numbered, one-piece plain stock and forearm, special shaped trigger guard, 2 3/4 lbs. Approx. 20,000 mfg. between 1920-27.

	N/A	$1,700	$1,500	$1,300	$1,050	$895	$750

MODEL 37 SINGLE SHOT – 12, 16, 20, 28 ga., or .410 bore, top-lever break-open action, all barrels are full choke. Note on pricing that there is a big difference between a 100% gun without a box and NIB condition. Not serial-numbered. Over 1,015,000 mfg. between 1936-63.

12 gauge	$450	$325	$250	$200	$125	$100	$90
16 gauge	$450	$325	$250	$200	$125	$100	$90
20 gauge	$495	$395	$325	$250	$150	$110	$90
28 gauge	$2,500	$1,825	$1,325	$995	$725	$575	$450
.410 bore	$650	$500	$450	$375	$325	$200	$150

If models are truly NIB, add $125-$175 to 100% condition values only, depending on gauge.

Add 20% for "Red Letter" models.

Add 15% for 32 in. barrel (12, 16, or 20 ga. only).

Most 28 ga. Model 37s have the "Red Letter."

* ***Model 37 Single Shot Youth/Boys/Red Dot*** – 20 ga. only, 26 in. barrel marked Mod. Choke on barrel, solid red factory pad, identifiable by red dot inset into metal that is visible when hammer is cocked.

	N/A	$500	$400	$325	$250	$195	$150

MODEL 40 SEMI-AUTO – 12 ga. only, long recoil action, 28 or 30 in. barrel, walnut stock, skeet model also, poorly designed, many recalled by Winchester. Approx. 12,000 mfg. 1940-41.

	$825	$675	$550	$450	$400	$300	$225

MODEL 41 BOLT ACTION – .410 bore, 2 1/2 in. chamber until 1933 when it changed to 3 in., bolt action, single shot, 24 in. round barrel bored F, one-piece plain walnut stock and forearm, not serialized, approx. 22,145 were mfg. 1920-34.

	$725	$650	$550	$500	$425	$350	$300

Add 15% for 3 in. chamber.

This model is rarely encountered with over 80% original condition.

MODEL 42 SLIDE ACTION – first pump specifically designed for the .410 bore, hammerless, 2 1/2 (introduced 1935) or 3 in. chamber, 26 or 28 in. barrel, plain walnut pistol grip stock with circular grooved forearm

MSR	100%	98%	95%	90%	80%	70%	60%

(modified 1947), invented by William Roemer, approx. 6 1/2 - 7 lbs. Approx. 164,800 mfg. in 4 grades between 1933-1963.

Add 30% to any Model 42 chambered for 2 1/2 in. shells.

Add 25% for factory installed Cutts compensator (no choke marking on barrel).

Add 25% for pre-war guns.

Subtract 50% for non-factory installed Cutts compensator (choke marked on barrel).

Special order features on field guns have captured much collector interest in recent years. Combinations of these features can add a considerable percentage to the base values listed. Special orders on rare variations are very desirable, and prices can double, or more than double, if the combination is right.

A note on Model 42 Vent. Ribs:

Early Model 42 vent. ribs were designed "Winchester Special Ventilated Rib" circa 1954 in the 125,000 ser. no. range. This rib had a wavy line matting on top of the rib, no stamping on the side, is known as the "Doughnut" post rib, and were in production until the end of 1957 with approx. ser. no. 149,000. The second variation Model 42 rib appears on guns in the approx. ser. no. range 141,000-149,000. This rib was made with both solid and hollow round posts. All parts for the vent. rib were made at the Winchester plant. A third variation was introduced at the end of 1957, when Winchester decided to send its Model 42 barrels to the Simmons Gun Specialty Co. in Kansas City for installation of the vent. ribs. In-the-white barrels were proofed in New Haven and marked on the left side so that the rib would not cover up the proofmark before shipment to Simmons. The ser. no. was not stamped on the receiver extension until the gun was completely assembled. This last variation, or oval post, appears on Model 42s starting at approx. ser. no. 150,000. This third variation is marked either "SIMMONS PATENTED" or "SIMMONS GUN SPECIALTY CO., KANSAS CITY, MO". The longer Simmons marking was stamped on the rib until the end of production.

* ***Model 42 Slide Action Standard Grade*** – 26 or 28 in. plain, solid rib or vent. rib (after market) barrel, plain walnut straight or pistol grip stock, walnut grooved forearm. Mfg. 1933-1963.

Plain barrel	**$2,275**	**$2,025**	**$1,800**	**$1,475**	**$1,375**	**$1,275**	**$1,100**
Solid rib	**$3,600**	**$3,150**	**$2,700**	**$2,350**	**$2,100**	**$2,000**	**$1,750**

A factory vent rib on this model is very rare and desirable, as only a very few have been encountered.

* ***Model 42 Slide Action Skeet Grade*** – 26 or 28 in. plain, solid rib or vent. rib barrel, select checkered walnut straight grip or pistol grip stock and checkered forearm extension, 4 different chokes (full, modified, skeet, or cylinder) during pre-war (approx. ser. no. 1-52,000), post-war (approx. ser. no. 52,000-164,000) had same chokes available through 1953, when cylinder choke was dropped, and improved cylinder was added.

Plain barrel	**$4,550**	**$4,050**	**$3,775**	**$3,275**	**$2,925**	**$2,600**	**$2,250**
Solid rib	**$5,900**	**$5,450**	**$5,000**	**$4,325**	**$3,875**	**$3,425**	**$2,975**
Vent rib	**$6,800**	**$6,300**	**$5,750**	**$5,000**	**$4,425**	**$3,925**	**$3,425**

MSR	100%	98%	95%	90%	80%	70%	60%

* *Model 42 Slide Action Trap Grade/Trap Grade Skeet* – first variation had small checkered forearm with one diamond in center, field choke (full, modified, or cylinder), second variation has large checkered forearm with 2 diamonds in center, both variations had 26 or 28 in. plain or solid rib barrel, select checkered walnut straight grip (one closed diamond on underside of grip) or pistol grip (one closed diamond on each side of grip) stock, usually choked skeet, stamped "TRAP" at bottom of receiver under the ser. no. Only 231 mfg.

	$15,000	$13,000	$11,750	$9,500	$8,000	$6,500	$5,000

Add 10% for small slide handle.

* *Model 42 Slide Action Deluxe Grade* – same configurations as Trap Grade, 20 LPI checkering, most are fitted with special vent. rib after 1954 in 3 styles: round post-donut base, round post, and rectangle post, pre-1954 mfg. had plain or solid rib barrel, 1946-1950 mfg. may have "DELUXE" stamp under ser. no. on receiver. Mfg. 1946-63.

» *Model 42 Slide Action Deluxe Grade Solid Rib*

	$15,000	$13,000	$11,500	$11,000	$10,500	$8,000	$7,500

» *Model 42 Slide Action Deluxe Grade Vent. Rib (factory)*

	$16,000	$14,750	$12,750	$11,500	$11,000	$8,500	$8,000

* *Model 42 Slide Action Pigeon Grade* – same configurations as Deluxe Grade, except has pigeon engraved on underside of mag. tube, most were factory engraved, very few mfg.

Must be appraised individually. Before purchasing any factory engraved Model 42, it is advised that a reputable dealer/collector be consulted.

MODEL 50 SEMI-AUTO – 12 or 20 ga., 3 shot, recoil-operated (non-recoiling barrel), 26-30 in. barrels, VR optional, steel frame or Feather Weight Model (aluminum receiver, FTW) introduced 1958. Over 196,000 mfg. between 1954-61, starting with serial number 1,000.

Standard Model	$650	$525	$450	$400	$350	$300	$250
Trap or Skeet Model	$1,300	$1,050	$950	$800	$700	$600	$500

Add $100 for VR (Simmons installed).

Add $50 for Feather Weight Model (denoted by "A" suffix in ser. no.).

Add $150 for 20 ga.

* *Model 50 Semi-Auto Pigeon Grade* – can be denoted by PIGEON stamped above the serial number on the barrel assembly, deluxe wood.

	$2,300	$2,100	$1,850	$1,625	$1,400	$1,200	$995

MODEL 59 SEMI-AUTO – 12 ga. only, 3 shot, short recoil operation, Win-lite (steel and fiberglass) ribless barrels, 26-30 in. barrel lengths, alloy receiver inscribed with hunting scenes, Versalite (first interchangeable choke tubes) option introduced 1961, 6 1/2 lbs. 82,085 mfg. between 1960-65.

	$750	$625	$500	$400	$300	$250	$200

Add 30% for barrel with all three choke tubes.

MSR	100%	98%	95%	90%	80%	70%	60%

Inspect carefully for either cracked receiver (by bolt handle cutout and over serial numbers), or separating fiberglass on end of barrel. Winchester also mfg. 20 and 14 gauges experimentally in this model, which are extremely rare and expensive.

* ***Model 59 Semi-Auto Pigeon Grade*** – mfg. 1962-1965.

$3,000	$2,500	$2,000	$1,600	$1,200	$1,000	$800

SHOTGUNS: POST-1964

Winchester introduced WinChokes in 1969.

Shotguns: Post-1964, Lever Action

MODEL 9410 TRADITIONAL – .410 bore, 2 1/2 in. chamber, lever action based on the Model 94 rifle, 24 in. round barrel with cylinder bore or Standard Invector chokes (new 2003), 9 shot tube mag., iron sights with TruGlo front and modified V adj. rear, checkered straight grip walnut stock and forearm, top tang safety became standard in 2003, approx. 6 3/4 lbs. Mfg. 2001-2006.

$995	$825	$675	$495	$400	$325	$250

Last MSR was $626.

Subtract approx. $50 if w/o Invector chokes.

* ***Model 9410 Traditional Semi-Fancy*** – similar to Model 9410 Traditional, except has checkered semi-fancy walnut stock and Standard Invector choke system. Mfg. 2004.

$1,350	$1,075	$875	$750	$575	$425	$325

Last MSR was $789.

* ***Model 9410 Traditional Packer*** – cylinder bored or Standard Invector chokes (new 2003, includes 3 chokes), 20 in. barrel, 5 shot, 2/3 mag., open sights, checkered semi-pistol grip walnut stock and forearm with sling swivel studs, also available in Packer Compact Model (12 1/2 in. LOP, new 2003), 6 1/4 - 6 1/2 lbs. Mfg. 2002-2006.

$995	$825	$675	$495	$400	$325	$250

Last MSR was $647.

Subtract approx. $50 if w/o standard Invector chokes (includes 3).

* ***Model 9410 Traditional Ranger*** – similar to Model 9410 Traditional, except has uncheckered hardwood stock and forearm, 24 in. barrel with fixed cylinder bore barrel, 6 3/4 lbs. Mfg. 2003-2006.

$825	$650	$525	$400	$325	$250	$200

Last MSR was $532.

* ***Model 9410 Traditional TS Custom Case Colored*** – similar to Model 9410 Traditional, case colored receiver, lever, crescent buttplate, lower tang, and barrel bands, deluxe straight grip checkered walnut stock and extended forearm, matte bluing, 24 in. round barrel, gold trigger, top safety, 7 lbs. Mfg. 2005 only.

$2,250	$1,800	$1,425	$1,150	$950	$800	$600

Last MSR was $1,418.

MSR	100%	98%	95%	90%	80%	70%	60%

Shotguns: Post-1964, Semi-Auto

Winchester introduced WinChokes in 1969.

MODEL 140 RANGER SEMI-AUTO - 12, 16, or 20 ga., entry level model. Disc.

	$275	$250	$220	$200	$175	$155	$140

MODEL 1400 SEMI-AUTO - 12, 16, or 20 ga., 26, 28, or 30 in. barrel, 2 3/4 in. chamber, alloy receiver, various chokes, gas operated, 2 shot mag., checkered pistol grip stock. Mfg. 1964-1981.

	$275	$250	$220	$200	$175	$155	$140
Vent. rib	$315	$265	$240	$220	$195	$165	$150

Add 33% for Winchester recoil reduction system (mfg. 1964-1970).

Note: In 1968 the model 1400 series was modified. The action release was improved and the checkering redesigned. From 1968-72, they were designated MKII, which was then dropped. The values for the later guns mfg. from 1968-73 may run approx. 10% higher - values shown are for guns mfg. from 1965-1968. A left-hand version was also available, and was disc. in 1973.

NEW MODEL 1400 WALNUT - 12 or 20 ga., 2 3/4 in. chamber, 22 (disc.), 26 (mfg. 1991-93), or 28 in. VR barrel, checkered walnut stock and forearm, WinChokes standard, 3 shot mag., rotary bolt system, 7-7 1/2 lbs. Mfg. 1989-94.

	$350	$290	$260	$240	$220	$190	$165

Last MSR was $419.

Add $15 for limited mfg. 1993 Quail Unlimited Model (2,500 mfg. 1993).

MODEL 1400 CUSTOM HIGH GRADE - 12 ga. only, 28 in. VR WinChoke barrel, special order only through the Custom Gun Shop, features deluxe hand checkered walnut and special engraving. Mfg. 1991-92.

	$1,295	$995	$750	N/A	N/A	N/A	N/A

Last MSR was $1,695.

MODEL 1400 SKEET GRADE - similar to 1400, 12 or 20 ga., with 26 in. VR barrel, skeet bore, select skeet style stock. Mfg. 1965-73.

	$425	$350	$300	$275	$220	$195	$165

MODEL 1400 TRAP GRADE - similar to 1400, with 30 in. full choke VR barrel, select trap style stock. Mfg. 1965-73.

	$360	$330	$305	$275	$220	$195	$165

MODEL 1400 DEER GUN - similar to 1400, with 22 in. barrel, rifle sights, 12 ga. only. Mfg. 1965-74.

	$265	$240	$220	$200	$175	$165	$140

MODEL 1400 SLUG HUNTER - 12 ga. only, 22 in. smooth bore cyl. or rifled Sabot choke-tubed barrel, drilled and tapped for scope, includes bases or iron sights, 7 1/4 lbs. Mfg. 1990-92.

	$355	$310	$270	$250	$225	$195	$165

Last MSR was $420.

MSR	100%	98%	95%	90%	80%	70%	60%

MODEL 1400 RANGER – 12 or 20 ga., gas operation, alloy receiver, 22 cyl. deer, 26 (mfg. 1991-93), or 28 in. WinChoke barrel, checkered walnut finished hardwood stock and forearm, VR became standard 1985, 7 1/4 lbs. Disc. 1994.

	$285	$235	$200	$180	$160	$140	$120

Last MSR was $377.

Add $53 for deer combo. (includes extra 22 in. cyl. bore barrel).
Subtract $40 without VR.

MODEL 1500 XTR – 12 or 20 ga., 2 3/4 inch only, 28 inch barrel, plain or VR, WinChoke tubes, gas operation. Mfg. 1978-82.

	$300	$260	$240	$220	$200	$180	$160

SUPER X MODEL 1 – 12 ga., 26, 28, or 30 in. VR barrel, various chokes, steel receiver, self compensating gas operation, checkered pistol grip stock and forearm. Mfg. 1974-1981.

	$500	$450	$400	$350	$300	$250	$225

SUPER X MODEL 1 SKEET – 12 ga., similar to Standard, with 26 in. skeet bore barrel, select skeet style stock. Mfg. 1974-1981.

	$695	$595	$500	$475	$450	$425	$400

Add 20% if NIB condition.

SUPER X MODEL 1 TRAP – 12 ga., similar to Standard, with 30 in. barrel, imp. mod. or full choke, select trap style stock.

	$595	$550	$475	$425	$415	$395	$350

Add 20% if NIB condition.

SUPER X MODEL 1 CUSTOM TRAP OR SKEET – 12 ga. only, limited production from the Custom Shop, deluxe checkered walnut stock and forearm, extensive scroll engraving on receiver, built to custom order. Limited mfg. 1987-92.

	$1,295	$925	$725	N/A	N/A	N/A	N/A

* ***Super X Model 1 Custom Trap or Skeet Engraved*** – 12 ga., features number 5 engraving pattern with 7 gold inlays. Disc.

	$2,395	$1,900	$1,350	N/A	N/A	N/A	N/A

Last MSR was $1,295.

Add $700 for factory gold inlays (8 flying ducks).

SUPER X2 3 IN. MAGNUM FIELD – 12 ga. only, 3 in. chamber, self-adjusting gas operation, 26 or 28 in. VR back-bored barrel with Invector chokes, 5 shot mag., choice of checkered walnut or black synthetic stock and forearm with recoil pad, high gloss blue or matte metal finish, approx. 7 1/4 - 8 lbs. Mfg. 1999-2004.

	$750	$650	$575	$525	$465	$400	$325

Last MSR was $874.

* ***Super X2 3 in. Magnum Field Light*** – 12 ga., 26 or 28 in. VR back-bored barrel with Invector Plus chokes, alloy receiver, checkered pistol grip walnut stock and forearm, 6 1/2 - 6 3/4 lbs. Mfg. 2005-2006.

	$835	$710	$600	$560	$500	$450	$375

Last MSR was $945.

MSR	100%	98%	95%	90%	80%	70%	60%

* ***Super X2 3 in. Magnum Field Sporting Clays*** – 12 ga., 28 or 30 in. VR back-bored barrel with Invector chokes, adj. stock using spacers, includes 2 gas pistons, checkered walnut or Signature Red Dura-Touch finished (new 2003) hardwood stock and forearm, approx. 8 lbs. Mfg. 2001-2007.

	$875	$730	$610	$560	$500	$450	$375

Last MSR was $999.

Add $16 for Signature Red Dura-Touch finish on stock and forearm.

* ***Super X2 3 in. Magnum Field Sporting Clays Signature II*** – 12 ga., 28, 30 or 32 (mfg. 2005 only) in. barrel, red anodized alloy receiver and forearm cap, two gas pistons provided, black metallic paint on stock and forearm, adj. stock spacers provided, approx. 8 lbs. Mfg. 2005-2006.

	$885	$735	$625	$575	$500	$450	$375

Last MSR was $1,015.

* ***Super X2 3 in. Magnum Field Composite*** – 12 ga., 26 or 28 in. VR barrels with three Invector chokes, black composite stock and forearm with Dura-Touch armor coating, matte metal finish, includes sling swivel studs, approx. 7 3/4 lbs. Mfg. 2004-2005.

	$775	$665	$585	$525	$465	$400	$325

Last MSR was $908.

* ***Super X2 3 in. Magnum Field Rifled Deer*** – 12 ga., 22 in. rifled barrel with cantilever scope base and TruGlo sights (rear sight folds down), black synthetic stock and forearm, 7 1/4 lbs. Mfg. 2002-2005.

	$800	$675	$585	$530	$455	$395	$325

Last MSR was $957.

* ***Super X2 2 3/4 in. Magnum Field Practical MK I*** – 12 ga., similar to Super X2 Practical MKII, except is 2 3/4 in. chamber, has regular TruGlo iron sights, and does not have Dura-Touch, cylinder bore Invector choke standard, 8 lbs. Mfg. 2003-2007.

	$960	$800	$675	$575	$500	$465	$435

Last MSR was $1,116.

* ***Super X2 3 in. Magnum Field Practical MK II*** – 12 ga., home defense configuration featuring black composite stock and forearm, black metal finish, 22 in. barrel with Invector choke system and removable LPA ghost ring sights, 8 shot extended mag., includes sling swivels, Dura-Touch armor coated composite finish became standard during 2003, 8 lbs. Mfg. 2002-2006.

	$1,075	$885	$715	$635	$550	$495	$440

Last MSR was $1,287.

Subtract 10% if w/o Dura-Touch finished stock and forearm.

SUPER X2 3 1/2 IN. MAG. COMPOSITE – 12 ga. only, 3 1/2 in. chamber, similar to Super X2, black synthetic stock and forearm with vent. recoil pad, Dura-Touch armor coated stock/forearm treatment became standard during 2003 for all models, 24 (disc. 2000), 26, or 28 in. VR back-bored barrel with Invector chokes, 7 1/2-8 lbs. Mfg. 1999-2005.

	$885	$725	$625	$565	$500	$450	$375

Last MSR was $1,027.

MSR	100%	98%	95%	90%	80%	70%	60%

* ***Super X2 3 1/2 In. Mag. Composite Universal Hunter*** – 12 ga., similar to Super X2 3 1/2 In. Mag., except has full coverage Mossy Oak Break-Up camo composite stock and forearm, 26 in. VR barrel with 3 Invector Plus chokes, including optional extended extra full (standard beginning 2006), TruGlo sights, 7 3/4 lbs. Mfg. 2002-2007.

$1,050 $875 $700 $600 $515 $455 $375

Last MSR was $1,252.

Subtract approx. 5% for standard Invector Plus chokes.

* ***Super X2 3 1/2 In. Mag. Composite Greenhead*** – 12 ga., similar to Super X2 3 1/2 In. Mag., except has green Dura-Touch stock and forearm for enhanced durability and non-slip hold during cold/wet conditions, 28 in. VR barrel, matte metal finish, 8 lbs. Mfg. 2002-2005.

$900 $740 $620 $565 $500 $450 $375

Last MSR was $1,036.

* ***Super X2 3 1/2 In. Mag. Composite Turkey*** – 12 ga., similar to Super X2 3 1/2 In. Mag., except has 24 in. VR barrel with TruGlo sights and extra full turkey choke tube, matte finish only, 7 1/2 lbs. Mfg. 1999-2002.

$880 $730 $615 $555 $495 $450 $375

Last MSR was $1,018.

During 2001-2002, this model incorporated a "Team NWTF" logo on the stock.

* ***Super X2 3 1/2 In. Mag. Composite Camo Turkey (NWTF)*** – 12 ga., similar configuration as regular Turkey, except has 100% Mossy Oak Break-Up or Mossy Oak Obsession camo treatment and TruGlo sights, 7 1/2 lbs. Mfg. 2000-2007.

$1,035 $850 $700 $550 $495 $425 $375

Last MSR was $1,236.

Beginning in 2001, this model incorporates a "Team NWTF" logo on the stock.

* ***Super X2 3 1/2 In. Mag. Composite Camo Waterfowl*** – 12 ga., similar to Super X2 3 1/2 In. Mag., except has 100% Mossy Oak Shadow Grass treatment, 28 in. VR back-bored barrel with Invector chokes, 8 lbs. Mfg. 1999-2005.

$1,000 $840 $685 $565 $495 $425 $375

Last MSR was $1,185.

SX3 (SUPER X3) 3 IN. MAGNUM WALNUT FIELD – 12 or 20 (new 2009) ga., 3 in. chamber, self-adjusting Active Valve gas operation, 26 or 28 in. VR barrel with Invector Plus chokes, variable checkered walnut stock with second generation Pachmayr Decelerator pad, adj. LOP, alloy receiver and 4 shot mag. tube, grey Perma-Cote Ultra Tough or Dura-Touch Armor coating (current) surface finish, 6 3/8 - 7 lbs. Mfg. 2006-2011.

$1,025 $875 $750 $650 $575 $500 $450

Last MSR was $1,220.

This model is also known as the SX3 (Super X3).

MSR	100%	98%	95%	90%	80%	70%	60%

* ***SX3 (Super X3) Compact Field*** – 12 or 20 ga., similar to Super X3 3 in. Magnum Walnut Field, except has shortened 13 in. LOP. Mfg. 2011 only.

	$1,025	$875	$750	$650	$575	$500	$450

Last MSR was $1,220.

* ***SX3 (Super X3) 3 in. Magnum Classic Field*** – 12 or 20 ga., similar to 3 in. Walnut Field, except has traditional diamond pattern checkering and non-adj. Decelerator recoil pad. Mfg. 2008-2009.

	$975	$850	$750	$650	$575	$500	$450

Last MSR was $1,159.

* ***SX3 (Super X3) 3 in. Flanigun Exhibition/Sporting*** – 12 or 20 ga., 28 or 30 (new 2010) in. VR barrel with Invector Plus chokes, black composite stock and forearm with Dura-Touch armor coating and red annodized frame and forearm cap, designed for Winchester exhibition shooter Patrick Flanigan, 7 1/4 lbs. Mfg. 2008-2010.

	$1,195	$995	$850	$725	$625	$550	$475

Last MSR was $1,479.

This model was featured as a 2009 SHOT Show Special in 12 ga. only, 30 in. VR barrel, TruGlo fiber optic front sight, three signature Invector Plus choke tubes, and Inflex Technology recoil pad.

* ***SX3 (Super X3) 3 in. Magnum Field Composite*** – 12 or 20 (new 2011) ga., similar to 3 in. Mag. Walnut Field, black composite stock and forearm, alloy receiver, 26 or 28 in. barrel with Invector Plus chokes, approx. 6 3/4 lbs. Mfg. 2006-2011.

	$975	$850	$725	$625	$525	$475	$425

Last MSR was $1,140.

Add $10 for 12 ga.

* ***SX3 (Super X3) 3 in. Magnum Field Cantilever Deer*** – 12 or 20 (new 2011) ga., 22 in. rifled barrel with Weaver style cantilever scope base and TruGlo sights, alloy receiver, black synthetic stock and forearm, approx. 7 1/2 lbs. Mfg. 2006-2011.

	$1,025	$895	$775	$650	$575	$500	$450

Last MSR was $1,200.

Add $20 for 12 ga.

SX3 BLACK FIELD – 12 or 20 ga., 3 in. chamber, 26 or 28 in. VR back bored barrel with three invector plus chokes, matte black aluminum alloy receiver with red accents, active valve system, satin finished walnut stock and forearm with cut checkering, Pachmayr Decelerator recoil pad, ambidextrous safety, drop out trigger, approx. 6-3/4 lbs. New 2012.

MSR $1,070	$950	$850	$750	$650	$575	$500	$425

Add $70 for 20 ga.

This model was originally featured as a SHOT Show Special in 2011.

* ***SX3 Black Field Compact*** – 12 or 20 ga., similar to SX3 Black Field, except has 24 (new 2014), 26, or 28 in. barrel, 13 in. LOP stock, approx. 6 -1/2 lbs. New 2012.

MSR $1,070	$950	$850	$750	$650	$575	$500	$425

Add $70 for 20 ga.

This model was originally featured as a 2010 SHOT Show Special.

MSR	100%	98%	95%	90%	80%	70%	60%

SX3 BLACK SHADOW – 12 or 20 ga., 3 in. chamber, 26 or 28 in. VR back bored barrel with three invector plus choke tubes, matte black synthetic stock with textured gripping surface and matching forearm, Inflex technology recoil pad, matte black receiver with red accents, ambidextrous safety, 6-3/4 - 7-1/4 lbs. New 2012.

MSR $1,000	$875	$775	$675	$600	$525	$425	$375

Add $70 for 20 ga.

This model was originally featured as a 2011 SHOT Show Special.

SX3 CANTILEVER BUCK – 12 or 20 ga., 3 in. chamber, 22 in. rifled barrel with TruGlo front sight and rear Weaver style cantilever, matte black synthetic stock with textured gripping surface and Inflex technology recoil pad, approx. 7-1/2 lbs. New 2012.

MSR $1,150	$995	$875	$750	$650	$575	$500	$425

Add $50 for 20 ga.

SX3 COMPOSITE SPORTING – 12 ga. 2 3/4 in. chamber, 4 shot mag., 28, 30, or 32 in. ported Perma-Cote gray barrel with vent. rib, extended signature Invector Plus choke tubes, TruGlo fiber optic sight and white mid-bead, active valve system, ambidextrous crossbolt safety, matte nickel plated receiver, signature Red Briley bolt handle, release button and magazine cap weight system, black synthetic stock with or without carbon fiber finish, Inflex technology recoil pad, includes shims and LOP spacers, 7 1/4-7 1/2 lbs. New 2016.

MSR $1,680	$1,450	$1,175	$1,000	$875	$750	$625	$550

Add $70 for carbon fiber finish.

SX3 WATERFOWL HUNTER – 12 or 20 ga., 3 in. chamber, 26 or 28 in. VR back bored barrel with three invector plus choke tubes, 100% Mossy Oak Duck Blind camo, TruGlo fiber optic front sight, Inflex technology recoil pad, active valve system, ambidextrous safety, drop out trigger, approx. 6 5/8 - 7 lbs. New 2012.

MSR $1,140	$995	$875	$750	$650	$575	$500	$425

SX3 UNIVERSAL HUNTER – 12 or 20 ga., 3 or 3 1/2 in. chamber, 26 or 28 in. VR back bored barrel with three invector plus shoke tubes, drop out trigger, TruGlo fiber optic front sight, Inflex technology recoil pad, ambidextrous safety, active valve system, 100% Mossy Oak Break-Up Infinity (disc. 2014) or Mossy Oak Break-Up Country (new 2015) camo coverage. New 2012.

MSR $1,240	$1,050	$900	$775	$675	$575	$500	$425

SX3 (SUPER X3) SPORTING – 12 ga. only, 2 3/4 in. chamber, 28, 30, or 32 in. ported VR barrel with 5 extended choke tubes and TruGlo front sight, checkered adj. comb walnut stock and forearm, Active Valve gas system, gun metal grey receiver finish, Pachmayr Decelerator recoil pad, approx. 7 1/2 lbs., includes red ABS hard case with Winchester logo. Mfg. 2011-2015.

	$1,450	$1,175	$1,000	$875	$750	$625	$550

Last MSR was $1,700.

This model was originally featured as a 2010 SHOT Show Special.

MSR	100%	98%	95%	90%	80%	70%	60%

SX3 (SUPER X3) 3 1/2 IN. MAGNUM COMPOSITE – 12 ga. only, 3 1/2 in. chamber, features black composite stock and forearm, alloy receiver, grey Perma-Cote Ultra Tough (disc.) or Dura-Touch Armor coating (current) surface finish, 26 or 28 in. VR barrel with Invector Plus chokes, 4 shot mag., approx. 7 1/4 lbs. Mfg. 2006-2011.

	$1,050	$925	$800	$675	$575	$525	$475

Last MSR was $1,280.

* ***SX3 (Super X3) 3 1/2 In. Magnum Composite Waterfowl*** – 12 or 20 (new 2011, 3 in. chamber) ga., similar to Super X3 3 1/2 In. Mag., except has 100% Mossy Oak New Shadow Grass (disc.) or Mossy Oak New Duck Blind (new 2007) treatment, 26 or 28 in. VR barrel with 3 choke tubes, approx. 6 1/2 (20 ga.) or 7 lbs. Mfg. 2006-2011.

	$1,225	$975	$825	$725	$625	$525	$450

Last MSR was $1,480.

Subtract $140 for 20 ga. (new 2011).

* ***SX3 (Super X3) 3 1/2 In. Magnum Composite All Purpose Field*** – 12 or 20 (new 2011, 3 in. chamber), similar to Super X3 3 1/2 In. Mag., except has 100% Mossy Oak New Break-Up (disc. 2009) or Mossy Oak Infinity (new 2010) camo treatment, 26 or 28 in. VR barrel with 3 choke tubes, approx. 6 1/2 (20 ga.) or 7 lbs. Mfg. 2006-2011.

	$1,225	$975	$825	$725	$625	$525	$450

Last MSR was $1,480.

* ***SX3 (Super X3) 3 1/2 in. Mag. NWTF Cantilever Extreme Turkey*** – 12 ga., 24 in. cantilever barrel with extra-full extended turkey choke tube, composite stock with full Mossy Oak New Break-Up camo treatment and Dura-Touch Armor coating, Active Valve system, Pachmayr Decelerator recoil pad, steel sling swivels, includes TruGlo deluxe red dot scope and Weaver style mount, includes hardshell case, approx. 7 1/2 lbs. Mfg. 2008-2010.

	$1,225	$1,000	$850	$725	$600	$525	$450

Last MSR was $1,539.

* ***SX3 (Super X3) 3 1/2 In. Mag. Gray Shadow*** – 12 ga., 3 1/2 in. chamber, gray Perma-Cote UT surface finish, 26 or 28 in. barrel, gray composite stock with Dura-Touch Armor coating, Active Valve System, three Invector-Plus chokes, sling swivel studs, red "W" embedded in stock, 7 - 7 1/4 lbs. Mfg. 2009.

	$1,050	$900	$800	$700	$625	$550	$475

Last MSR was $1,299.

This model was originally featured as a 2008 SHOT Show Special.

SX3 BLACK SHADOW 3-1/2 IN. MAG. – 12 ga., 3-1/2 in. chamber, otherwise similar to the SX3 3 in. Black Shadow, 7 1/4 lbs. New 2012.

MSR $1,070	$925	$800	$700	$600	$500	$400	$350

SX3 WATERFOWL HUNTER 3-1/2 IN. MAG. – 12 ga., 3-1/2 in. chamber, otherwise similar to SX3 3 in. Waterfowl Hunter, approx. 7 1/8 lbs. New 2012.

MSR $1,200	$1,050	$925	$825	$700	$600	$500	$400

MSR	100%	98%	95%	90%	80%	70%	60%

SX3 ULTIMATE SPORTING ADJUSTABLE – 12 ga., 2 3/4 in. chamber, 4 shot mag., 28, 30, or 32 in. ported Perma-Cote gray barrel with vent. rib, extended signature Invector Plus choke tubes, TruGlo fiber optic sight and white mid-bead, active valve system, ambidextrous crossbolt safety, matte nickel plated receiver, signature Red Briley bolt handle, release button and magazine cap weight system, satin oil finish Grade II/III walnut stock with adj. comb and cut checkering, Pachmayr Decelerator recoil pad, 7 1/4-7 1/2 lbs. New 2016.

MSR $1,870	$1,575	$1,275	$1,050	$925	$800	$700	$600

SX3 UNIVERSAL HUNTER 3-1/2 IN. MAG. – 12 ga., 3-1/2 in. chamber, otherwise similar to SX3 Universal Hunter 3 in., 7-7 1/8 lbs. New 2012.

MSR $1,240	$1,025	$875	$750	$650	$575	$500	$425

SX3 (SUPER X3) NWTF CANTILEVER (EXTREME) TURKEY – 12 (3 1/2 in.) or 20 (3 in.) ga., 24 in. cantilever barrel with extra-full extended turkey choke tube and TruGlo front sight, composite stock with full Mossy Oak New Break-Up Infinity (disc. 2014) or Mossy Oak Break-Up Country (new 2015) camo treatment and Dura-Touch Armor coating, Active Valve system, Inflex technology recoil pad, steel sling swivels, approx. 7 1/2 lbs. New 2011.

MSR $1,200	$1,050	$925	$825	$700	$600	$500	$400

SX3 3 1/2 IN. MAG. LONG BEARD – 12 ga., 3 1/2 in. chamber, 24 in. barrel with Briley X-full Long Beard Invector Plus extended choke tube, TruGlo fiber-optic front sight, fully adj. folding rear sight, Weaver style cantilever scope mount rail design, pistol grip stock with 3 interchangeable recoil pads and comb pieces, 100% coverage Realtree Xtra green leaf (disc. 2014) or Mossy Oak Break-Up Country (new 2015) camo finish, 7 1/2 lbs. New 2014.

MSR $1,270	$1,075	$950	$825	$700	$600	$500	$425

Shotguns: Single Barrel, 1968-1980 mfg.

MODEL 370 – 12, 16, 20, 28 ga., or .410 bore, 28-32 in. full choke plain barrel, replaced the Model 37, top lever break open, exposed hammer, plain pistol grip stock. Approx. 221,578 were mfg. between 1968-73.

12 ga.	$150	$125	$100	$90	$85	$80	$75
16 ga.	$175	$150	$110	$90	$85	$80	$75
20 ga.	$195	$165	$130	$110	$90	$85	$75
28 ga.	$275	$225	$175	$140	$120	$100	$85
.410 bore	$275	$225	$175	$140	$120	$100	$85

The Model 370 was mfg. in Winchester's Canadian plant in Cobourg, Ontario.

MODEL 370 YOUTH – similar to 370, with 26 in. barrel, 12 1/2 in. stock, with recoil pad.

	$175	$145	$110	$95	$85	$80	$75

MODEL 37A – single barrel shotgun, 26-36 in. full choke barrel, concave hammer spur, gold plated trigger, updated checkering pattern on pistol

MSR	100%	98%	95%	90%	80%	70%	60%

grip and bottom of forearm, roll engraved receiver, optional 36 in. goose barrel, 5 1/2-6lbs. Approx. 391,168 mfg. between 1973-80 in the Winchester plant in Cobourg, Ontario.

12 ga.	$150	$125	$100	$90	$85	$80	$75
16 ga.	$150	$125	$100	$90	$85	$80	$75
20 ga.	$150	$125	$100	$90	$85	$80	$75
28 ga.	$225	$195	$150	$130	$110	$90	$80
.410 bore	$275	$225	$175	$140	$120	$100	$85

Add 15% for 36 in. goose barrel (12 ga. only)

MODEL 37A YOUTH – similar to 37A, except 20 ga. or .410 bore with 12 1/2 in. LOP stock.

$175 $145 $110 $95 $85 $80 $75

MODEL 840 – various gauges, mfg. in Canada until 1980.

$140 $110 $95 $85 $75 $65 $55

MODEL 1370 SLAGBLASTER – 12 ga., 26 in. heavy barrel, shoots special Winchester/Western CE8Z industrial ammunition with extended 3 oz. zinc slug (rare), industrial sales only - used to clean slag from steel kilns, 9 lbs. Mfg. in Canada, disc.

$750 $700 $650 $575 $525 $450 $400

SHOTGUNS: SLIDE ACTION, 1964-CURRENT

Winchester introduced WinChokes in 1969.

U.S. Repeating Arms closed its New Haven, CT manufacturing facility on March 31, 2006. There may be some speculation on recently manufactured Model 1300 shotguns. All Model 1300 last MSRs listed are from the Winchester 2006 price sheet.

MODEL 12 SUPER PIGEON GRADE – 12 ga., slide action, 26, 28, or 30 in. barrel, VR, any choke, hand honed action, engine turned breech block and loading flap, "B" checkering and No. 5 engraving, custom order grade walnut stock. Limited production between 1964-72.

$3,750 $3,275 $2,650 $2,275 $1,995 $1,650 $1,400

Subtract 20% for Super Pigeon Grades mfg. 1984-85 (480 total).

MODEL 12 FIELD GRADE – 12 ga., slide action, 26, 28, or 30 in. VR barrel, various chokes, jeweled bolt, hand checkered, checkered select walnut stock. Mfg. 1972-75, "Y" ser. no. prefix.

$750 $650 $600 $550 $500 $450 $400

In 1984, Y series Model 12s were once again available through a private contract with U.S.R.A. Co. which included engraving on Grades 1A 1C and 2-5. These guns were available in either Field, Trap, or Skeet configurations. Since there was no manufacturer's suggested retail, Model 12 values shown are established by analyzing the sales of the two private contractors - no more of these variations are available.

* ***Model 12 Field Grades 1-A, 1-B, & 1-C*** – light engraving depicting dogs or ducks. Disc.

$1,425 $1,250 $1,025 $875 $785 $695 $600

Last MSR was $1,375.

MSR	100%	98%	95%	90%	80%	70%	60%

* *Model 12 Field Grades 2 & 3* - engraving features large duck and dog game scenes on receiver flats. Disc.

	$1,875	$1,650	$1,500	$1,300	$1,150	$900	$800

Last MSR was $1,695.

* *Model 12 Field Grade 4* - more elaborate game scene engraving than Grades 2 & 3. Disc.

	$2,200	$1,875	$1,600	$1,400	$1,200	$1,050	$950

Last MSR was $1,995.

* *Model 12 Field Grade 5* - elaborate game scene engraving with style B checkering. Disc.

	$2,750	$2,300	$1,900	$1,600	$1,350	$1,200	$995

Last MSR was $2,450.

Also available with gold inlays - add $1,000 to values.

* *Model 12 Field Grade 3 Barrel Set* - grade 5 engraving with gold inlays and two extra barrels. Disc.

	$5,995	$5,495	$4,795	$4,295	$3,995	$3,495	$2,795

Last MSR was $6,000.

MODEL 12 SKEET GRADE - similar to Field Grade, with 26 in. VR skeet bore barrel, skeet style stock, with recoil pad. Mfg. 1972-75.

	$1,195	$995	$895	$750	$650	$550	$500

See listings under Model 12 Field Grade for engraved values.

MODEL 12 TRAP GRADE - similar to Field grade, with 30 in. VR full choke barrel, trap style stock, straight or Monte Carlo, recoil pad. Mfg. 1972-80.

	$1,095	$950	$850	$750	$650	$500	$450

See listings under Model 12 Field Grade for engraved values.

MODEL 12 DU - 800 mfg. during 1975 for auction at Ducks Unlimited chapter banquets. Please refer to the Ducks Unlimited listing in the D section.

MODEL 12 LIMITED EDITION

* *Model 12 Limited Edition Grade I 20 Ga.* - 20 ga. only, 2 3/4 in. chamber only, reproduction of the famous Winchester Model 12 with slight design improvements, 26 in. VR barrel bored modified, 5 shot mag., high post floating rib, walnut stock and forearm with semi-gloss finish, takedown, 7 lbs. 4,000 mfg. by Miroku 1993-95.

	$995	$825	$650	N/A	N/A	N/A	N/A

Last MSR was $879

* *Model 12 Limited Edition Grade IV 20 Ga.* - similar specifications to Grade I, except has select walnut checkered 22 lines per inch with high gloss finish, extensive game scene engraving including multiple gold inlays. 1,000 mfg. 1993-95.

	$1,500	$1,250	$995	N/A	N/A	N/A	N/A

Last MSR was $1,431.

MSR	100%	98%	95%	90%	80%	70%	60%

MODEL 42 HIGH GRADE LIMITED EDITION - .410 bore, 26 in. full choke VR barrel, Grade V-VI wood with special scroll and gold border engraving, 850 mfg. 1993 only.

	100%	98%	95%	90%	80%	70%	60%
	$1,850	$1,425	$1,100	N/A	N/A	N/A	N/A

Last MSR was $1,617.

MODEL 120 RANGER - 12, 16, or 20 ga., entry level model, VR and WinChokes. Disc.

	100%	98%	95%	90%	80%	70%	60%
	$200	$180	$165	$140	$110	$100	$90

MODEL 1200 FIELD GRADE - 12, 16, or 20 ga., 26, 28, or 30 in. barrel, alloy receiver, various chokes, checkered pistol grip stock, pad. Mfg. 1964-1981.

	100%	98%	95%	90%	80%	70%	60%
	$200	$180	$165	$140	$110	$100	$90
Vent. rib	$220	$205	$195	$165	$140	$110	$100
WinChoke	$240	$215	$200	$190	$180	$160	$140

Add 33% for Winchester recoil reduction system (mfg. 1966-1970).

MODEL 1200 MAGNUM - similar to 1200, chambered for 12 or 20 ga., 3 in. magnum shells. Mfg. 1964-80.

	100%	98%	95%	90%	80%	70%	60%
	$210	$190	$175	$165	$140	$110	$100
Vent. rib	$240	$215	$200	$185	$150	$140	$110

MODEL 1200 SKEET GUN - similar to 1200, 12 or 20 ga., 26 in. VR barrel, skeet bore, 2 shot mag. and select style stock. Mfg. 1965-74.

	100%	98%	95%	90%	80%	70%	60%
	$325	$275	$235	$200	$165	$140	$120

MODEL 1200 TRAP GUN - similar to 1200, with 12 ga., VR, 30 in. full choke barrel, select trap style stock. Mfg. 1965-74.

	100%	98%	95%	90%	80%	70%	60%
	$295	$275	$250	$195	$165	$140	$120
WinChoke	$330	$305	$275	$250	$220	$165	$140

MODEL 1200 DEER GUN - similar to 1200, with 22 in. barrel, rifle sights, 12 ga. only. Mfg. 1965-74.

	100%	98%	95%	90%	80%	70%	60%
	$250	$200	$165	$110	$100	$85	$75

MODEL 1200 POLICE STAINLESS - 12 ga. only, 18 in. barrel, 7 shot mag. Disc.

	100%	98%	95%	90%	80%	70%	60%
	$250	$195	$165	$125	$105	$90	$75

MODEL 1200 DEFENDER - 12 ga. only, 18 in. cylinder bore barrel, 7 shot mag., 6 lbs. Disc.

	100%	98%	95%	90%	80%	70%	60%
	$250	$200	$180	$155	$140	$125	$110

MODEL 1300 FEATHERWEIGHT - 12 or 20 ga., 3 in. chamber, takedown, 26 (new 1991) or 28 in. barrel, 5 shot, plain or VR (became standard 1990), WinChoke tubes, checkered walnut stock and grooved forearm, alloy frame, recoil pad, 6 3/4 - 7 1/8 lbs. Mfg. 1978-93.

	100%	98%	95%	90%	80%	70%	60%
	$300	$260	$230	$195	$175	$160	$145

Last MSR was $374.

Subtract $30 without VR.

This model had an "XTR" suffix until 1989. Older Model 1300 Featherweights had roll-engraving but no premiums are being asked at this time.

MSR	100%	98%	95%	90%	80%	70%	60%

MODEL 1300 WALNUT FIELD – 12 or 20 (disc. 1994) ga., 3 in. chamber, 26 or 28 in. VR barrel with WinChokes (includes 3), checkered satin (disc. 2003) or gloss finished (new 2004) walnut stock and forearm, approx. 7 1/4 - 7 1/2 lbs. Mfg. 1994-2006.

	$350	$250	$200	$160	$140	$120	$110

Last MSR was $444.

Beginning 2003, Winchester started engraving "Speed Pump" on receiver on all Model 1300 variations.

* *Model 1300 Walnut Black Shadow Field* – 12 or 20 (new 1996) ga., 3 in. chamber, 26 or 28 in. (12 ga. only) VR WinChoke barrel, black composite stock and forearm, 6 3/4 - 7 1/4 lbs. Mfg. 1995-2006.

	$275	$210	$170	$135	$120	$110	$95

Last MSR was $357.

* *Model 1300 Walnut Field Sporting* – 12 ga., 3 in. chamber, 24 (compact) or 28 in. VR barrel with 5 WinChokes, satin finished checkered walnut full length or compact (13 in. LOP) stock and forearm with radiused recoil pad, TruGlo front sight, matte metal finish, 6 3/4 or 7 1/2 lbs. Mfg. 2002-2006.

	$350	$255	$205	$165	$135	$120	$110

Last MSR was $444.

* *Model 1300 Walnut Field Advantage Camo* – 12 ga. only, 28 in. barrel with choke tubes, full coverage. Advantage Camo. Mfg. 1997.

	$340	$265	$235	$195	$165	$145	$125

Last MSR was $432.

* *Model 1300 Walnut Field New Shadow Grass* – 12 ga. only, 26 or 28 in. VR barrel with 3 WinChokes, 100% Mossy Oak New Shadow Grass camo coverage, approx. 7 lbs. Mfg. 2004-2006.

	$365	$275	$215	$180	$150	$130	$115

Last MSR was $472.

MODEL 1300 UPLAND SPECIAL FIELD – 12 or 20 (new 2000) ga., 3 in. chamber, features gloss finished (new 2004) or satin finished (disc. 2003) checkered straight grip walnut stock and forearm, solid recoil pad, 24 in. VR barrel with choke tube, blue only, 6 3/4 lbs. Mfg. 1999-2006.

	$350	$255	$205	$165	$135	$120	$110

Last MSR was $444.

MODEL 1300 CUSTOM HIGH GRADE – while advertised, this model never went into production. Advertised retail was $1,395.

MODEL 1300 WATERFOWL – 12 ga. only, 3 in. chamber, 28 or 30 (disc.) in. VR barrel, matte finished metal, choice of low luster walnut finish or brown Win-Tuff wood stock, recoil pad, camo sling, and swivels, WinChokes standard, 7 lbs. Mfg. 1984-1991.

	$295	$260	$235	$200	$180	$165	$150

Last MSR was $367.

MSR	100%	98%	95%	90%	80%	70%	60%

MODEL 1300 TURKEY GUN – 12 ga. only, 3 in. chamber, 22 in. VR barrel, WinChoked, walnut stock and forearm with low luster finish, metal surfaces have matte finish, supplied with camouflaged fabric sling, 6 3/8 lbs. Mfg. 1985-88.

	$290	$265	$235	$200	$180	$165	$150

Last MSR was $348.

* ***Model 1300 Turkey Gun Win-Cam*** – similar to Model 1300 Turkey Gun, except has greenish laminated hardwood stock and forearm. Mfg. 1987-93.

	$350	$295	$250	$200	$180	$165	$150

Last MSR was $435.

* ***Model 1300 Turkey Gun Win-Cam Combo Pack*** – 12 ga., supplied with 22 and 30 in. VR non-glare finished barrels, greenish laminated hardwood stock and forearm, camo sling, matte finished metal. Mfg. 1987-88 only.

	$375	$330	$290	$260	$230	$200	$185

Last MSR was $425.

* ***Model 1300 Turkey Gun Ladies-Youth Win-Cam Turkey Gun*** – 20 ga. only, 3 in. chamber, 22 in. VR barrel, green camo laminate shortened stock and forearm, includes sling and National Wild Turkey Federation engraving, 6 lbs. Mfg. 1992 only.

	$340	$295	$250	$200	$180	$165	$150

Last MSR was $411.

* ***Model 1300 Turkey Gun Win-Cam NWTF Series I-IV*** – 12 or 20 ga., Series I was released 1989 (12 ga. only) and included special receiver engraving featuring National Wild Turkey Federation motifs, Series II was released 1990 with a choice of either 12 (disc.) or 20 ga. Ladies/Youth model, Series III was released 1991-92, Series IV was released 1993. Disc. 1994.

	$365	$300	$250	$200	$180	$165	$150

Last MSR was $458.

MODEL 1300 TURKEY - SYNTHETIC STOCK – 12 or 20 (mfg. 1996-99, Black Shadow only) ga., 3 in. chamber, 22 in. VR barrel with choke tube, choice of 2 color Realtree camo patterns on synthetic stock and forearm, full camo coverage available in Realtree or Advantage (new 1996), or non-glare black (Black Shadow) finish on all surfaces, approx. 6 3/4 lbs. Mfg. 1994-2000.

* ***Model 1300 Turkey Synthetic Stock Black Shadow Finish*** – disc. 2000.

	$260	$195	$160	$135	$120	$110	$95

Last MSR was $328.

* ***Model 1300 Turkey Synthetic Stock Mossy Oak Break-Up*** – 12 ga. only, 3 in. chamber, 22 in. VR barrel with TruGlo sights, high density X-full turkey choke tube, 100% Mossy Oak coverage on wood and metal, 6 3/4 lbs. Mfg. 2000 only.

	$375	$295	$260	$225	$200	$185	$170

Last MSR was $459.

This model was also available with iron sights and rifled sabot choke tube for deer hunting - add approx. $30.

MSR	100%	98%	95%	90%	80%	70%	60%

* ***Model 1300 Turkey Synthetic Stock RealTree/Advantage Camo Finish*** – RealTree covered synthetic stock and forearm or full coverage camo. Disc. 1998.

	$290	$240	$180	$150	$130	$115	$100

Last MSR was $370.

Add $62 for full coverage camo.

Add $40 for full coverage without sling (disc. 1997).

Add $40 for smoothbore barrel (Advantage full camo only).

MODEL 1300 UNIVERSAL HUNTER/TURKEY – 12 ga. only, 3 in. chamber, 26 in. VR barrel with 3 WinChokes, full coverage standard or New Mossy Oak Break-Up (new 2003) camo, with or w/o TruGlo 3-dot sights, composite stock and forearm, 7 lbs. Mfg. 2002-2006.

	$400	$350	$300	$255	$200	$165	$140

Last MSR was $517.

Subtract 5% if w/o TruGlo sights (Hunter Model).

MODEL 1300 NWTF TURKEY MODELS – 12 ga. only, 3 in. chamber, 18 (Short Turkey, new 2002) or 22 in. barrel, choice of Black Shadow (black synthetic stock and forearm with non-glare metal finish and extra full choke tube, mfg. 2001 only), Turkey Superflauge with full coverage TreBark Superflauge (mfg. 2001) or Mossy Oak Break-Up camo with TruGlo sights, Buck & Tom Superflauge with full coverage TreBark Superflauge (mfg. 2001) or Mossy Oak Break-Up (new 2002) camo with 2 choke tubes including rifled sabot, or Short Turkey (18 in. barrel with rifled sights and full coverage Mossy Oak Break-Up camo) configurations, "Team NWTF" logo printed on stock, 6 3/4 lbs. Mfg. 2001-2006.

	$425	$360	$260	$225	$175	$150	$125

Last MSR was $514.

Subtract approx. $160 for Black Shadow configuration.

Add $42 for Buck & Tom Superflauge configuration.

MODEL 1300 LADIES-YOUTH – 20 ga. only, 3 in. chamber, 22 in. VR barrel, shortened stock dimensions, walnut stock with recoil pad and rearward positioned, grooved forearm, 6 1/4 lbs. Mfg. 1992 only.

	$315	$260	$220	$180	$165	$150	$135

Last MSR was $355.

MODEL 1300 SLUG HUNTER – 12 ga. only, 3 in. chamber, 22 in. rifled or smooth bore barrel with iron sights, checkered stock and forearm, satin walnut finish or brown laminate stock (Win-Tuff). Supplied with camo fabric sling and rings and bases. Mfg. 1988-disc.

	$360	$300	$250	$200	$180	$165	$150

Last MSR was $445.

Add $10 for smooth bore barrel with Sabot rifled tubes (disc. 1992).

Add $4 for "Whitetails Unlimited" Model (new 1991).

MODEL 1300 WALNUT DEER – 12 ga. only, 3 in. chamber, 22 in. rifled barrel, non-glare metal surfaces, rifle sights, checkered walnut stock with recoil pad and forearm, 7 1/4 lbs. Mfg. 1994-1999.

	$350	$285	$255	$225	$200	$185	$170

Last MSR was $429.

MSR	100%	98%	95%	90%	80%	70%	60%

* ***Model 1300 Walnut Deer Black Shadow*** – 12 or 20 (mfg. 1996-97, reintroduced 2000) ga., 3 in. chamber, 22 in. smoothbore (12 ga. only, disc. 2003) or rifled (new 1996) barrel with IC WinChoke, matte black stock, forearm, and metal parts, rifle sights, drilled and tapped receiver, approx. 6 3/4 lbs. Mfg. 1994-2006.

$300	$225	$175	$150	$125	$115	$95

Last MSR was $382.

Add $44 for Cantilever scope mount, available in 12 ga. only (new 2000).

Add $77 for deer combo package that includes 22 in. cyl. bore (disc. 1998) or rifled (new 2000) barrel and 28 in. VR WinChoke barrels.

Subtract approx. $25 for smoothbore barrel (disc. 2003).

* ***Model 1300 Walnut Deer Ranger*** – 12 or 20 (Ranger regular or compact) ga., 3 in. chamber, 22 in. rifled barrel with rifle or TruGlo sights, smaller dimensions on 20 ga. Deer Ranger Compact (13 in. LOP, disc. 2005), brown composite stock and forearm, non-glare finish, 6 3/4 lbs. Mfg. 2000-2006.

$305	$230	$170	$145	$125	$110	$100

Last MSR was $396.

* ***Model 1300 Walnut Deer Full Advantage Camo*** – 12 ga. only, 3 in. chamber, choice of 22 in. rifled or smoothbore barrel, entire gun is in Full Advantage camo pattern, drilled and tapped receiver, iron sights, 7 lbs. Mfg. 1995-98.

$350	$295	$260	$225	$200	$185	$170

Last MSR was $432.

Subtract $22 for smoothbore barrel.

MODEL 1300 RANGER – 12 or 20 ga., 3 in. chamber, 22 cyl. or rifled (deer only, disc.), 24 1/8 cyl. (disc. deer barrel), 26 (mfg. 1991-98), 28, or 30 (disc. 1992) in. plain or VR barrel, walnut finished hardwood stock, alloy receiver, approx. 7 1/4 lbs. Mfg. 1983-2004.

$285	$215	$170	$135	$120	$110	$95

Last MSR was $367.

Subtract $40 without VR or WinChokes.

This model was also available in a deer combination package which included either a 22 in. rifled or smoothbore deer barrel and a 28 in. VR WinChoke barrel in either 12 or 20 ga. (disc.). - add approx. 25% to values listed.

* ***Model 1300 Ranger Gloss*** – 12 or 20 ga., 3 in. chamber, 26 or 28 in. VR barrel, gloss finished checkered hardwood stock and forearm, 7 1/4 - 7 1/2 lbs. Limited mfg. 2006.

$300	$225	$180	$140	$125	$110	$95

Last MSR was $391.

» ***Model 1300 Ranger Gloss Compact*** – similar to Model 1300 Ranger Gloss, except has 22 or 24 in. barrel and 13 in. LOP. Limited mfg. 2006.

$285	$215	$170	$135	$120	$110	$95

Last MSR was $366.

MSR	100%	98%	95%	90%	80%	70%	60%

* *Model 1300 Ranger Ladies/Youth Model* – 20 ga. only, 3 in. chamber, 22 in. VR barrel, shorter stock dimensions - 13 in. LOP and rearward positioned forearm. Disc. 1998.

	$285	$235	$200	$170	$150	$125	$110

Last MSR was $309.

Subtract $40 if without WinChoke and VR.

* *Model 1300 Ranger Compact* – 12 or 20 ga., 3 in. chamber, features shorter dimensions (13 LOP), 22 (20 ga. only) or 24 (12 ga. only) in. VR barrel with WinChoke and TruGlo sights, uncheckered hardwood stock and grooved forearm, blue only, approx. 6 3/4 lbs. Mfg. 1999-2005.

	$300	$225	$175	$140	$120	$110	$95

Last MSR was $391.

MODEL 1300 CAMP DEFENDER – 12 ga. only, 3 in. chamber, 8 shot mag., 22 in. barrel with rifle sights and WinChoke, choice of black synthetic (disc. 2000) or hardwood (new 2001) stock and forearm, matte metal finish, 6 7/8 lbs. Mfg. 1999-2004.

	$300	$230	$180	$150	$125	$110	$100

Last MSR was $392.

MODEL 1300 DEFENDER – 12 or 20 (disc. 1996, reintroduced 2001) ga., 3 in. chamber, available in Police (disc. 1989), Practical (new 2005), Marine, and Defender variations, 18 or 24 (mfg. 1994-98) in. cyl. bore barrel, 5 (disc. 1998), 7 (disc. 1998), or 8 shot mag., matte metal finish, choice of hardwood (disc. 2001), composite (matte finish), or pistol grip (matte finish, 12 ga. only) stock, TruGlo sights became standard 1999, 5 3/4 - 7 lbs. Disc. 2006.

	$270	$210	$160	$130	$110	$95	$85

Last MSR was $341.

Add $13 for short pistol grip and full length stocks.

Add approx. $100 for Combo Package (includes extra 28 in. VR barrel - disc. 1998).

* *Model 1300 Defender NRA* – 12 or 20 ga., 18 in. barrel with removable TruGlo fiber optic front sight, composite stock, 8 shot mag., features NRA medallion on pistol grip, also available in 12 ga. combo with pistol grip stock, 6 1/4 - 6 1/2 lbs. Limited mfg. 2006.

	$285	$215	$175	$140	$120	$110	$95

Last MSR was $364.

Add $13 for combo with pistol grip and full length stock.

* *Model 1300 Defender Practical* – 12 ga. only, 3 in. chamber, 8 shot mag., 22 in. barrel with TruGlo adj. open sights, designed for practical shooting events, black synthetic stock and forearm. Mfg. 2005.

	$300	$230	$170	$145	$125	$110	$100

Last MSR was $392.

» *Model 1300 Defender Practical NRA* – 12 ga. only, 3 in. chamber, 8 shot mag., 22 in. barrel with TruGlo sights, black synthetic stock and forearm,

MSR	100%	98%	95%	90%	80%	70%	60%

Winchoke system, adj. open sights, NRA logo grip cap, 6 1/2 lbs. Limited mfg. 2006.

	$315	$240	$180	$150	$130	$110	$100

Last MSR was $414.

* *Model 1300 Defender Stainless Coastal Marine* - 12 ga. only, 18 in. cyl. bore stainless steel barrel and mag. tube, a Sandstrom 9A phosphate coating was released late 1989 to give long lasting corrosion protection to all receiver and internal working parts, Dura-Touch armor coating stock treatment added 2004, 6 shot mag., synthetic pistol grip (disc. 2001) or full black stock configuration, approx. 6 3/8 lbs. Mfg. 2002-2005.

	$465	$380	$275	$225	$195	$165	$140

Last MSR was $575.

» *Model 1300 Defender Stainless Coastal Marine NRA* – 12 ga. only, 18 in. nickel plated stainless steel barrel, anodized aluminum alloy receiver and plated parts for corrosion resistance, Dura-Touch Armor coating on composite stock, 7 shot mag., sling swivel studs, removable TruGlo fiber optic front sight, 6 1/2 lbs. Limited mfg. 2006.

	$480	$390	$280	$230	$200	$165	$140

Last MSR was $598.

* *Model 1300 Lady Defender* - 20 ga. only, 3 in. chamber, choice of synthetic regular or pistol grip stock, 4 (disc. 1996) or 7 shot mag., 18 in. cyl. bore barrel (new 1996), 5 3/8 lbs. Disc. 1998.

	$235	$190	$150	$120	$105	$90	$80

Last MSR was $290.

SPEED PUMP FIELD - 12 ga., 3 in. chamber, side ejection, four lug rotary bolt, 26 or 28 in. VR barrel with Invector Plus chokes, choice of gloss finished checkered walnut or black synthetic stock and forearm, approx. 7 1/4 lbs. Mfg. by Miroku during 2008.

	$295	$250	$215	$200	$185	$170	$155

Last MSR was $349.

Add $50 for checkered walnut stock and forearm.

SPEED PUMP DEFENDER - 12 ga., 3 in. chamber, side ejection, 5 shot mag., 18 in. plain barrel with fixed cylinder choke, black composite stock with non-glare finish and ribbed forearm. Mfg. by Miroku during 2008.

	$240	$210	$190	$170	$150	$135	$120

Last MSR was $299.

SXP (SUPER X PUMP) BLACK SHADOW DEER - 12 ga., 3 in. chamber, 4 shot mag., 22 in. fully rifled barrel, black synthetic stock with textured gripping surfaces, Inflex technology recoil pad, TruGlo fiber optic front and adj. rear sights, receiver mounted Picatinny rail, rotary bolt, drop out trigger, crossbolt safety, 6 7/8 lbs. New 2013.

MSR $520	$450	$400	$350	$300	$265	$235	$195

This model was originally featured as a 2012 SHOT Show Special.

MSR	100%	98%	95%	90%	80%	70%	60%

SXP (SUPER X PUMP) BLACK SHADOW FIELD – 12 or 20 (new 2015) ga., 3 or 3-1/2 (new 2012) in. chamber, 26 or 28 in. VR barrel with 3 Invector Plus choke tubes, rotary bolt with dual steel action slide bars, black pistol grip composite stock, non-glare matte metal finish with red accents, crossbolt trigger guard safety, styling similar to Super X3 semi-auto, Inflex recoil pad, approx. 6 3/4 -7 lbs. New 2009.

MSR $380	$325	$275	$240	$215	$185	$170	$150

Add $50 for 3-1/2 in. chamber (new 2012).
Add $20 for 20 ga. (new 2015).

SXP EXTREME DEER – 12 ga., 3 in. chamber, 22 in. rifled barrel with fiber optic front and adj. rear sights, alloy receiver, black synthetic pistol grip stock with two interchangeable comb pieces, Inflex recoil pad, non-glare matte metal finish with red receiver accents, 7 lbs. New 2016.

MSR $560	$475	$415	$360	$315	$275	$240	$200

SXP EXTREME DEER HUNTER – 12 ga., 3 in. chamber, 22 in. rifled barrel with fiber optic front and adj. rear sights, alloy receiver, pistol grip stock with two interchangeable comb pieces, Inflex recoil pad, 100% camo finish on barrel and stock/forearm, 7 lbs. New 2016.

MSR $620	$525	$450	$395	$350	$300	$275	$250

SXP (SUPER X PUMP) FIELD – 12 or 20 (new 2015) ga., 3 in. chamber, 4 shot mag., 26 or 28 in. barrel, full, mod., or IC Invector plus choke tubes, checkered satin finished stock and forearm with premium recoil pad, brass bead front sight, drop out trigger, crossbolt safety, 6 3/4-7 1/8 lbs. New 2013.

MSR $400	$350	$315	$285	$250	$220	$195	$175

Add $30 for 20 ga. (new 2015).

* ***SXP (Super X Pump) Field Compact*** – 12 or 20 (new 2015) ga., similar to SXP Field, except has 24, 26, or 28 in. barrel and 13 in. LOP. New 2014.

MSR $400	$350	$315	$285	$250	$220	$195	$175

Add $30 for 20 ga. (new 2015).

SXP LONG BEARD – 12 ga., 3 or 3 1/2 in. chamber, alloy receiver, 4 shot mag., 24 in. barrel with Invector Plus extra-full Long Beard turkey choke tubes, Truglo fiber optic adj. sights, crossbolt safety, synthetic pistol grip stock with textured gripping surfaces and two interchangeable comb pieces and LOP spacers, Inflex Technology recoil pad, Mossy Oak Break-Up Country camo finish, 7 1/4 lbs. New 2016.

MSR $530	$450	$400	$365	$335	$300	$265	$235

Add $30 for 3 1/2 in. chamber.

SXP TURKEY HUNTER – 12 or 20 (new 2015) ga., 3 or 3-1/2 in. chamber, 4 or 5 (20 ga.) shot mag., 22 (disc. 2014) or 24 in. VR barrel with TruGlo sights, 100% Mossy Oak Break-Up Infinity (disc. 2014) or Mossy Oak Break-Up Country (new 2015) camo coverage, Inflex technology recoil pad, 6 1/4-6 5/8 lbs. New 2012.

MSR $520	$450	$400	$365	$335	$300	$265	$235

Add $30 for 20 ga.

MSR	100%	98%	95%	90%	80%	70%	60%

SXP UNIVERSAL HUNTER - 12 or 20 ga., 3 or 3 1/2 in. chamber, 4 shot mag., 24, 26, or 28 in. barrel, Invector Plus choke tubes, alloy receiver, TruGlo Long Beard fiber optic front sight, crossbolt safety, synthetic stock with textured gripping surfaces, 100% Mossy Oak Break-Up Country camo finish, 6 1/2-7 lbs. New 2016.

MSR $470	$400	$360	$315	$265	$215	$180	$160

Add $40 for 3 1/2 in. chamber or 20 ga.

SXP (SUPER X PUMP) WATERFOWL HUNTER - 12 or 20 (new 2016) ga., 3 or 3-1/2 (new 2012) in. chamber, 100% Mossy Oak Duck Blind (disc. 2012) or non-glare Mossy Oak Shadow Grass Blades (new 2013) camo coverage, 26 or 28 in. VR barrel with 3 Invector-Plus choke tubes, speed-plug 3 shot adaptor, Inflex recoil pad, approx. 6 3/4-7 lbs. New 2011.

MSR $460	$395	$350	$300	$250	$200	$175	$150

Add $40 for 20 ga. (new 2016) or 3-1/2 in. chamber (new 2012).

SXP (SUPER X PUMP) TRAP - 12 ga., 3 in. chamber, 30 or 32 in. VR (5/16 in.) barrel with back-bored invector plus choke system, 4 shot mag., drop out trigger group, fiber optic front sight and ivory mid-bead, checkered Monte Carlo stock and forearm with Inflex Technology recoil pad, matte black finish, approx. 7 1/2 lbs. New 2015.

MSR $480	$425	$365	$315	$265	$235	$210	$185

* ***SXP (Super X Pump) Trap Compact*** - 12 ga., similar to SXP Trap, except has 28 or 30 in. barrel and 13 in. LOP. New 2015.

MSR $480	$425	$365	$315	$265	$235	$210	$185

SXP (SUPER X PUMP) DEFENDER - 12 or 20 (new 2015) ga., 3 in. chamber, 18 in. fixed cylinder bore barrel, non-glare metal finish, 5 shot mag., deep groove forearm, black composite pistol grip stock, 6 1/4 lbs. New 2009.

MSR $350	$295	$265	$230	$200	$175	$150	$125

Add $30 for 20 ga. (new 2015).

SXP (SUPER X PUMP) ULTIMATE DEFENDER - 12 ga., 3 in. chamber, 18 in. barrel with extended ported door-breacher choke tube, 4 shot mag., drop out trigger group, ghost ring rear sight and protected front blade front sight, black synthetic stock with textured gripping surfaces and Inflex technology recoil pad, includes receiver Picatinny rail and 2 additional rails in front of forearm, 7 1/2 lbs. New 2015.

MSR $500	$425	$375	$335	$300	$275	$250	$225

SXP (SUPER X PUMP) MARINE DEFENDER - 12 or 20 (new 2016) ga., 3 in. chamber, 18 in. barrel with Invector Plus cylinder choke tube, black synthetic stock with textured gripping surfaces, Inflex technology recoil pad, non-glare matte black alloy drilled and tapped receiver with hard chrome barrel and mag. tube, tactical ribbed forearm, includes both brass bead and TruGlo fiber optic front sights, drop out trigger, crossbolt safety, 4-lug rotary bolt, 6 1/4 lbs. New 2013.

MSR $400	$350	$315	$285	$250	$220	$195	$175

Add $30 for 20 ga. (new 2016).

MSR	100%	98%	95%	90%	80%	70%	60%

SXP (SUPER X PUMP) ULTIMATE MARINE DEFENDER - 12 ga., 3 in. chamber, 18 in. barrel with extended porter breacher choke tube, 4 shot mag., drop out trigger group, ghost ring rear sight with protected front sight blade, includes receiver Picatinny rail and 2 additional rails in front of forearm, matte hard chrome plating on barrel and mag., 7 1/2 lbs. New 2015.

MSR $540	$465	$415	$375	$335	$300	$275	$250

SHOTGUNS: O/U - RECENT PRODUCTION

Model 101 dates of manufacture and serialization data can be found in the SERIALIZATION section in the back of this text.

In November of 1987 Olin/Winchester disc. the Model 101. Classic Doubles (listed separately in this text) imported this model under their own trademark until approx. 1990. With the discontinuance of the Model 101 and its many variations, both dealers and collectors have created a lot more demand for this model recently. As a result, prices have escalated and the scramble is on to try and pick off those rare and desirable variations. Since there have been a lot of limited editions and production changes in the 101 O/U series, it could very well be that this model might become very collectible in upcoming years (as happened to the Model 12).

Note: Model 101 and Model 96 Xpert guns were made by Olin Kodensha located in Tochigi, Japan.

Add 10% for the following discontinued Model 101s listed in this section if in NIB condition only.

MODEL 91 - 12 ga. only, mfg. by Laurona in Spain for international sales including Europe, SST, ejectors optional, VR, distinguishable by black chrome finish on metal parts. Disc.

Prices are difficult to evaluate because of limited importation domestically. In some regions they are bought as medium priced field guns ($550-$650), while in others they are sold as a rare Winchester O&U ($900-$1,100).

MODEL 96 XPERT FIELD GRADE - 12 or 20 ga., similar action to Model 101, 3 in. chambers, auto ejectors, SST, various barrel lengths and chokes, action similar to 101, no engraving, checkered pistol grip stock and forearm. Mfg. 1976-82.

	$875	$775	$650	$550	$475	$425	$375

Add 10% for 20 ga.

This model has become known as the "Poor Man's 101".

MODEL 96 XPERT SKEET GRADE - 2 3/4 in. chambers, similar to Field Grade, with 27 in. skeet barrels, skeet style stock. Mfg. 1976-82.

	$925	$850	$725	$600	$500	$450	$410

Add 10% for 20 ga.

MODEL 96 XPERT TRAP GRADE - 12 ga. only, 2 3/4 in. chambers, similar to Field, 30 in. imp. mod./full or full/full choke, trap style stock. Mfg. 1976-82.

	$875	$775	$650	$550	$475	$425	$375

MODEL 99 - 12 ga., DT, no engraving. Disc.

	$700	$575	$525	$470	$430	$395	$360

MSR	100%	98%	95%	90%	80%	70%	60%

MODEL 101 FIELD VARIATION – 12, 20 ga., or .410 bore, 26, 28, or 30 in. barrels, various chokes, boxlock, auto ejectors, SST, engraved receiver, checkered American walnut pistol grip stock. Mfg. 1963-87.

Values assume WinChokes (standard since 1983) - subtract $60 if without.

* ***Model 101 Field Variation Older Production*** – checkered walnut stock and forearm, ejectors, SST, blue metal with light engraving on receiver, various barrel lengths, w/o choke tubes.

	$995	$850	$725	$625	$585	$550	$500

Add 50% for 28 ga. or .410 bore. Add 20% for 20 ga.

* ***Model 101 Field Variation 25th Anniversary Model*** – 12 ga., 32 in. F/M barrels, 2 3/4 in. chambers, engraved "1 of 101" with silver inlays, cased. Mfg. 1988.

	$5,000	$4,500	$4,000	$3,500	$3,000	$2,000	$1,500

Last MSR was $3,500.

* ***Model 101 Field Variation Special*** – 12 ga., 3 in. chambers, VR, 27 in. barrels with WinChokes, blue receiver with scroll engraving, ejectors, 7 lbs. Disc. 1987.

	$1,350	$1,225	$995	$875	$775	$695	$600

Last MSR was $1,185.

* ***Model 101 Field Variation Lightweight*** – 12 or 20 ga., similar to regular Field Grade, except has coin finished receiver, vent. barrels, and solid rubber recoil pad, w/o WinChokes, 6 1/2 - 7 lbs. Disc. 1987.

	$1,200	$1,100	$1,000	$900	$800	$600	$500

Add 20% for 20 ga.

Last MSR was $1,425.

* ***Model 101 Field Variation Waterfowl Model*** – 12 ga. only, 3 in. chambers, 30 or 32 (disc.) in. WinChoked barrels, VR, matte blue receiver with moderate engraving, low gloss walnut stock with vent. recoil pad, 7 3/4 lbs. Disc. 1987.

	$1,895	$1,700	$1,500	$1,250	$1,050	$800	$700

Last MSR was $1,570.

* ***Model 101 Field Variation Grade 2 Barrel Hunting Set*** 12 or 20 ga. barrels, both with WinChokes, 26 in. barrels - 20 ga., 28 in. barrels - 12 ga., scroll engraved, blue receiver with game scene engraving and borders, cased. Mfg. 1984-87.

	$3,300	$2,800	$2,600	$2,400	$2,200	$2,000	$1,800

Last MSR was $2,345.

* ***Model 101 Field Variation Quail Special*** – 12, 20 (disc.1984), 28 (new 1987) ga., or .410 bore (new 1987), 25 1/2 in. WinChoke barrels, straight grip stock, vent. barrels and rib, coin finished receiver with game scene engraving, 6 3/4 lbs, 500 of each ga. were mfg. Imported 1984-86.

12 ga.	$2,900	$2,495	$2,250	$1,995	$1,750	$1,550	$1,450
20 ga.	$3,500	$3,100	$2,650	$2,200	$1,850	$1,750	$1,650
28 ga.	$5,250	$4,500	$3,950	$3,600	$3,200	$2,700	$2,500
.410 bore	$4,500	$3,850	$3,250	$2,800	$2,350	$1,900	$1,800

Last MSR was $1,950.

All 28 ga. models are baby frames.

MSR	100%	98%	95%	90%	80%	70%	60%

* ***Model 101 Field Variation National Wild Turkey Federation Commemorative*** – features golden turkeys on receiver sides, 27 in. VR barrels with choke tubes, only 300 mfg.

	$3,000	$2,400	$1,900	$1,700	$1,500	$1,300	$1,000

Original issue price was $1,950.

* ***Model 101 Field Variation American Flyer Live Bird*** – 12 ga. only, 28 or 29 1/2 (new 1988) in. separated barrels with special competition VR, blue frame with gold wire borders and pigeon inlay, 8 - 8 1/2 lbs. Imported 1987 only.

	$2,595	$2,275	$1,950	$1,775	$1,600	$1,425	$1,300

Last MSR was $2,910.

Add $925 for Combo Model (with extra set of 28 & 29 1/2 in. barrels with WinChokes - 45 mfg.).

Add $265 for 29 1/2 in. barrel with WT4 choke tubes.

Approx. 200 of this model were mfg.

MODEL 101 MAGNUM – similar to 101 Field, 12 or 20 ga., 3 in. Mag. chambering, recoil pad, 30 in. barrels, full and mod., or full and full choke. Mfg. 1966-81.

	$1,300	$1,100	$1,000	$800	$700	$600	$500

Add 20% for 20 ga.

MODEL 101 SKEET VARIATION – similar to 101 Field, with 26 1/2 (12 or 20 ga.) or 28 (28 ga. or .410 bore) in. skeet bored barrels, skeet style stock. Mfg. 1966-84.

	$1,200	$1,000	$825	$770	$700	$650	$595

Add 50% for 28 ga. or .410 bore.

Add 30% for 20 ga.

MODEL 101 THREE GAUGE SKEET SET – similar to Skeet 101, with 20, 28 ga., and .410 bore barrels, cased. Mfg. 1974-84.

	$3,800	$3,475	$3,150	$2,850	$2,600	$2,250	$1,900

MODEL 101 TRAP VARIATION – 12 ga. only, 30 or 32 in. barrels with normal or wide VR, imp. mod. and full or full and full chokes, trap style stock. Mfg. 1966-84.

	$1,320	$1,100	$935	$825	$715	$660	$605

MODEL 101 SINGLE BARREL TRAP – similar to O/U Trap, with 32 or 34 in. F or IM choke barrel, Monte Carlo trap style stock. Mfg. 1967-71.

	$880	$660	$550	$495	$385	$360	$330

Add 100% for an extra O/U barrel (Trap Set).

MODEL 101 PIGEON GRADE (XTR) – 12, 20, 28 ga. or .410 bore (disc. 1986), vent. barrels, deluxe engraved silver receiver version of 101, select checkered wood. Mfg. 1974-87.

MSR	100%	98%	95%	90%	80%	70%	60%

* ***Model 101 Pigeon Grade Lightweight Field Model*** – lightweight variation, WinChokes standard, 28 ga. baby frame has 27 in. barrels, 6 1/2 - 7 lbs. Disc. 1987.

	100%	98%	95%	90%	80%	70%	60%
12 ga.	$2,195	$2,000	$1,800	$1,450	$1,350	$1,250	$1,150
20 ga.	$2,700	$2,350	$2,000	$1,800	$1,700	$1,600	$1,500
28 ga. standard	$3,750	$3,300	$2,900	$2,500	$2,200	$2,100	$1,700
28 ga. baby frame	$5,000	$4,650	$4,250	$3,800	$3,350	$2,750	$2,500
.410 bore	$3,500	$3,250	$2,925	$2,500	$2,200	$2,100	$1,700

Last MSR was $1,950.

Subtract 5% if without WinChokes (available in all gauges).

* ***Model 101 Pigeon Grade Lightweight recent mfg.*** – 20 ga. only, 27 in. barrels only with WinChokes, previously manufactured guns that have been photo-chemically engraved and gold plated, 101 (total mfg.) shotguns were sold by Guns Unlimited Inc. located in Omaha, NE 1995-96.

$2,495	$2,200	$2,000	$1,800	$1,600	$1,500	$1,300

Last MSR was $1,795.

* ***Model 101 Pigeon Grade Lightweight two barrel set*** – includes either 12/20 ga. with WinChokes (28 in. barrels on 12 ga. and 27 in. on 20 ga.) or 28 ga./.410 bore (27 in. barrels, 28 ga. has WinChokes; .410 bore has fixed M/F chokes), 250 sets mfg. serial numbered HS1-HS250. Disc. 1986.

$3,595	$3,350	$2,950	$2,750	$2,300	$2,150	$1,900

Last MSR was $2,500.

Add 30% for 28 ga./.410 bore combo.

* ***Model 101 Pigeon Grade 3 barrel set*** – coin finished Pigeon Grade frame, approx. 250 mfg.

$4,750	$4,350	$3,900	$3,400	$2,750	$2,450	$2,250

* ***Model 101 Pigeon Grade Featherweight*** – 12 or 20 ga., English straight stock, 25 1/2 in. barrels bored IC/IM, 6 1/2 - 6 3/4 lbs. Disc. 1987.

$1,950	$1,750	$1,450	$1,275	$950	$850	$750

Last MSR was $1,580.

Add 20% for 20 ga.
Add 20% for WinChokes.

* ***Model 101 Pigeon Grade Skeet*** – 12, 20, 28 ga., or .410 bore.

$1,850	$1,650	$1,450	$1,225	$1,100	$875	$775

Add 25% for 20 ga.
Add 50% for 28 ga. or .410 bore.

* ***Model 101 Pigeon Grade Trap (Disc.)*** – 12 ga. only, vent. barrels and rib, coin finish receiver with fine scroll engraving, engraved pigeon on floorplate, WinChoke standard, 8 1/4 lbs. Disc. 1985.

$1,550	$1,350	$1,100	$925	$825	$725	$650

Last MSR was $1,475.

Subtract 15% if w/o WinChokes.

MSR	100%	98%	95%	90%	80%	70%	60%

* *Model 101 Pigeon Grade Super* - 12 ga. only, blue receiver with elaborate engraving including multiple gold inlays, extra select walnut with fleur-de-lis checkering on stock and forearm, WinChoke standard, 7 1/2 lbs. Imported 1985-87 only.

	$5,000	$4,800	$4,500	$3,800	$3,000	$2,750	$2,200

Last MSR was $4,590.

MODEL 101 PIGEON GRADE TRAP (CURRENT) - 12 ga., 2 3/4 in. chambers, engraved nickel finished action, choice of 30 or 32 in. 10mm VR ported barrels with Invector Plus choking and TruGlo interchangeable fiber optic front sights, checkered Grade III/IV walnut with adj. comb, adj. trigger shoe, approx. 7 1/2 lbs., includes ABS hard case. Mfg. in Belgium. New 2008.

MSR $2,520	$2,150	$1,825	$1,575	$1,350	$1,075	$900	$750

Add $160 for adj. comb.

MODEL 101 PIGEON SPORTING - 12 ga., 30 or 32 in. ported barrels, 2 3/4 in. chambers, 10mm rib, gloss finished checkered Grade II/III walnut stock with adj. comb, five choke tubes, adj. trigger, silver Nitride receiver with light scroll engraving, TruGlo front sight, includes hard case, 7 - 7 1/4 lbs. Mfg. 2009-2010.

	$2,275	$1,850	$1,625	$1,375	$1,100	$900	$825

Last MSR was $2,619.

MODEL 101 DIAMOND GRADE - Trap or Skeet O/U, 12 (Trap only), 20, 28 ga., or .410 bore, vent. barrels and rib, WinChoke standard on Trap - add $75 on Skeet model (disc.1986), select hand checkered walnut, engraved satin-finish receiver. Trap model has extra high VR. Skeet model has raised rib and muzzle vents.

* *Model 101 Diamond Grade Standard Trap* - 12 ga. only, 30 or 32 in. vent. barrels, 8 3/4 - 9 lbs. Disc. 1987.

	$1,700	$1,500	$1,275	$1,100	$900	$780	$640

Last MSR was $1,860.

* *Model 101 Diamond Grade Unsingle Trap* - 12 ga. only, lower single barrel, 32 or 34 in. barrel, extended rib. Disc. 1986.

	$1,900	$1,675	$1,425	$1,200	$1,000	$800	$600

Last MSR was $1,760.

Add $60 for WinChoke.

* *Model 101 Diamond Grade Oversingle Trap* - 12 ga. only, WinChokes, 34 in. upper barrel only, 8 1/2 lbs. Imported 1986-87 only.

	$2,100	$1,795	$1,600	$1,425	$1,200	$995	$895

Last MSR was $2,145.

* *Model 101 Diamond Grade Oversingle Combo* - includes one set of O/U barrels and an oversingle barrel, cased. Imported 1987 only.

	$2,950	$2,725	$2,500	$2,250	$2,000	$1,800	$1,600

Last MSR was $3,550.

Add $275 for ATA Trap set.

MSR	100%	98%	95%	90%	80%	70%	60%

* ***Model 101 Diamond Grade Trap Combo*** - 12 ga. only, includes a set of 30 or 32 in. vent. O/U barrels and a 32 or 34 in. high ribbed unsingle (lower) barrel, standard or Monte Carlo stock, approx. 9 lbs. Disc. 1987.

	$2,950	$2,600	$2,325	$1,975	$1,800	$1,600	$1,400

Last MSR was $2,940.

* ***Model 101 Diamond Grade Standard Skeet*** - 12, 20, 28 ga., or .410 bore, 27 1/2 in. vent. barrels and competition rib, 6 1/2 - 7 1/4 lbs. Disc. 1987.

	$1,725	$1,525	$1,300	$1,125	$950	$850	$700

Last MSR was $1,950.

Add 30% for 28 ga. or .410 bore.
Add 20% for 20 ga.

Certain design features may increase/decrease the values of this model.

* ***Model 101 Diamond Grade Four Gauge Skeet Set*** - includes 12, 20, 28 ga., and .410 bore 27 1/2 in. separated barrel assemblies, cased. Imported 1985-87 only.

	$4,500	$4,000	$3,500	$3,000	$2,800	$2,500	$2,000

Last MSR was $5,025.

* ***Model 101 Diamond Grade Sporting Clay*** - 12 ga. only, marked Diamond Sporter, 28 in. barrels with WinChokes, designed for Sporting Clay competition. Disc. 1987.

	$2,250	$1,875	$1,550	$1,225	$1,025	$875	$725

Last MSR was $1,965.

MODEL 101 150TH COMMEMORATIVE - 12 ga., 3 in. chamber, 28 in. high gloss blued barrel, Invector Plus choke tubes, white front bead sight, deep relief scroll engraving with gold embellishments on the silver Nitride finished receiver, trigger guard, top lever, forearm bracket, latch lever, and safety barrel selector, includes the Winchester 150th Anniversary logo and the WRA scroll trademark, gloss finished high Grade IV/V walnut stock with cut checkering, white line spacer Pachmayr Decelerator recoil pad, 7 lbs. New 2016.

MSR $3,070	$2,750	$2,500	$2,250	$2,000	$1,850	$1,700	$1,550

MODEL 101 SPORTING - CURRENT MFG. (SELECT) - 12 ga., 28, 30, or 32 in. lightweight ported barrels, 2 3/4 in. chambers, ejectors, Invector-Plus chokes with 5 Signature extended choke tubes, traditional 101 styling with low profile blue engraved receiver, high-gloss Grade II/III walnut stock and forearm, adj. SST, Pachmayr Decelerator pad, 10mm broadway rib, white mid-bead and TruGlo front sight, 7 1/4 - 7 1/2 lbs. Mfg. by FN in Belgium. New 2007.

MSR $2,380	$2,075	$1,775	$1,525	$1,250	$995	$875	$800

This model was featured as a SHOT Show Special for 2006 and 2008.

Select was dropped from this model's nomenclature beginning 2008.

MSR	100%	98%	95%	90%	80%	70%	60%

MODEL 101 FIELD - CURRENT MFG. (SELECT) – 12 ga., 26 or 28 in. lightweight barrels, 3 in. chambers, ejectors, Invector-Plus flush chokes with three choke tubes, blue receiver with deep relief engraving, high-gloss Grade II/III walnut stock and forearm, adj. SST, vented Pachmayr Decelerator pad, 10mm broadway rib, brass bead front sight, 7 1/4 - 7 1/2 lbs. Mfg. by FN in Belgium. New 2007.

MSR $1,900	$1,675	$1,350	$1,150	$995	$875	$775	$675

Select was dropped from this model's nomenclature beginning 2008.

MODEL 101 DELUXE FIELD (SELECT) – 12 ga. only, 3 in. chambers, 26, 28, or 30 in. barrels, ejectors, oil finished Grade II checkered walnut stock and forearm, Pachmayr Decelerator pad, adj. SST, Invector-Plus chokes and three Signature flush choke tubes, silver nitride receiver with engraving, includes hard case, 7 - 7 1/2 lbs. Mfg. by FN in Belgium. Mfg. 2007-2010.

	$1,395	$1,150	$950	$850	$750	$650	$575

Last MSR was $1,679.

Select was dropped from this model's nomenclature beginning 2009.

MODEL 101 LIGHT – 12 ga., 3 in. chambers, 26 or 28 in. barrels, Grade II/III checkered gloss finished walnut stock and forearm, engraved aluminum alloy receiver with quail and pheasants, springer spaniel on bottom, Pachmayr Decelerator pad, three Invector-Plus choke tubes, 6 - 6 1/4 lbs. Mfg. 2009-2010.

	$1,725	$1,475	$1,250	$1,050	$925	$800	$675

Last MSR was $2,039.

This model was originally featured as a 2008 SHOT Show Special.

501 GRAND EUROPEAN – Trap or Skeet, 12 or 20 (Skeet only) ga., 27, 30, or 32 in. vent. barrels and rib, extra select hand checkered walnut with oil finish, Schnabel forearm, extensive scroll engraving on satin-finished receiver. Mfg. 1981-1986.

	$2,300	$2,100	$2,000	$1,800	$1,600	$1,400	$1,200

Last MSR was $1,720.

Add 20% for 20 ga. Skeet.

* ***501 Grand European Featherweight*** – 20 ga. only, straight grip stock, 25 1/2 in. VR barrels, 5 3/4 lbs. Disc. 1986.

	$3,150	$2,750	$2,500	$2,175	$1,900	$1,700	$1,500

Last MSR was $1,720.

PRESENTATION GRADE – 12 ga. only, available in both Trap and Skeet models, blue action extensively engraved with gold inlays, special crotch walnut, 27 (Skeet) or 30 in. vent. barrels, hand checkered, silver wire borders on perimeter of receiver. Imported 1984-87 only.

	$3,950	$3,395	$3,075	$2,400	$2,000	$1,800	$1,600

Last MSR was $3,840.

Subtract 10% for Trap Model.

MSR	100%	98%	95%	90%	80%	70%	60%

MODEL 1001 FIELD GRADE - 12 ga. only, 3 in. chambers, boxlock action, 28 in. VR (8mm) barrel with WinPlus chokes, blue metal featuring 40% engraving coverage, Grade I stock and forearm, high luster finish, mfg. in Italy by Marocchi 1993, disc. 1998.

	$975	$795	$725	$650	$595	$550	$495

Last MSR was $1,099.

* ***Model 1001 Field Grade Sporting Clays*** - 12 ga. only, 2 3/4 in. chambers, 28 or 30 in. VR (10mm) vent. barrels with WinPlus chokes, full engraving (includes scroll and flying W with clay bird), silver nitride receiver with remaining parts blue, Grade II-III stock and forearm, satin finish, mfg. in Italy by Marocchi 1993, disc. 1998.

	$1,075	$925	$795	$725	$650	$595	$550

Last MSR was $1,253.

* ***Model 1001 Field Grade Sporting Clays Lite*** - 12 ga. only, 3 in. chambers, blue finish, 28 in. VR barrels with WinPlus chokes, checkered walnut stock and forearm, gold SST, 7 lbs. Mfg. 1995-98.

	$1,000	$795	$725	$650	$595	$550	$495

Last MSR was $1,153.

MODEL G5500 SPORTER - 12 ga. only, marked Sporter, 28 or 30 in. barrels with fixed chokes (bored IC/M, IM/F, or XF/F) or WinChokes.

	$1,795	$1,475	$1,275	$1,075	$900	$780	$640

Add 20% for WinChokes.

MODEL G6500 SPORTER - 12 ga. only, marked Sporter, barrels and chokes same as G5500.

	$2,295	$1,925	$1,625	$1,400	$1,225	$1,050	$900

Add 20% for WinChokes.

SELECT FIELD (SUPREME) - 12 ga. only, 3 in. chambers, low profile boxlock action with dual tapered locking lugs positioned between the barrels, SST, ejectors, game scene engraved receiver, 26 (new 2001) or 28 in. 6mm VR back-bored barrels with Invector Plus choking (high polish barrels became standard in 2005), redesigned barrels in 2003, checkered walnut stock and forearm, blue action and barrels, barrel selector on safety switch, approx. 7 lbs. Mfg. 2000-2005.

	$1,265	$1,025	$900	$800	$700	$600	$500

Last MSR was $1,498.

During 2004, this model's nomenclature was changed from Supreme Select Field to Select Field.

SELECT WHITE FIELD TRADITIONAL/EXTREME - 12 ga. only, 3 in. chambers, 26 or 28 in. barrels, engraved low profile silver nitride receiver, walnut stock with oval (Extreme) or standard (Traditional) checkering, Invector-Plus choke system, 7 - 7 1/4 lbs., mfg. by Miroku. Limited mfg. 2006.

	$1,295	$1,050	$900	$800	$700	$600	$500

Last MSR was $1,533.

MSR	100%	98%	95%	90%	80%	70%	60%

SELECT ELEGANCE (SUPREME) – 12 ga. only, 3 in. chambers, grey game scene engraved low profile receiver with dual locking pin design, choice of regular checkered (Traditional Elegance) or oval checkered (Extreme Elegance, new 2004) Grade III walnut stock and Schnabel forearm, 26 or 28 in. non-ported barrels with Invector Plus choke system (high polish barrels became standard in 2005), includes red hardshell case, approx. 7 lbs., mfg. by FN Belgium. Mfg. 2003-2006.

$1,950 $1,625 $1,275 $995 $875 $775 $675

Last MSR was $2,320.

SELECT MIDNIGHT – 12 ga. only, 3 in. chambers, 26 or 28 in. barrels, high gloss blued receiver with gold bird accents on both sides and bottom, satin finished Grade II/II walnut stock with oval checkering pattern, deluxe recoil pad, approx. 7 lbs., limited mfg. by Miroku 2006 only.

$1,995 $1,650 $1,300 $1,025 $900 $800 $700

Last MSR was $2,380.

SUPREME SELECT SPORTING – 12 ga. only, 2 3/4 in. chambers, satin finished bi-tone receiver w/o engraving, 28 or 30 in. 10mm VR back-bored barrels with porting, redesigned barrels in 2003, SST with adj. trigger shoe system, sharply checkered walnut stock and Schnabel style forearm, approx. 7 1/2 lbs. Mfg. 2000-2003.

$1,200 $995 $900 $800 $700 $600 $500

Last MSR was $1,406.

SELECT ENERGY SPORTING – 12 ga. only, 2 3/4 in. chambers, 28, 30, or 32 in. ported and vented side rib high polish barrels with Invector Plus chokes (high polish barrels became standard in 2005), marked "Select Energy Sporting" on contrasting chrome finished receiver, 10mm VR, select American walnut stock with oval checkering and palm swell, with or w/o adj. cheekpiece, adj. trigger shoe, TruGlo front sight, approx. 7 1/2 lbs., mfg. by Miroku 2004-2006.

$1,635 $1,425 $1,125 $965 $855 $750 $650

Last MSR was $1,950.

Add $165 for adj. comb stock.

SELECT ENERGY TRAP – 12 ga. only, 2 3/4 in. chambers, 30 or 32 in. VR barrels with Invector Plus chokes (high polish barrels became standard in 2005), similar features as the Select Energy Sporting, features oval checkering on stock and forearm, palm swell, TruGlo front sight, Monte Carlo or adj. comb stock with solid recoil pad, approx. 7 1/2 lbs., made by FN in Belgium. Mfg. 2004-2007.

$1,635 $1,425 $1,125 $965 $855 $750 $650

Last MSR was $1,948.

Add $164 for adj. comb stock.

SELECT PLATINUM FIELD – 12 ga. only, 3 in. chambers, 26 or 28 in. barrels, ejectors, oil finished Grade II/III checkered walnut stock and Schnabel forearm, Invector-Plus chokes and three Signature extended

MSR	100%	98%	95%	90%	80%	70%	60%

choke tubes, adj. SST, silver nitride receiver with deep relief engraving, includes hard case, 7 - 7 1/2 lbs. Mfg. by FN in Belgium. Mfg. 2007-2008.

	100%	98%	95%	90%	80%	70%	60%
	$1,975	$1,650	$1,300	$1,025	$900	$800	$700

Last MSR was $2,359.

This model was featured as a SHOT Show Special during 2006.

SELECT PLATINUM SPORTING – 12 ga. only, 2 3/4 in. chambers, 28, 30, or 32 in. ported barrels, ejectors, oil finished Grade II/III checkered walnut stock and forearm, Invector-Plus chokes and five Signature extended choke tubes, silver nitride receiver with light game scene engraving, adj. SST system, 10mm broadway rib, mid-bead and TruGlo competition front sight, includes hard case, approx. 7 - 7 1/2 lbs. Mfg. by FN in Belgium. Mfg. 2007-2008.

	100%	98%	95%	90%	80%	70%	60%
	$2,200	$1,925	$1,650	$1,400	$1,200	$1,000	$875

Last MSR was $2,625.

SHOTGUNS: RECENT PRODUCTION SxS

Values for recently manufactured side-by-sides assume NIB condition - subtract 10%-15% if without box, warranty card, and original shipping container (with packing materials).

MODEL 21: RECENT/CURRENT MFG. – between 1960-1987, Model 21 production was limited to high grades, built to special order only, and 1987 was the last year Winchester carried Model 21 pricing in its catalog. On custom shop guns mfg. 1960-1969, there is no Winchester name on the barrels, but the Winchester proof mark is on the water table, along with a designation "Model 21" or "New Haven, CT" plus the ser. no. On Model 21s produced from 1969-1988, the water tables are stamped as already noted, and the designation "Model 21 - Winchester" is stamped on the top of the left barrel adjacent to the rib, next to the receiver. Connecticut Shotgun Manufacturing Company is currently manufacturing Model 21 shotguns (marked "Model 21" only), including Grades 21-1, 21-5, 21-6, Grand American, and the Royal Exhibition. These guns are not marked "Winchester", and will not letter from the Cody Firearms Museum. Please refer to the Connecticut Shotgun Manufacturing Company listing for more information regarding these newer custom Model 21s. Also refer to previously mfg. Winchester Model 21 listings under SHOTGUNS: 1879-1963.

Add 25% for 16 or 20 ga.

Add $1,500 for vent. rib.

* ***Model 21 Custom Built*** – standard model with no engraving.

	100%	98%	95%	90%	80%	70%	60%
	$8,000	$7,000	$5,000	N/A	N/A	N/A	N/A

Last MSR was $8,100.

* ***Model 21 Custom Grade*** – includes No. 6 engraved receiver and VR.

	100%	98%	95%	90%	80%	70%	60%
	$12,500	$10,500	$9,000	N/A	N/A	N/A	N/A

Last MSR was $11,080.

MSR	100%	98%	95%	90%	80%	70%	60%

* ***Model 21 Pigeon Grade*** – single set of barrels, No. 6 engraved, w/o gold inlays, 37 mfg. total in 12, 16, and 20 ga.

	$21,000	$19,000	$16,000	N/A	N/A	N/A	N/A

* ***Model 21 Grand American Grade*** – includes 2 sets of barrels with forearms, No. 6 engraved with gold inlays, cased. Must letter from CFM.

	$28,500	$23,000	$19,500	N/A	N/A	N/A	N/A

Last MSR was $22,745.

* ***Model 21 Grand American Small Gauge*** – 28 ga. or .410 bore. Must letter from CFM.

	$39,000	$31,000	$24,500	N/A	N/A	N/A	N/A

Last MSR was $34,460.

Add 25% for 28 ga./.410 bore combo.

* ***Model 21 Grand American ("1 of 8" set)*** – includes 20, 28 ga., and .410 bore VR barrels. Only 4 of 8 sets actually mfg. Must letter from CFM.

	N/A	$65,000	$45,000	N/A	N/A	N/A	N/A

Last MSR was $55,000.

* ***Model 21 Grand Royal (2 barrel set)*** – the highest grade of Model 21s ever produced, originally made in a .410 bore 2 barrel set for John Olin, only 4 others were ever manufactured, and all were 2 barrel sets.

Extreme rarity precludes accurate pricing on this model.

MODEL 22 – 12 ga. only, subcontracted by Winchester and manufactured in Spain by Laurona circa 1975 for international sales including Europe, field configuration only with 28 in. barrels, DT, oil finished checkered walnut stock and semi-beavertail forearm, matted rib, black-chrome finish on metal parts, hand engraved receiver, limited mfg.

	$1,200	$995	$825	$700	$600	$525	$475

MODEL 23 XTR – 12 or 20 ga., 3 in. chambers, 25 1/2, 26, 28, or 30 in. barrels, various chokes, single trigger, VR, auto ejectors, scroll engraved, silver grey satin finish, blue barrel, checkered select walnut stock and forearm, first commercial gun to employ interchangeable chokes. Mfg. 1978-disc.

* ***Model 23 Grade 1***

	$1,900	$1,750	$1,600	$1,350	$1,100	$950	$800

Add 20% for 20 ga.
Subtract 10% for fixed chokes.

* ***Model 23 XTR Pigeon Grade*** – standard weight model, 6 1/2 - 7 lbs, coin finished receiver with scroll engraving. WinChoke option became standard in 1986. Disc. 1986.

	$2,300	$2,100	$1,850	$1,600	$1,300	$1,100	$900

Last MSR was $1,460.

Add 20% for 20 ga.
Subtract 10% if w/o WinChokes.

MSR	100%	98%	95%	90%	80%	70%	60%

* *Model 23 XTR Pigeon Grade Lightweight* – 25 1/2 in. barrels only bored IM/IC (12 ga.) or IC/M (20 ga.) or with WinChokes, 6 1/4 - 6 3/4 lbs., coin finished receiver with bird scene engraving, English stock. Disc. 1986.

	$2,495	$2,150	$1,925	$1,750	$1,250	$1,000	$800

Last MSR was $1,420.

Add 15% for 20 ga.
Subtract 10% if w/o WinChokes.

MODEL 23 PIGEON GRADE DUCKS UNLIMITED – 12 or 20 ga., 500 mfg. in 1981 (12 ga.), and 500 mfg. in 1983 (20 ga.), 1981 12 ga. serialization is 81-DU-XXX, 1983 20 ga. serialization is 83-DU-XXX, cased.

	$2,500	$2,300	$2,200	$2,000	$1,800	$1,500	$1,200

Add 20 % for 20 ga. (1983 mfg.).

MODEL 23 GOLDEN QUAIL SERIES – 12 ga. (1986), 20 ga. (1984), 28 ga. (1985), or .410 bore (1987), 25 1/2 in. solid rib barrels bored IC/M, monoblocs are marked "IC/M" but the barrels are marked "Q1/Q2", coin finished receiver with one gold inlay on floorplate, beavertail forearm, straight grip English stock with recoil pad. Only 500 mfg. each year per gauge. Disc. 1987.

12 ga.	$2,995	$2,775	$2,500	$2,150	$1,850	$1,475	$1,325
20 ga.	$3,400	$3,100	$2,700	$2,300	$1,975	$1,750	$1,475
28 ga. (20 ga. frame)	$4,750	$4,350	$3,950	$3,650	$3,300	$2,900	$2,450
410 bore (small frame)	$4,750	$4,350	$3,950	$3,650	$3,300	$2,900	$2,450

Last MSR was $1,950.

MODEL 23 LIGHT DUCK – 20 ga., blue receiver and 28 in. barrels F/F, select walnut, 8 1/2 lbs. Limited edition, 500 mfg., introduced 1985.

	$2,895	$2,400	$2,075	$1,775	$1,350	$1,100	$975

Last MSR was $1,660.

MODEL 23 HEAVY DUCK – 12 ga., 30 in. barrels, F/F, blue receiver, select walnut, 8 1/2 lbs. Limited edition, 500 mfg. 1984 only.

	$2,995	$2,895	$2,695	$2,495	$2,195	$1,895	$1,595

MODEL 23 CUSTOM 2 BARREL SET – interchangeable 20 and 28 ga. 26 in. barrels, blue engraved receiver with gold inlays, "B" checkering on stock and forearm, leather cased with accessories, only 500 sets mfg. 1986. Disc. 1987.

	$5,975	$5,325	$4,975	$4,075	$3,525	$3,375	$3,075

Last MSR was $4,625.

MODEL 23 GRANDE CANADIAN – 12 or 20 ga., 25 1/2 in. barrels with fixed chokes, coin finished receiver with oak leaf engraving and one gold leaf inlay on receiver bottom, English AAA select walnut stock with beavertail forearm, 51 mfg. in 12 ga., 450 mfg. in 20 ga., approx. 50 two-gun sets were also offered with cases (approx. ser. nos. 1-51).

	$2,850	$2,400	$1,950	$1,700	$1,500	$1,250	$1,125
Cased set	$6,750	$6,050	$5,150	$4,450	$4,000	$3,450	$3,000

Add 20% for 20 ga.

MSR	100%	98%	95%	90%	80%	70%	60%

MODEL 23 CUSTOM - 12 ga. only, 27 in. WinChoke barrels, high luster bluing, no engraving, SST, ejectors, solid red rubber recoil pad, 7 lbs. Imported 1987 only.

	100%	98%	95%	90%	80%	70%	60%
	$2,800	$2,600	$2,400	$2,200	$1,900	$1,600	$1,200

Last MSR was $1,975.

MODEL 23 CLASSIC SERIES - 12, 20, 28 ga., or .410 bore, 26 in. VR barrels, single trigger, deluxe hand-checkered walnut stock and beavertail forearm, solid recoil pad, brass nameplate, gold inlay on bottom of receiver, ebony inlay in forearm, 5 3/4 - 7 lbs. Imported 1986-1987 only.

	100%	98%	95%	90%	80%	70%	60%
12 ga.	$2,650	$2,375	$2,100	$1,825	$1,400	$1,250	$1,150
20 ga.	$2,950	$2,550	$2,225	$1,900	$1,675	$1,395	$1,295
28 ga. (small frame)	$5,400	$5,000	$4,000	$3,500	$3,000	$2,500	$2,250
.410 bore (small frame)	$4,495	$4,100	$3,600	$3,350	$3,100	$2,750	$2,400

Last MSR was $1,975.

100% values assume NIB for this model.

The 28 ga. on this model features a smaller frame, and was the only 28 ga. small frame produced in the Model 23 Series.

FACTORY WINCHESTER COMMEMORATIVES: U.S. PRODUCTION

During the course of a year, we receive many phone calls, emails, and letters on Winchester non-factory special editions and limited editions which do not appear in this section. It should be noted that a factory commemorative issue is a gun that has been manufactured, marketed, factory cataloged, and sold through the auspices of the specific trademark. There have literally been hundreds of non-factory special and limited editions which, although mostly made by Winchester (some were subcontracted), were not marketed or retailed by Winchester. These guns are NOT considered Winchester factory commemoratives in this publication, and for the most part, do not have the desirability factor that the factory commemoratives have. Non-factory cataloged special/limited editions are not listed in this text, because there are literally hundreds of them and collector interest is not as great as for the factory commemoratives. Remember, the least your special/limited edition can be worth is a little more than the standard edition value. Do not concentrate on the rarity or you will be disappointed.

Typically, special and limited editions are made for distributors and typically manufactured by sub-contract for an organization, state, special event, personality, etc. and are typically sold and marketed through a distributor to dealers, or a company/individual to those people who want to purchase them. These special editions may or may not have a retail price and many times, the demand may be regional with values decreasing rapidly in other areas of the country. Also, most special/limited editions do not have alphabetical prefixes/suffixes within their serial ranges. Desirability is the key to determining values on these editions.

As a reminder on commemoratives, especially for the beginning collector, here are a few facts applicable to all manufacturers of commemoratives. Commemoratives were guns specifically designed as a reproduction of an historically famous gun model, or as a tie-in with historically famous persons or events. They are generally of very excellent quality and often embellished with select woods and finishes such as silver, nickel, or gold plating. Obviously, they are manufactured to be instant collectibles and to be pleasing to the eye. As with firearms in general, not all commemorative models have achieved collector status, although most enjoy an active market. Consecutive-numbered pairs as well as collections based on the same serial number will bring a premium. Remember that handguns usually are in some type of wood presentation case, and that rifles may be cased or in packaging with graphics styled to the particular theme of the collectible.

The original factory packaging and papers should always accompany the firearm as they are necessary to realize full value. All commemorative firearms should be absolutely new, unfired, and as issued since any obvious use or wear removes it from collector status and lowers its value significantly. Many owners have allowed their commemoratives to sit in their boxes and plastic bags (could be serious if there is moisture where storage occurs) for years without inspecting them for corrosion or oxidation damage. Periodic inspection should be implemented to ensure no damage occurs - this is important, since even light "freckling" created from touching the metal surfaces can reduce values significantly. A fired gun with obvious wear or without its original packaging can lose as much as 50% of its normal value - many used commemoratives get sold as "fancy shooters" with little, if any, premiums being asked.

The values listed reflect actual prices paid recently through dealer offerings, at gun shows, and both online and brick and mortar auctions. In some regions it may be possible to purchase a Winchester 94 commemorative made in substantial quantity for a slight premium over a standard production Winchester 94. Because of this, prices could fluctuate over 25% depending on the geographic location of purchase or sale.

A final note on factory commemoratives: One of the characteristics of commemoratives/special editions is that over the years of ownership, most of the original amount manufactured stays in the same NIB condition. Thus, if supply always is constant and in one condition, demand has to increase before price appreciation can occur. Many commemorative dealers have told me that recent changes in overseas currency rates have made domestic guns less expensive to own - for Europeans especially. For this reason, more commemoratives are being sold overseas resulting in less supply for the domestic market. After almost 50 years of factory commemoratives and non-factory commemorative/special editions, the performance of these older guns can now be accurately analyzed and the appreciation (or depreciation) can be compared against other purchases of equal vintage. A definitive series of articles has been written on Commemoratives and how they have performed as investments against other traditional economic items - please visit www.bluebookofgunvalues.com click on the Blogs & Gun of the Week tab - S.P. Fjestad's Lethal Blogging - Archived Articles - then click on Commemorative Firearms - Beauty or the Beast Parts 1-4. You be the judge.

U.S. Repeating Arms announced in 1990 that they would once again resume the production of factory commemorative firearms.

There are no factory records available on Winchester Commemoratives from the Buffalo Bill Historical Center, and as a result, no factory letters are available.

100%	Issue Price	Qty. Made

1964 WYOMING DIAMOND JUBILEE 94 CARBINE – ser. no. range WJ1- WJ1500.

$1,200	$100	1,501

1966 CENTENNIAL '66 RIFLE – no ser. no. prefix or suffix.

$695	$125	N/A

1966 CENTENNIAL '66 CARBINE – total mfg. of both the rifle and carbine was 102,309, no ser. no. prefix or suffix.

$695	$125	102,309

Add $50-$75 over individual prices for consecutively serial numbered rifle and carbine set.

1966 NEBRASKA CENTENNIAL 94 RIFLE – ser. no. range NC1- NC2500.

$1,200	$100	2,500

1967 CANADIAN '67 CENTENNIAL RIFLE – no ser. no. prefix or suffix.

$650	$125	N/A

1967 CANADIAN '67 CENTENNIAL CARBINE – total mfg. of both the rifle and carbine was 90,301, no ser. no. prefix or suffix.

$650	$125	90,301

Add $50-$75 over individual prices for consecutively serial numbered rifle and carbine set.

1967 ALASKAN PURCHASE CENTENNIAL CARBINE – ser. no. range AP1- AP1500, w/rack.

$1,495	$125	1,501

1968 ILLINOIS SESQUICENTENNIAL 94 CARBINE – ser. no. range IS1- IS37468.

$595	$110	37,468

1968 BUFFALO BILL RIFLE "1 OF 300" PRES. – ser. no. range WCF1- WCF300.

$3,995	$1,000	300

1968 BUFFALO BILL RIFLE – ser. no. range WC1- WC112923.

$695	$130	N/A

1968 BUFFALO BILL CARBINE – total mfg. of both the rifle and carbine was 112,923, ser. no. range WC1- WC112923.

$695	$130	112,923

Add $50-$75 over individual prices for consecutively serial numbered rifle and carbine set.

1969 GOLDEN SPIKE CARBINE – ser. no. range GS1- GS69996.

$700	$120	69,996

1969 THEO. ROOSEVELT RIFLE – ser. no. range TR1- TR52386.

$695	$135	N/A

1969 THEO. ROOSEVELT CARBINE – total mfg. of both the rifle and carbine was 52,386, ser. no. range TR1- TR52386.

$695	$135	52,386

1970 COWBOY COMMEMORATIVE CARBINE – ser. no. range CB1- CB27549.

$750	$125	27,549

100%	Issue Price	Qty. Made

1970 COWBOY CARBINE "1 OF 300" – ser. no. range NCHF1- NCHF300.

$3,995	$1,000	300

1970 LONE STAR RIFLE – ser. no. range LS1- LS38385.

$695	$140	N/A

1970 LONE STAR CARBINE – total mfg. of both the rifle and carbine was 38,385, ser. no. range LS1- LS38385.

$695	$140	38,385

1971 NRA CENTENNIAL MUSKET – ser. no. range NRA1- NRA47380, not all shipped.

$695	$150	23,400

1971 NRA CENTENNIAL RIFLE – ser. no. range NRA1- NRA47380, not all shipped.

$695	$150	21,000

1974 TEXAS RANGER CARBINE – ser. no. range RA151- RA5000.

$795	$135	4,850

1974 TEXAS RANGER PRESENTATION – ser. no. range RA1- RA150.

$3,995	$1,000	150

1976 U.S. BICENTENNIAL CARBINE – ser. no. range USA1- USA19999.

$795	$325	19,999

1977 WELLS FARGO – ser. no. range WFC1- WFC19999.

$795	$350	19,999

1977 "LIMITED EDITION I" – ser. no. range 77L1- 77L1500.

$1,595	$1,500	1,500

1977 LEGENDARY LAWMEN – ser. no. range LL1- LL19999.

$895	$375	19,999

1978 ANTLERED GAME CARBINE – ser. no. range AG1- AG19999.

$895	$375	19,999

1979 LEGENDARY FRONTIERSMAN RIFLE – ser. no. range LF1- LF19999.

$895	$425	19,999

1979 "LIMITED EDITION II" – ser. no. range 78L1- 78L1500.

$1,595	$1,750	1,500

1979 MATCHED SET ONE OF ONE THOUSAND – ser. no. range MC1- MC1000 and MR1- MR1000.

$3,000	$3,000	1,000

1980 "OLIVER WINCHESTER" – ser. no. range OFW1- OFW1999.

$895	$375	19,999

1981 U.S. BORDER PATROL - MEMBERS MODEL – ser. no. range USBP1- USBP800.

$995	$695	800

1981 JOHN WAYNE – ser. no. range JW1- JW49000.

$1,595	$600	49,000

100%	Issue Price	Qty. Made

Optional accessories were also available for this model: the gun rack with leather insert is currently selling for approx. $395 and the leather scabbard is trading for $395.

1981 "DUKE" – ser. no. range DUKE1- DUKE1000.

$3,995	$2,250	1,000

1981 JOHN WAYNE "1 OF 300" SET – ser. no. range JWM1- JWM300 and JWDM1-JWDM300.

$7,500	$10,000	300

1982 ANNIE OAKLEY – ser. no. range AOK1- AOK6000.

$1,500	$699	6,000

1982 OKLAHOMA DIAMOND JUBILEE – ser. no. range ODJ-1 - ODJ-1001.

$1,750	$2,250	1,001

1982 AMERICAN BALD EAGLE - SILVER – ser. no. range ABE1984-ABE4784.

$795	$895	2,800

1982 AMERICAN BALD EAGLE - GOLD – ser. no. range ABE1782-ABE1983.

$4,000	$2,950	200

1983 CHIEF CRAZY HORSE – ser. no. range CCH1- CCH19999.

$895	$600	19,999

1984 WINCHESTER-COLT COMMEMORATIVE SET – 1 each of the Model 1894 Carbine and Colt Peacemaker, serial numbered 1 WC-4440 WC., .44-40 WCF cal., elaborate gold etching, cased.

$3,000	$3,995	2,300

Approx. 2,300 sets were actually put together in this combination. Some sets were split up with individual prices being discounted. Colt SAAs have been selling individually in the $1,350-$1,495 range.

1985 BOY SCOUTS 75TH ANNIVERSARY – Model 9422 action, .22 cal., rifle configuration, 6 1/4 lbs.

* *1985 Boy Scouts 75th Anniversary* – 15,000 mfg., serial numbered BSA 1 - BSA 15,000, roll engraved, antique pewter receiver, hooded front sight.

$1,350	$495	15,000

* *1985 Eagle Scouts 75th Anniversary* – 1,000 mfg., serial numbered EAGLE 1 - EAGLE 1,000, receiver has triple level gold etching, select American walnut stock and forearm, gold-plated lever, hammer, and forearm cap.

$6,000	$1,710	1,000

1985 MODEL 94 TEXAS SESQUICENTENNIAL – .38-55 WCF cal., available in carbine or rifle.

100%	Issue Price	Qty. Made

* *1985 Model 94 Texas Sesquicentennial Rifle* - 24 in. round barrel, elaborate gold etching, includes Bowie knife, oak cased, 586 mfg, ser. no. range TSR1- TSR586.

$2,995	$2,995	586

* *1985 Model 94 Texas Sesquicentennial Carbine* - 18 1/2 in. round barrel, gold finished receiver and barrel bands, roll engraved receiver, 2,600 mfg., serial numbered TEX1 -TEX2600.

$995	$695	2,600

* *1985 Model 94 Texas Sesquicentennial Rifle/Carbine Set* - includes one each of the Model 94 rifle and carbine, Bowie knife, 150 mfg., ser. no. range Carbine: TEXM1- TEXM150 and Rifle: TSRM1- TSRM150.

$6,500	$7,995	150

1986 120TH ANNIVERSARY MODEL 94 CARBINE - .44-40 WCF cal. only, 20 in. barrel, large loop type finger lever, crescent buttplate, deluxe checkered walnut stock and forearm, extensive gold etching on barrel and framesides, 1,000 mfg. ser. no. WRA001-WRA1000.

$995	$995	1,000

1986 STATUE OF LIBERTY MODEL 94 - Model 94 rifle in .30-30 Win. cal. with octagon barrel, extensive C. Giovanelli scroll engraving with multiple 22Kt. gold inlays, deluxe walnut with fine checkering, also includes 29 in. hand-carved wooden statue of the Statue of Liberty, serial numbers can range from SL001-SL100, while 100 were scheduled to be produced, only 62 were mfg. on a special order basis only, and the customer could pick out the serial number. This model is a USRAC factory commemorative.

$10,000	$6,500	62

Must have matching carved statue.

1987 U.S. CONSTITUTION 200th ANNIVERSARY - .44-40 WCF cal., 20 in. octagon barrel, deluxe checkered walnut, crescent buttplate, full coverage master engraving, No more than 50 guns were to be mfg., the serial number is the name of the state and is done in gold on the top of the tang, cased in a leather luggage style case.

$20,000	$12,000	19

This model was distributed exclusively by Cherry's, located in Greensboro, NC.

1990 WYOMING CENTENNIAL - .30-30 Win. cal., 20 in. round barrel, deluxe checkered walnut, engraved by Bottega C. Giovanelli, coin finished receiver. Originally advertised as an issue of 999 guns, the Winchester strike caused the edition to be reduced in size to only 500 pieces. Serial numbered WYC001-WYC500.

$1,750	$895	500

This model was distributed exclusively by Cherry's, located in Greensboro, NC.

	100%	Issue Price	Qty. Made

1991 125th ANNIVERSARY – .44-40 WCF cal., 24 in. octagon barrel, deluxe checkered walnut, crescent style buttplate, engraving by Bottega C. Giovnaelli utilizing some of Winchester's most historic engraving patterns, includes walnut display case. Serial numbered from WRAC001-WRAC125. Serial numbers were made to order.

$7,500	$4,995	61

This model was distributed exclusively by Cherry's, located in Greensboro, NC.

1992 KENTUCKY BICENTENNIAL – .30-30 Win. cal., lever action, 20 in. round barrel, receiver, lever and hammer casehardened and lacquered by Doug Turnbull, semi-fancy checkered American walnut stock, optional display case. Serial numbered KY001-KY500.

$1,750	$995	500

This model was distributed exclusively by Cherry's, located in Greensboro, NC.

1992 ARAPAHO – .30-30 Win. cal., 20 in. round barrel, checkered walnut stock, lever, receiver and barrel bands gold plated, etched receiver scenes by Baron technology, optional display case. Originally advertised as uncheckered, Winchester made the mistake of checkering all the wood when it was on the production line. The advertisement showed the gun as uncheckered but all guns were delivered as checkered. Serial number ARAP001-ARAP500.

$1,750	$895	500

This model was distributed exclusively by Cherry's, located in Greensboro, NC.

1993 NEZ PERCE MODEL 94 CARBINE – .30-30 Win. cal., 20 in. round barrel, receiver, lever, and barrel bands nickel plated, etched receiver scenes done by Baron Technology, includes suede leather soft case with trim and a branded head and shoulders image of Chief Joseph. Serial numbered NEZ001-NEZ600.

$1,750	$950	600

This model was distributed exclusively by Cherry's, located in Greensboro, NC.

1995 FLORIDA SESQUICENTENNIAL 94 CARBINE – .30-30 Win. cal., 20 in. round barrel, brushed gold plate on the receiver, lever and barrel bands, scenes are roll dyed with hand touch up by Bottega C. Giovanelli. All 500 receivers were mfg., but not all of these receivers were used to make the Florida guns. Other special issue receivers were used that bear this serial number as the reception to this commemorative was poor, optional presentation case. Serial numbered FL001-FL500.

$1,750	$1,195	350

This model was distributed exclusively by Cherry's, located in Greensboro, NC.

	100%	Issue Price	Qty. Made

1996 WILD BILL HICKOK RIFLE – .45 LC cal., 20 in. round barrel, "John Wayne" style lever loop, receiver, lever, and bands are brushed nickel, left side of the receiver features a full coverage engraving pattern, right side of the receiver has his famous engraved 1851 Navy Colts, surrounded by scrollwork, a banner with his birth and date of death along with his famous "Dead Man's Hand" (Aces & Eights), deluxe uncheckered walnut. Serial numbered WBH001-WBH350.

	100%	Issue Price	Qty. Made
	$1,750	$1,195	350

This model was distributed exclusively by Cherry's, located in Greensboro, NC.

WINCHESTER COMMEMORATIVES: NON-DOMESTIC - 1970 TO DATE

Between 1970-1982, Winchester Model 94 Commemoratives were made by Cooey, located in Cobourg, Ontario, Canada.

1970 NORTHWEST TERRITORIES (CANADIAN) – ser. no. range NWT501- NWT3106.

	100%	Issue Price	Qty. Made
	$1,150	$150	2,500

1970 NORTHWEST TERRITORIES DELUXE (CANADIAN) – ser. no. range NWT1- NWT500.

	100%	Issue Price	Qty. Made
	$1,650	$250	500

1973 YELLOW BOY (SOLD IN EUROPE ONLY) – ser. no. range YB1- YB4903.

	100%	Issue Price	Qty. Made
	$1,500	$150	4,903

1973 M.P.X. (MADE ESPECIALLY FOR A MOVIE) – ser. no. range MPX1-MPX32.

	100%	Issue Price	Qty. Made
	$7,500	$78	32

1973 R.C.M.P. (CANADIAN) – ser. no. range RCMP1- RCMP10442, not all shipped.

	100%	Issue Price	Qty. Made
	$995	$190	9,500

1973 R.C.M.P. MEMBERS ISSUE (CANADIAN) – ser. no. range MP1-MP5100, not all shipped.

	100%	Issue Price	Qty. Made
	$995	$190	4,850

1973 R.C.M.P. PRESENTATION - (CANADIAN) – ser. no. range RCMP1P-RCMP10P.

	100%	Issue Price	Qty. Made
	$11,500	N/A	10

1974 APACHE (CANADIAN) – ser. no. range AC1- AC10200, not all shipped.

	100%	Issue Price	Qty. Made
	$995	$150	8,600

1975 KLONDIKE GOLD RUSH (CANADIAN) – ser. no. range KGR1-KGR10200.

	100%	Issue Price	Qty. Made
	$995	$230	10,200

1975 K.G.R. (DAWSON CITY ISSUE) - (CANADIAN) – ser. no. range D1KGR- D25KGR.

	100%	Issue Price	Qty. Made
	$8,500	N/A	25

1975 COMANCHE (CANADIAN) – ser. no. range CC1- CC11511.

	100%	Issue Price	Qty. Made
	$995	$230	11,511

100%	Issue Price	Qty. Made

1976 SIOUX (CANADIAN) - ser. no. range SU1- SU12000, not all shipped.

$995	$280	10,000

1976 LITTLE BIG HORN (CANADIAN) - ser. no. range LBH1- LBH11000.

$995	$230	11,000

1977 CHEYENNE .44-40 WCF CAL. (CANADIAN) - .44-40 WCF Cal., ser. no. range CH1- CH13000, not all shipped.

$995	$300	11,225

1977 CHEYENNE .22 LR CAL. (CANADIAN) - .22 LR Cal., ser. no. range CHF1- CHF8221, not all shipped.

$1,350	$320	5,000

1978 CHEROKEE .30-30 WIN. CAL. (CANADIAN) - .30-30 Win. Cal., ser. no. range CK1- CK9000.

$995	$385	9,000

1978 CHEROKEE .22 LR CAL. (CANADIAN) - .22 LR cal., ser. no. range CHF1- CHF4286, not all shipped.

$1,350	$385	3,950

1978 ONE OF ONE THOUSAND (SOLD IN EUROPE ONLY) - no ser. no. prefix or suffix.

$9,995	$5,000	250

This model was not advertised in the U.S.

1980 ALBERTA DIAMOND JUBILEE (CANADIAN) - ser. no. range ADJ301- ADJ3000.

$995	$650	2,700

1980 A.D.J. DELUXE PRESENTATION (CANADIAN) - ser. no. range ADJ1- ADJ300.

$1,795	$1,900	300

1980 BAT MASTERSON CARBINE - ser. no. range BM1-BM8000.

$995	$650	8,000

1980 SASKATCHEWAN DIAMOND JUBILEE (CANADIAN) - ser. no. range SDJ301- SDJ3000.

$995	$695	2,700

1980 S.D.J. DELUXE PRESENTATION (CANADIAN) - ser. no. range SDJ1- SDJ300.

$1,795	$1,995	300

1981 U.S. BORDER PATROL - ser. no. range BP1- BP1000.

$995	$1,195	1,000

1981 CALGARY STAMPEDE (CANADIAN) - ser. no. range CS1- CS1000.

$1,795	$2,200	1,000

1981 CANADIAN PACIFIC CENTENNIAL (CANADIAN) - ser. no. range CPC301- CPC3000.

$895	$800	2,700

100%	Issue Price	Qty. Made

1981 CANADIAN PACIFIC CENTENNIAL PRESENTATION (CANADIAN) – ser. no. range CPC1- CPC300.

$1,795	$2,200	300

1981 CANADIAN PACIFIC (EMPL.) - (CANADIAN) – ser. no. range CP1-CP2000.

$895	$800	2,000

1981 JOHN WAYNE (CANADIAN) – ser. no. range CJW1- CJW1000.

$1,595	$995	1,000

1982 GREAT WESTERN ARTIST I – no ser. no. prefix or suffix.

$1,595	$2,200	999

1982 GREAT WESTERN ARTIST II – no ser. no. prefix or suffix.

$1,595	$2,200	999

1986 SECOND SERIES EUROPEAN 1 OF 1,000 – mfg. for European sales only 1986, ser. no. range N/A.

$9,995	$6,000	150

1992 ONTARIO CONSERVATION – this model was marketed in Canada only, ser. no. range 001CO - 400CO.

$1,595	$1,195	400

SHOT SHOW SPECIALS

Since 2006 Winchester has introduced SHOT (Shooting, Hunting, Outdoor Trade) Show Specials annually for its dealers who attend the SHOT Show. These are typically variations of existing models, but with different features, finishes, calibers/gauges, etc. These guns can only be ordered during the SHOT Show, and the quantity depends on the amount of dealer orders received during the show. Unfortunately, the quantity of each SHOT Show Special variation is not available. If a SHOT Show Special is well received by the dealers, it may go into production as a standard model. If this happens, these variations can be found in the regular categories. These SHOT Show Specials are not Limited or Special Editions. Models listed in this section have only the MSRs at the time of their releases, and secondary values must be based off the variation from which they are derived. SHOT Show Specials that appear under the various sub-categories are listed in alphabetical order.

SHOT SHOW SPECIAL LISTINGS: RIFLES

SHOT Show Specials manufactured during 2008-2015 will appear alphabetically according to category. For complete model descriptions and information, please visit our website at www.bluebookofgunvalues.com. Unfortunately, Winchester does not have records on the quantities produced on these SHOT Show Special models. **Rifles: Bolt Action:** Model 70 Alaskan Stainless Laminate (2012 - $1,470), Model 70 Coyote Varmint Suppressor Ready (2012 - $1,130), Model 70 Coyote Varmint Suppressor Ready Stainless (2012 - $1,330), Model 70 Extreme Weather (2013 - $1,240), Model 70 Featherweight 7x57 (2013 - $920), Model 70 Featherweight .257 Roberts (2012 - $880), Model 70 Featherweight .280 Rem. (2015 - $940), Model 70 Featherweight Stainless (2010/2011 - $1,069-$1,099), Model 70 Sporter RMEF (2013 - $920, 2014 - $950), Model 70 Stealth (2010 - $939), Model 70 Super Grade Maple

(2015 - $1,600-$1,640), Model 70 Super Grade Short Action Standard Calibers (2014 - $1,300, 2015 - $1,360), Model 70 Super Grade .264 Win. (2012 - $1,340), Model 70 Super Grade Special Limited Edition (2008 - $2,399), Wildcat Bolt Action 22 (2006 - $230), XPR Hunter Mossy Oak Break-Up Country (2015 - $600), XPR Scope Combo (2015 - $710). **Rifles: Lever Action:** Model 71 Standard (2011 - $1,469), Model 73 Sporter Case Hardened (2013 - $1,580, 2014/2015 - $1,740), Model 73 Sporter Octagon Pistol Grip (2015 - $1,470), Model 92 Large Loop Carbine (2011 - $1,199), Model 92 Sporter Case Hardened (2011 - $1,269), Model 92 Trapper (2011 - $1,069), Model 1886 Deluxe Case Hardened (2015 - $1,740), Model 1886 Short Rifle (2012 - $1,340), (2012 - $1,340), Model 1892 Deluxe Octagon (2012 - $1,670), Model 1892 Short (2009/2010 - $1,029). **Rifles: Single Shot:** Model 1885 Black Powder Cartridge Rifle (2010 - $2,669), Model 1885 High Wall 125TH Anniversary (2010 - $1,599), Model 1885 High Wall Hunter ($2014 - $1,600), Model 1885 High Wall Hunter WSM Calibers - (2006 - $1,085), Model 1885 High Wall Safari Octagon (2010 - $1,399), Model 1885 High Wall Traditional Hunter (2012 - $1,670), Model 1885 Low Wall Hunter Rimfire Octagon (2013 - $1,470), Model 1885 Low Wall (2009 - $1,069), Model 1885 Low Wall Octagon (2012 - $1,400), Model 1885 Traditional Sporter Case Hardened (2011 - $1,449), Model 1895 Saddle Ring Carbine (2006 - $1,399).

SHOT SHOW SPECIAL LISTINGS: SHOTGUNS

SHOT Show Specials manufactured during 2008-2015 will appear alphabetically according to category. For complete model descriptions and information, please visit our website at www.bluebookofgunvalues.com. Unfortunately, Winchester does not have records on the quantities produced on these SHOT Show Special models. **Shotguns: Over/Under:** Select Field II (2006 - $1,533), Select Model 101 With Full Coverage Mossy Oak Duck Blind (2007 - $2,239), **Shotguns: Semi-Auto:** Super X2 Special Field (2006 - $910), Super X3 With Full Coverage Mossy Oak Brush (2007 - $1,216), SX3 Composite Sporting Carbon Fiber (2015 - $1,740), SX3 Composite Sporting (2015 - $1,680), SX3 Coyote (2014 - $1,200), SX3 Rifled Deer Cantilever Camo (2010 - $1,269), SX3 Waterfowl Realtree MAX-4 (2012/2013 - $1,130-$1,200), SX3 Ultimate Sporting Adjustable (2015 - $1,870), SX3 Waterfowl Realtree MAX-5 (2014 - $1,140-$1,200, 2015 - $1,200). **Shotguns: Slide Action:** SXP Buck/Bird Combo (2013 & 2015- $630), SXP Camp & Field Combo (2011/2012/2013/2014/2015 - $480), SXP Compact Field (2013 - $440), SXP Extreme Defender (2013 - $520, 2014 - $560), SXP Desert Defender (2015 - $380-$400), SXP Extreme Deer (2015 - $560), SXP Extreme Deer Hunter (2015 - $620), SXP Extreme Marine Defender (2013 - $580, 2014 - $620), SXP Trap (2014 - $480), SXP Trap Compact (2014 - $480), SXP Waterfowl Realtree MAX-4 (2012/2013 - $460-$500), SXP Waterfowl Realtree MAX-5 (2014 & 2015 - $460-$500), SXP Waterfowl Mossy Oak Shadow Grass Blades (2015 - $500), SXP Ultimate Defender (2014 - $500), SXP Ultimate Marine Defender (2014 - $540).

*	Banned due to 1994-2004 Crime Bill (may be current again)
5R	Five (groove) Rifling
A	Standard Grade Walnut
A.R.M.S.	Atlantic Research Marketing Systems
A2	AR-15 Style/Configuration w/fixed carry handle
A3	AR-15 Style/Configuration w/detachable carry handle
AA	Extra Grade Walnut
AAA	Best Quality Walnut
ACB	Advanced Combat Bolt (LWRC)
ACP	Automatic Colt Pistol
ACR	Adaptive Combat Rifle
ACS	MAGPUL Adaptable Carbine/Storage (stock)
adj.	Adjustable
AE	Automatic Ejectors or Action Express
AECA	Arms Export Control Act
AFG	MAGPUL Angled Fore Grip
AK	Avtomat Kalashnikova rifle
AMU	Army Marksman Unit
AOW	Any Other Weapon (NFA)
appts.	Appointments
AR	Armalite Rifle
ASAP	MAGPUL Ambi Sling Attachment Point
ATACS	Advanced Tactical Concealment System (camo pattern)
ATR	All Terrain Rifle (Mossberg)
ATS	All Terrain Shotgun (Mossberg)
AWB	Assault Weapons Ban
AWR	Alaskan/African Wilderness Rifle
B	Blue
BAC	Browning Arms Company
BAD	MAGPUL Battery Assist Device (bolt catch lever)
BAN/CRIME BILL ERA	Mfg. between Nov. 1989 - Sept. 12, 2004
BAR	Browning Automatic Rifle
BASR	Bolt Action Sniper Rifle (H&K)
BB	Brass Backstrap
BBL	Barrel
BLR	Browning Lever Rifle
BMG	Browning Machine Gun
BOSS	Ballistic Optimizing Shooting System
BOSS-CR	BOSS w/o Muzzle Brake
BP	Buttplate or Black Powder
BPE	Black Power Express
BPS	Browning Pump Shotgun
BR	Bench Rest
BT	Beavertail
BT	Browning Trap shotgun
BUIS	Back-Up Iron Sight(s)
c.	Circa
C/B 1994	Introduced Because of 1994 Crime Bill
CAD	Computer Assisted Design
cal.	Caliber
CAR	Colt Automatic Rifle or Carbine
CAWS	Close Assault Weapons System
CB	Crescent Buttplate
CC	Case Colors
CCA	Colt Collectors Association
CDP	Custom Defense Package
CF	Centerfire
CFR	Code of Federal Regulations
CH	Cross Hair
CLMR	Colt Lightning Magazine Rifle
CMS	Cowboy Mounted Shooter
CMV	Chrome Moly Vanadium Steel
CNC	Computer Numeric Controlled (machining/machinery)
COMM.	Commemorative
COMP	Compensated/Competition
CQB	Close Quarter Battle
CQC	Close Quarter Combat
C-R	Curio-Relic
CRF	Controlled Round Feed
CRPF	Controlled Round Push Feed
CSAT	Combat Shooting & Tactics (accessories)
CTF	Copper/Tin Frangible (bullet)
CTG/CTGE	Cartridge
CTR	MAGPUL Compact/Type Restricted (stock)
CYL/C	Cylinder
DA	Double Action
DA/SA	Double Action/Single Action
DAGR	Dual aperture Gunsite rifle scope
DAK	Double Action Kellerman Trigger (SIG)
DAO	Double Action Only
DB	Double Barrel
DBM	Detachable Box Magazine
DCM	Director of Civilian Marksmanship
DI	Direct Impingement Gas System, see Glossary
DIGS	Delayed Impingement Gas System, see Glossary
DISC or disc.	Discontinued
DMR	Designated Marksman Rifle (U.S Army, LWRC)

DPMS Defense Procurement Manufacturing Services
DSL Detachable Side Locks
DST Double Set Triggers
DT Double Triggers
DWM DeutscheWaffen and Munitions Fabriken
EGLM Enhanced Grenade Launcher Module (FNH)
EJT Ejector or Ejectors
EMAG MAGPUL Export MAGazine
EMP Enhanced Micro Pistol (Springfield Inc.)
EXC Excellent
EXT Extractor or Extractors
F Full Choke
F&M Full & Modified
FA Forearm
FAL Fusil Automatique Leger
FBT Full Beavertail Forearm
FC Full Choke
FDE Flat Dark Earth (finish color)
FDL Fleur-de-lis
FE Forend/Fore End
FFL Federal Firearms License
FIRSH Free Floating Integrated Rail System Handguard
FK Flat Knob
FKLT Flat Knob Long Tang
FM Full Mag
FMJ Full Metal Jacket
FMOS Full Mass Operating System
FN CAL FN Carabine Automatique Leger
FN GP FN Grande Puissance (pistol)
FN LAR Fabrique Nationale Light Automatic Rifle
FN Fabrique Nationale
FNAR FN Automatic Rifle
FNC Fabrique Nationale Carabine
FNH USA Fabrique Nationale Herstal (U.S. sales and marketing)
FNH Fabrique Nationale Herstal
FOL Foliage (finish)
FPS Feet Per Second
g. Gram
ga. Gauge
GCA Gun Control Act
GIO Gas Impingement Operation
G-LAD Green Laser Aiming Device
GOVT Government
GPO Gas Piston Operation
gr. Grain
H&H Holland & Holland
HAMR High accuracy multi-range rifle scope
HB Heavy Barrel
H-BAR H(eavy)-BARrel, AR-15/M16
HC Hard Case
HK Heckler und Koch
HMR Hornady Magnum Rimfire
HP High Power (FN/Browning pistol)
HP Hollow Point
HPJ High Performance Jacket
I Improved
IAR Infantry Automatic Rifle (LWRC)
IC Improved Cylinder
ICORE International Confederation of Revolver Enthusiasts
ILS Integral Locking System (North American Arms)
IM Improved Modified
IMI Israel Military Industries
in. Inch
intro. Introduced
IOM Individual Officer Model (FNH model suffix)
IPSC International Practical Shooting Confederation
ISSF International Shooting Sports Federation
ITAR International Traffic (in) Arms Regulation
IVT Italian Value-Added Tax
JCP Joint Combat Pistol
KAC Knight's Armament Co.
KMC Knight's Manufacturing Co.
KSG Kel Tec Shotgun
L Long
LBA Lightning Bolt Action (Mossberg)
LBC Les Baer Custom (Inc.)
lbs. Pounds
LC Long Colt
LCW Lauer Custom Weaponry
LDA Light Double Action (PARA USA INC.)
LEM Law Enforcement Model or Modification
LEO Law Enforcement Only
LMT Lewis Machine and Tool (Company)
LOP Length of Pull
LPA Lightning Pump Action (Mossberg)
LPI Lines Per Inch
LR Long Rifle
LT Long Tang or Light
LTR Light Tactical Rifle (Rem.)
LTRK Long Tang Round Knob

LWRC Land Warfare Resources Corporation
LWRC Leitner-Wise Rifle Company, Inc.
LXX Trigger by Weatherby (new 2016)
M (MOD.) Modified Choke
M&P Military & Police
M-4 Newer AR-15/M16 Carbine Style/ Configuration
Mag. Magnum Caliber
mag. Magazine
MARS Modular Accessory Rail System
MBUS MAGPUL Back-Up Sight
MC Monte Carlo
MCS Modular Combat System (Rem.)
MFG or Mfg. Manufactured/manufacture
MIAD MAGPUL Mission Adaptable (grip, other)
mil see Glossary
mil-dot See Glossary
Mil-Spec Mfg. to Military Specifications
Mil-Std Mfg. to Military Standards
MK Mark
mm Millimeter
MOA Minute of Angle
MOE MAGPUL Original Equipment
MOS Modular Optic System (Glock)
MOUT Military Operations (on) Urbanized Terrain
MR Matted Rib
MS2 MAGPUL Multi Mission Sling System
MSR Manufacturer's Suggested Retail or Modern Sporting Rifle
MVG MAGPUL MOE Vertical Grip
MWS Modular Weapons System
N Nickel
N/A Not Applicable or Not Available
NATO North Atlantic Treaty Org.
NE Nitro Express
NFA National Firearms Act (U.S. 1934)
NIB New in Box
NM National Match
no. Number
NP New Police
NP3/NP3 Plus Nickel-Phosphorus (firearm coating)
NSST Non Selective Single Trigger
NVD Night Vision Device
O/U Over and Under
OA Overall
OAL Overall Length
OB Octagon Barrel
OBFM Octagon Barrel w/full mag.
OBO Or Best Offer
OCT Octagon
ODG Olive Drab Green (finish color)
ORB Oil-Rubbed Bronze finish (Sig Sauer)
ORC Optics Ready Carbine
oz. Ounce
P Police (Rem. rifle/shotgun)
P99AS Pistol 99 Anti Stress (trigger, Walther)
PAD Personal Anti-recoil Device (Savage)
Para. Parabellum
PBR Patrol Bolt Rifle (FNH)
PDA Personal Defense Assistant (PARA USA INC.)
PFFR Percantage of factory finish remaining
PG Pistol Grip
PGF Precision Guided Firearm
PK Pistol Kompact (Walther)
PMAG MAGPUL Polymer MAGazine
POR/P.O.R. Price on Request
POST-'89 Paramilitary mfg. after Federal legislation in Nov. 1989
POST-BAN Refers to production after Sept. 12, 2004
PPC Pindell Palmisano Cartridge
PPD Post Paid
PPK Police Pistol Kriminal (Walther 1931 design)
PPKs Police Pistol Kriminal (Walther 1968 design)
PPQ Police Pistol Quick (defense trigger, Walther)
PRE-'89 Paramilitary mfg. before Federal legislation in Nov. 1989
PRE-BAN Mfg. before September 13, 1994 per C/B or before Nov. 1989.
PRS/PRS2 MAGPUL Precision Rifle/Sniper (stock)
PSD Personal Security Detail rifle (LWRC)
PSG Prazision Schutzen Gewehr (H&K rifle)
PSR Precision Shooting Rifle (FNH)
PXT Power Extractor Technology (PARA USA INC.)
QD Quick Detachable
RACS Remington Arms Chassis System
RAS Rail Adapter System
RB Round Barrel/Round Butt
RCM Ruger Compact Magnum
RCMP Royal Canadian Mounted Police
RDS Rapid Deployment Stock
REC Receiver
Rem. Remington
Rem. Mag. Remington Magnum

REPR	Rapid Engagement Precision Rifle (LWRC)
RF	Rimfire
RFB	Rifle Forward (ejection) Bullpup
RFM	Rim Fire Magnum
RIS	Rail Interface system
RK	Round Knob
RKLT	Round Knob Long Tang
RKST	Round Knob Short Tang
RMEF	Rocky Mt. Elk. Foundation
RMR	Rimfire Magnum Rifle (Kel Tec)
RPD	Ruchnoy Pulemyot Degtyaryova (machine gun)
RR	Red Ramp
RSA	MAGPUL Rail Sling Attachment
RSUM	Remington Short-Action Ultra Magnum
RUM	Remington Ultra Magnum
RVG	MAGPUL Rail Vertical Grip
S	Short
S&W	Smith & Wesson
S/N	Serial Number
SA	Single Action
SAA	Single Action Army
SAAMI	Sporting Arms and Ammunition Manufacturers' Institute
SABR	Sniper/Assaulter Battle Rifle (LWRC)
SAE	Selective Automatic Ejectors
SAO	Single Action Only
SAS	SIG Anti Snag (pistol models)
SASS	Single Action Shooting Society or (U.S. Army) Semi Automatic Sniper System
SAUM	Short Action Ultra Magnum
SAW	Semiautomatic Assault Weapon
SAW	Squad Automatic Weapon
SB	Shotgun butt or Steel backstrap
SBR	Short Barrel Rifle
SCAR	Special (Operations Forces) Combat Assault Rifle (FNH)
SCW	Sub Compact Weapon (Colt)
SDT	Super Dynamic Technology (PARA USA INC.)
ser.	serial
SFO	Striker Fire Operation
SG	Straight Grip
SIG	Schweizerische Industriegesellschaft
SIM	Special Impact Munition
SK	Skeet
SLP	Self Loading Police (FNH shotgun)
SMG	Submachine Gun
SMLE	Short Magazine Lee Enfield Rifle
SNT	Single Non-Selective Trigger
SOCOM	Special Operations Command
SOPMOD	Special Operations Peculiar Modification
SP	Special Purpose
SPC	Special Purpose Cartridge
SPEC	Special
SPEC-OPS	Special Operations
SPG	Semi-Pistol Grip
Spl.	Special
SPLLAT	Special Purpose Low Lethality Anti Terrorist (Munition)
SPR	Special Police Rifle (FNH), Special Purpose Rifle
SPS	Special Purpose Synthetic (Remington)
SPS	Superalloy Piston System (LWRC)
sq.	Square
SR	Solid Rib
SRC	Saddle Ring Carbine
SRT	Short Reset Trigger
SS	Single Shot or Stainless Steel
SSA	Super Short Action
SSR	Sniper Support Rifle (FNH)
SST	Single Selective Trigger
ST	Single Trigger
SUR	Sport Utility Rifle - see Glossary
SWAT	Special Weapons Assault Team
SWAT	Special Weapons and Tactics
SxS	Side by Side
TB	Threaded Barrel
TBA	To be Announced
TBM	Tactical Box Magazine
TD	Take Down
TDR	Target Deployment Rifle (Rem.)
TFO	Tritium Fiber Optic (Sig Sauer)
TGT	Target
TH	Target Hammer
TIR	Target Interdiction Rifle (Rem.)
TPS	Tactical Police Shotgun (FNH)
TRP	Tactical Response Pistol (Springfield Inc.)
TRPAFD	Take Red Pen Away From Dave!
TS	Target Stocks
TSOB	Scope Mount Rail Weaver Type
TSR XP USA	Tactical Sport Rifle - Extreme Performance Ultra Short Action (FNH)
TSR XP	Tactical Sport Rifle - Extreme Performance (FNH)
TT	Target Trigger

TTR	Tactical Target Rifle (PARA USA INC.)
TWS	Tactical Weapons System (Rem.)
UBR	MAGPUL Utility/Battle Rifle (stock)
UCIW	Ultra Compact Individual Weapon (LWRC)
UCP	Universal Combat Pistol (H&K)
UIT	Union Internationale de Tir
UMC	Union Metallic Cartridge Co.
UMP	Universal Machine Pistol (H&K)
URX	Upper Receiver Extending (free floating barrel system, Knight's Armament)
USA	Ultra Safety Assurance (Springfield Inc.)
USAMU	U.S. Army Marksmanship Unit
USC	Universal Self-Loading Carbine (H&K)
USG	United States Government (FNH model suffix)
USP	Universal Self-Loading Pistol (H&K)
USPSA	United States Practical Shooting Association
USR	Urban Sniper Rifle (Rem.)
USSOCOM	U.S. Special Operations Command
VAT	Value Added Tax
Vent.	Ventilated
VG	Very Good
VR	Ventilated Rib
VTAC	Viking Tactics, Inc. (accessories)
VTR	Varmint Triangular Profile Barrel (Remington)
w/	With
w/o	Without
WBY	Weatherby
WC	Wad Cutter
WCF	Winchester Center Fire
WD	Wood
WFF	Watch For Fakes
WIN	Winchester
WMR	Winchester Magnum Rimfire
WO	White Outline
WRA	Winchester Repeating Arms Co.
WRF	Winchester Rim Fire
WRM	Winchester Rimfire Magnum
WSL	Winchester Self-Loading
WSM	Winchester Short Magnum
WSSM	Winchester Super Short Magnum
WW	World War
X (1X)	1X Wood Upgrade or Extra Full Choke Tube
XD	Extreme Duty (Springfield Inc.)
XDM	Extreme Duty M Factor (Springfield Inc.)
XX (2X)	2X Wood Upgrade or Extra Extra Full Choke Tube
XXX (3x)	3X Wood Upgrade
YHM	Yankee Hill Machine

CONTACT INFORMATION

WINCHESTER - REPEATING ARMS

Administrative Offices

275 Winchester Avenue
Morgan, UT 84050-9333
Customer Service Toll Free: 800-333-3288
Parts & Service Toll Free: 800-945-1392
Fax: 801-876-3737
Website: www.winchesterguns.com

Winchester Parts and Service

3005 Arnold Tenbrook Rd.
Arnold, MO 63010-9406
Toll Free: 800-322-4626
Fax: 636-287-9751

WINCHESTER/OLIN

Models 101 & 23 only (Disc.)

Attn: Shotgun Customer Service
427 N. Shamrock Street
East Alton, IL 62024
Fax: 618-258-3393
Website: www.winchester.com

WINCHESTER RIFLES SERIALIZATION

The following Winchester serial numbers appear courtesy of U.S. Repeating Arms, New Haven, CT. I would like to thank U.S. Repeating Arms and Mr. Pardee for making these production figures available.

Shipping rooms records at the factory indicate the following serial numbers were assigned to guns at the end of the calendar year. Polishing Room SNA (Serial Number Application date) column information comes from the Polishing Room Ledgers.

For additional information including factory letters contact the Cody Firearms Museum. Factory letters for Lever Action rifles are $70 and for Model 21 SxS shotguns are $85.

Buffalo Bill Buffalo Bill Center of the West
Attn: Cody Firearms Museum
720 Sheridan Ave.
Cody, WY 82414

In the spring of 2005, the Cody Firearms Museum began a research project involving the Winchester Repeating Arms Company production through the comparison of shipping records (used by the Cody Firearms Museum for Winchester factory letters) and the recently received polishing room records. The little known Winchester polishing room Serial Number Application Records (SNAs) (used in many works of George Madis) documents many Winchester firearms receiver serialization circa 1873 to 1964. The following overview appears courtesy of David Kennedy former Robert W. Woodruff Curator of the Cody Firearms Museum at the Buffalo Bill Historical Center in Cody, Wyoming. The SNAs data assembled from this research is labeled Polishing Room SNAs and included with the U.S. Repeating Arms serialization below.

"Mr. A. E. Hertel, who has had charge of numbering guns practically since the Company started, has 30-odd books in which he has kept track of the gun numbers. These are most valuable records and it seems desirable to place these in a vault. I would therefore suggest that Miss Hall be asked to see Mr. Hertel and make proper arrangements for filing them in the Contract Files, and in a manner so that they can be readily referred to by Mr. Hertel in case questions arise."

This memo from Edwin Pugsley to R.C. Swanton, dated January 22, 1934, preserved a very important part of firearms history. Moved into a vault in location 1-A-3 (Building 1, Tract A, Floor 3) within the Winchester Factory, the books mentioned and the data they contain hold a little-seen insight into the production history of the Winchester Repeating Arms Company. This insight will allow researchers, in time, to create a more accurate understanding of the rate of production, the time spent by parts in the warehouse, and even an approximate understanding of the number of parts retained as a surplus at a given time.

The Serial Number Application Records (SNAs), each a small notebook with most measuring 3.5 in.x6 in., have the model name written on or, more often, punched out of the brown cover. Most pages contain two columns. The left column lists the date and the right column lists the last serial number processed within a group of guns.

I had the privilege of researching these SNAs and their contents while employed as the Robert W. Woodruff Curator of the Cody Firearms Museum at the Buffalo Bill Historical Center (BBHC) in Cody, Wyoming. The SNAs booklets from Winchester's Polishing Room are currently held by the McCracken Research Library at the BBHC as part of MS 20-Winchester Repeating Arms Co. Office Files Collection.

These SNAs maintained by the Polishing Room of the Winchester Repeating Arms Company, contain dates and related serial numbers. Arranged in a series of small booklets, the information contained within gives a new view into the history of the Winchester Repeating Arms Company. Being the only step in which we know the parts were processed in a consecutively numbered manner, this appears to be the closest we can achieve to determining the date of manufacture for these firearms given current primary sources.

The models represented by these records run the gamut from the Model 1866 (starting at serial number 135668) to the end of production of the Model 12 shotgun (serial number 1970885). While the shipping records held by the Cody Firearms Museum end generally in the period 1907-1920, SNAs include production of the World War I-era Model 1917 and the World War II-era M1 Carbine – known internally as the Model 31. Many other models appear in the records in addition to those listed above.

Although some researchers and historians may not be familiar with these SNAs, the data contained in them have appeared in several reports and books on the subject of firearms, and with little in the way of an uproar. House's *The Winchester Model 52* and both The *Winchester Model 42 Shotgun* and *Winchester Slide-Action Rifles, Volume I*, by Ned Schwing include production information from the Hertel's records. Dave Riffle's *The Greatest Hammerless Shotgun Ever Built: The Model 12 – 1912-1964*, while not referencing the serial number applications, references similar information that can be corroborated by these data.

The great question to ask at this point is, "Why Bother? We have had production numbers from Winchester available for most of a century!" This is correct, in a way. Winchester published their sales numbers several times, internally and externally. Unfortunately, sales figures and productions did not always match and were, in some instances, creating more questions than they answered. As these numbers were used again and again in many books (*The History of Winchester Firearms* - numerous editions, *The Winchester Book* - and others by George Madis, and, yes, the *Blue Book of Gun Values*), confusing situations arose when specific small samples were examined or when Winchester production data on individual guns failed to agree with the previously published information. The SNAs can help smooth out some of these bumps. While some of these clarifications may be familiar to the expert, much of this is news to the collector.

Model 1885 Late Production - Information regarding production of the Model 1885 has been troublesome simply as a result of discrepancies between other sources and those in the SNAs. The positive side of this error is that the entire production of this gun after 1901 is older than has been previously understood - sometimes by seven or eight years.

Model 1890 Early Production - This information has not been accurate or available the years prior to 1908 or after 1932. We now have access to reliable data for the entire range of production from 1890 to 1947 - serial numbers 1 to 854747.

Models 1893 & 1897 Transition - The confusion with this pair of early Winchester slide action shotguns comes from where serialization ended for the Model 1893 and began for the Model 1897 and, more importantly, when. The previous understanding of this production taught that the Model 1897 was serially numbered separate from the Model 1893 and that production of the Model 1897 was more than 30,000 in its first year of production. In fact, the Model 1897 simply continued the serialization of the 1893. Annual production of this Model did not surpass 30,000 until 1900 - the first Winchester to reach this mark since the Model 1873.

Models 1892 & 1894 Antique Status - An area of concern for collectors of early Model 1892s and 1894s was the three to five year difference between the earlier-known production dates and the dates provided in Factory Letters from the Cody Firearms Museum. A commonly given reason was, "Oh, that's OK. This must have sat in a parts bin in the warehouse all this time." There is always this possibility. However, individual guns show up in the shipping books only two days to two weeks after serialization. There are some that take longer and there are no known instances of warehouse "Date In" records that precede SNAs dates.

As for the parts bin theory, Winchester would have required storage for the parts of more than 100,000 guns (sometimes 145,000 or more) on any given day during 1896 to 1903 - a period in which Winchester made 370,000-400,000 guns of these two models, depending on the source. This number of excess parts is the difference between the previously understood production numbers and the numbers provided in the SNAs (and supported by the shipping records).

Regarding the BATFE and any interest in 150,000 no-longer-antique guns, there is no change in their level of interest - which is practically none. The only interest that law enforcement has held and will likely continue to hold is in guns illegally modified to short-barrel rifle configuration (barrels less than 16 inches). As for the dating of these firearms, Cody seldom receives calls from the BATFE's Firearms Technology Branch. Your run-of-the-mill antique gun collector doesn't come up on their radar as much as your run-of-the-mill biker gang.

Model 1894 "Spruce Guns" - 1,800 Model 1894 carbines were delivered to the U.S. Army in January 1918, in order to protect spruce production in the Pacific Northwest. These guns are typically in the serial number range 835,xxx to 853,xxx. By the previous reckoning, production occurred in 1918 and 1919, largely after their understood delivery. The SNAs show the production to have taken place during 1916, 1917, and 1918, clarifying the situation.

Model 1897 & 1912 Trench Guns - Collectors of WWI and II Winchester trench guns have scratched their collective heads when comparing guns verified by the connoisseur to the previously understood production dates. This confusion was increased when delivery dates on military records preceded the understood production date by several years - often after the war in question. The SNAs give clear evidence that most of these guns were produced during wartime - and in many cases before!

Model 1894 PCMR Carbines - Similar to the "Spruce Guns" of World War I, 3,000 Model 1894 carbines were used in the Pacific coast forests during World War II. The Canadian Military purchased them in order to equip the Pacific Coast Militia Rangers, a volunteer unit tasked with patrolling the coast in preparation for a Japanese invasion. These guns, ordered in 1942, are all believed to have been manufactured in the 1,300,XXX serial range (based on known guns). As with the "Spruce Guns," this is problematic, placing the guns in a nether region of apparently unrecorded Winchester production during the War.

However, the SNAs place production in 1941, preceding the order date.

Many other models that cannot be listed here...

The question on the lips of many is, "How can I get access to this information?" Prior to the writing of this article, the answer would involve a trip to Cody, Wyoming, to visit America's premier gun museum (my apologies - I am biased in this respect).

Fortunately for the gun collecting public, the Cody Firearms Museum recently announced that these records would be made available (and for a small fee) through the Cody Firearms Museum Records Office starting in spring 2011. A list of models and fee structure is available from the Records Office. Contact information can be found on the Buffalo Bill Historical Center webpage (www.bbhc.org).

A short biography of Mr. Hertel is in *The Winchester Model 52: Perfection in Design*, Herbert Houze (Iola, WI: Krause Publications), Pg. 166. In 1918, he was listed in the Winchester Record as being one of Winchester's "25-year men" with a hire date of May 10, 1884. By the time he left the company, Hertel had worked at Winchester for over a half-Century ("The Winchester Record", Vol. 1, No. 2, August 30, 1918, Pg. 7).

MS 20, Winchester Repeating Arms Company Office Files, Serial Number Application Books, folder 1.

MODEL 1866

YEAR	APPROX. LAST NO.
1866	12476 to 14813
67	15578
68	19768
69	29516
70	52527
71	88184
72	109784
73	118401
74	125038
75	125965
76	131907
77	148207
78	150493
79	152201
80	154379
81	156107
82	159513
1883	162376
84	163649
85	163664
86	165071
87	165912
88	167155
89	167401
90	167702
91	169003
92	NONE
93	169007
94	169011

MODEL 1866, cont.

YEAR	APPROX. LAST NO.
95	NONE
96	NONE
97	169015
98	170100
99	DISCONTINUED

MODEL 1873

YEAR	APPROX. LAST NO.
1873	1 to 126
74	2726
75	11325
76	23151
77	23628
78	27501
79	41525
80	63537
81	81620
82	109507
83	145503
84	175126
85	196221
86	222937
87	225922
88	284529
89	323220
90	363220
91	405026
92	441625
93	466641
94	481826
95	499308
96	507545
97	513421
98	525922
99	541328
1900	554128
01	557236
02	564557
03	573957
04	588953
05	602557
06	613780
07	NONE
08	NONE
09	630385
10	656101
11	669324
12	678527
13	684419
14	686510
15	688431
16	694020
17	698617
18	700734
19	702042
No last # available	
20, 21, 22, 23,	720609

MODEL 1876

YEAR	APPROX. LAST NO.
1876	1 to 1429
77	3579
78	7967
79	8971
80	14700
81	21759
82	32407
83	42410
1884	54666

MODEL 1876, cont.

YEAR	APPROX. LAST NO.
85	58714
86	60397
87	62420
88	63539
89	NONE
90	NONE
91	NONE
92	63561
93	63670
94	63678
95	NONE
96	63702
97	63869
98	63871

MODEL 1885 SINGLE SHOT

YEAR	APPROX. LAST NO.	POLISHING ROOM SNA
1885 -	1 to 375	no entry
86 -	6841	8193
87 -	18328	20006
88 -	30571	30132
89 -	45019	37662
90 -	N/A	45109
91 -	53700	54099
92 -	60371	60305
93 -	69534	66163
94 -	N/A	71024
95 -	73771	74649
96 -	78253	77255
97 -	78815	80877
98 -	84700	82492
99 -	85086	85257
1900 -	88501	88302
01 -	90424	91733
02 -	92031	94738
03 -	92359	96553
04 -	92785	98953
05 -	93611	102084
06 -	94208	104603
07 -	95743	107063
08 -	96819	108004
09 -	98097	109327
10 -	98506	110870
11 -	99012	112555
12 -	N/A	113267
13 -	100352	114726

No further serial numbers were recorded until the end of 1923. Last No. known was: 139700

MODEL 1886

YEAR	APPROX. LAST NO.	POLISHING ROOM SNA
1886 -	1 to 3211	3528
07	14728	12497
88 -	28577	28609
89 -	38401	38652
90 -	49723	51068
91 -	63601	63738
92 -	73816	74898
93 -	83261	85144
94 -	94543	97034
95 -	103708	107346
96 -	109670	111243
97 -	113997	115106
98 -	119192	118646
99 -	120571	120795
1900 -	122834	No further entries

MODEL 1886, cont.

YEAR	APPROX. LAST NO.
01 -	125630
02 -	128942
03 -	132213
04 -	135524
05 -	138838
06 -	142249
07 -	145119
08 -	147322
09 -	148237
10 -	150129
11 -	151622
12 -	152943
13 -	152947
14 -	153859
15 -	154452
16 -	154979
17 -	155387
18 -	156219
19 -	156930
20 -	158716
21 -	159108
22 -	159337

No further serial numbers were recorded until the discontinuance of the Model 1886 which was in 1935 at serial no. 159994.

MODEL 1890

Records on the Model 1890 are somewhat incomplete. Factory records indicate the following serial numbers were assigned to guns at the end of the calendar year beginning with 1908. Actual records on the firearms which were manufactured between 1890 and 1907 will be available from the "Cody Firearms Museum," located at the "Buffalo Bill Historical Center."

YEAR	APPROX. LAST NO.	POLISHING ROOM SNA
1890	N/A	245
91 -	N/A	10884
92 -	N/A	16454
93 -	N/A	25954
94 -	N/A	32554
95 -	N/A	40218
96 -	N/A	46525
97 -	N/A	55855
98 -	N/A	64748
99 -	N/A	80268
1900 -	N/A	100554
01 -	N/A	127181
02 -	N/A	154985
03 -	N/A	186724
04 -	N/A	228104
05 -	N/A	276637
06 -	N/A	302204
07 -	N/A	349947
08 -	NONE	398006
09 -	393427	431483
10 -	423567	450000
11 -	451264	484700
12 -	478595	509100
13 -	506936	527500
14 -	531019	562400
15 -	551290	594300
16 -	570497	608741
17 -	589204	612979
18 -	603438	617978
19 -	630801	649452
20 -	NONE	678928

MODEL 1890, cont.

YEAR	APPROX. LAST NO.	POLISHING ROOM SNA
21 -	634783	679313
22 -	643304	683470
23 -	654837	693040
24 -	664613	701941
25 -	675774	711462
26 -	687049	736246
27 -	698987	767898
28 -	711354	795605
29 -	722125	824623
30 -	729015	837448
31 -	733178	844278
32 -	734454	846022
33 -	N/A	846524
34 -	N/A	848044
35 -	N/A	848584
36 -	N/A	848936
37 -	N/A	No further entries

The Model 1890 was discontinued in 1932, however, a clean up of the production run lasted another 8+ years and included another 14-15,000 guns. Our figures indicate approximately 849,000 guns were made.

MODEL 1892

YEAR	APPROX. LAST NO.	POLISHING ROOM SNA
1892 -	1 to 23701	7121
93 -	35987	22804
94 -	73508	38744
95 -	106721	53616
96 -	144935	67853
97 -	159312	85930
98 -	165431	103328
99 -	171820	129983
1900 -	183411	155567
01 -	191787	183683
02 -	208871	209770
03 -	253935	233451
04 -	278546	280321
05 -	315425	324168
06 -	376496	366950
07 -	437919	413705
08 -	476540	471652
09 -	522162	512627
10 -	586996	581623
11 -	643483	645931
12 -	694752	694420
13 -	742675	747502
14 -	771444	776016
15 -	804622	799690
16 -	830031	811052
17 -	853819	841881
18 -	870942	854878
19 -	903649	881258
20 -	906754	917240
21 -	910476	No further entries
22 -	917300	
23 -	926329	
24 -	938641	
25 -	954997	
26 -	973896	
27 -	990883	
28 -	996517	
29 -	999238	
30 -	999730	
31 -	1000727	
32 -	1001324	

MODEL 1894

Records at the factory, and in some years, estimates, indicate the following serial numbers were assigned to guns at the end of the calendar year.

YEAR	APPROX. LAST NO.	POLISHING ROOM SNA
1894 -	1 to 14579	1674
95 -	44359	14222
96 -	76464	18571
97 -	111453	33108
98 -	147684	53941
99 -	183371	80148
1900 -	204427	103932
01 -	233975	137058
02 -	273854	168420
03 -	291506	204565
04 -	311363	249782
05 -	337557	291706
06 -	378878	331895
07 -	430985	381524
08 -	474241	429757
09 -	505831	449102
10 -	553062	479073
11 -	599263	534429
12 -	646114	591281
13 -	703701	645304
14 -	756066	722280
15 -	784052	825186
16 -	807741	840846
17 -	821972	873425
18 -	838175	882032
19 -	870762	895365
20 -	880627	926851
21 -	908318	935778
22 -	919583	951501
23 -	938539	964709
24 -	953198	974121
25 -	978523	987148
26 -	997603	997938
27 -	1027571	1012753
28 -	1054465	1038665
29 -	1077097	1060899
30 -	1081755	1071420
31 -	1084156	1079689
32 -	1087836	1088141
33 -	1089270	1092328
34 -	1091190	1095364
35 -	1099605	1099625
36 -	1100065	1119104
37 -	1100679	1158835
38 -	1100915	1198405
39 -	1101051	1216165
40 -	1142423	1259563
41 -	1191307	1313301
42 -	1221289	1343183
43 -	N/A	no entry
44 -	N/A	1343196
45 -	N/A	1352066
46 -	N/A	No further entries
47 -	N/A	
48 -	1500000	
49 -	1626100	
50 -	1724295	
51 -	1819800	
52 -	1910000	
53 -	2000000	
54 -	2071100	
55 -	2145296	
56 -	2225000	
57 -	2290296	

MODEL 1894, cont.

YEAR	APPROX. LAST NO.
58 -	2365887
59 -	2410555
60 -	2469821
61 -	2500000
62 -	2551921
63 -	2586000
*1964	2700000 - 2797428
65 -	2894428
66 -	2991927
67 -	3088458
68 -	3185691
69 -	3284570
70 -	3381299
71 -	3557385
72 -	3806499
73 -	3929364
74 -	4111426
75 -	4277926
76 -	4463553
77 -	4565925
78 -	4662210
1979 -	4826596
80 -	4892951
81 -	5024957
82 -	5103248
83-	N/A
84-	5309432
85-	5362944
86-	5409249
87-	5463790
88-	5517897
89-	5574822
90-	5615397
91-	6008296

Model 1894 facts.

** During 1964 the Model 94 surpassed serial number 2,700,000.*

**Serial number 1,000,000 was presented to President Calvin Coolidge in 1927.*

**Serial number 1,500,000 was presented to President Harry S. Truman in 1948.*

**Serial number 2,500,000 and 3,000,000 were presented to the Winchester Gun Museum, now located in Cody, Wyoming.*

**Serial number 3,500,000 was not constructed until 1979 and was sold at auction in Las Vegas, Nevada.*

**Serial number 4,000,000 - whereabouts unknown at this time.*

**Serial number 4,500,000 - shipped to Italy by Olin in 1978. Whereabouts unknown.*

**Serial number 5,000,000 - in New Haven, not constructed as of March 1983.*

MODEL 9422

YEAR	APPROX. LAST NO.
1972 -	F48558
73 -	F121182
74 -	F169044
1975 -	F229666
76 -	F293472
77-	F323197
78-	F367976
79-	F398044
80-	F431532
81-	F489918
82-	F527632
83-	F531722
84-	F539305
85-	F550843
86-	F557835
87-	F571623
88-	F590039
89-	F605281
90-	F617848
91-	F633224
92-	F646000
93-	F658316
94-	F671391

MODEL 1895

YEAR	APPROX. LAST NO.	POLISHING ROOM SNA
1895 -	1 to 287	56
96 -	5715	2783
97 -	7814	5734
98 -	19871	19567
99 -	26434	24311
1900 -	29817	29808
01 -	31584	34615
02 -	35601	39459
03 -	42514	43963
04 -	47805	48444
05 -	54783	52099
06 -	55011	56688
07 -	57351	62041
08 -	60002	64326
09 -	60951	68094
10 -	63771	72565
11 -	65017	76030
12 -	67331	80423
13 -	70823	84889
14 -	72082	99264
15 -	174233	211410
16 -	377411	400166
17 -	389106	403773
18 -	392731	403791
19 -	397250	405391
20 -	400463	409662
21 -	404075	412928
22 -	407200	416355
23 -	410289	419730
24 -	413276	420874
25 -	417402	421337
26 -	419533	423100
27 -	421584	423370
28 -	422676	423779
29 -	423680	424651
30 -	424181	424662
31 -	425132	425523
32 -	425825	425825
33 -	N/A	425881

MODEL 1903

YEAR	APPROX. LAST NO.
1903 -	N/A
04 -	6944
05 -	14865
06 -	23097
07 -	31852
08 -	39105
09 -	46496
10 -	54298
11 -	61679
12 -	69586
13 -	76732
14 -	81776
15 -	84563
16 -	87148
17 -	89501
18 -	92617
19 -	96565
20 -	N/A
21 -	97650
22 -	99011
23 -	100452
24 -	101688
25 -	103075
26 -	104230
27 -	105537
28 -	107157
29 -	109414
30 -	111276
31 -	112533
32 -	112992

This model was discontinued in 1932, however, a clean up of parts was used for further production of approximately 2000 guns. Total production was approx. 126,000 rifles through 1936.

MODEL 1905

YEAR	APPROX. LAST NO.
1905 -	1 to 5659
06 -	15288
07 -	19194
08 -	20385
09 -	21280
10 -	22423
11 -	23503
12 -	24602
13 -	25559
14 -	26110
15 -	26561
16 -	26910
17 -	27297
18 -	27585
19 -	28287
20 -	29113

MODEL 1906

YEAR	APPROX. LAST NO.	POLISHING ROOM SNA
1906 -	1 to 52278	55911
07 -	89147	96820
08 -	114138	134258
09 -	165068	187450
10 -	221189	250850
11 -	273355	304600
12 -	327955	355400
13 -	381922	422600
14 -	422734	458300
15 -	453880	497200
16 -	483805	500700
17 -	517743	523127
18 -	535540	538247
19 -	593917	604917
20 -	N/A	652563
21 -	598691	652584
22 -	608011	652780
23 -	622601	663549
24 -	636163	670684
25 -	649952	683119
26 -	665484	685999
1927 -	679892	No further entries
28 -	695915	
29 -	711202	
30 -	720116	
31 -	725978	
32 -	727353	

A clean up of production took place for the next few years (approx. 1932-1937) with a record of production reaching approximately 848,000.

MODEL 1907

YEAR	APPROX. LAST NO.
1907 -	1 to 8657
08 -	14486
09 -	19707
10 -	23230
11 -	25523
12 -	27724
13 -	29607
14 -	30872
15 -	32272
16 -	36215
17 -	38235
18 -	39172
19 -	40448
20 -	N/A
21 -	40784
22 -	41289
23 -	41658
24 -	42029
25 -	42360
26 -	42688
27 -	43226
28 -	43685
29 -	44046
30 -	44357
31 -	44572
32 -	44683
33 -	44806
34 -	44990
35 -	45203
36 -	45482
37 -	45920
38 -	46419
39 -	46758
40 -	47296
41 -	47957

MODEL 1907, cont.

YEAR	APPROX. LAST NO.
42 -	48275
43 -	N/A
44 -	N/A
45 -	48281
46 -	48395
47 -	48996
48 -	49684
**49 -	50662
**50 -	51640
**51 -	52618
**52 -	53596
**53 -	54574
**54 -	55552
**55 -	56530
**56 -	57508
**57 -	58486

** Actual records on serial numbers stops in 1948. The serial numbers ending each year from 1948 to 1957 were derived at by taking the last serial number recorded (58486) and the last number from 1948, (49684) and dividing the years of production (9), which relates to 978 guns each year for the nine year period.

MODEL 1910

YEAR	APPROX. LAST NO.
1910 -	1 to 4766
11 -	7695
12 -	9712
13 -	11487
14 -	12311
15 -	13233
16 -	13788
17 -	14255
18 -	14625
19 -	15665
20 -	N/A
21 -	15845
22 -	16347
23 -	16637
24 -	17030
25 -	17281
26 -	17696
27 -	18182
28 -	18469
29 -	18893
30 -	19065
31 -	19172
32 -	19232
33 -	19281
34 -	19338
35 -	19388
36 -	19445

A cleanup of production continued into 1937 when the total of the guns was completed at approximately 20,786

MODEL 1911 S.L.

YEAR	APPROX. LAST NO.
1911 -	1 to 3819
12 -	27659
13 -	36677
14 -	40105
15 -	43284
16 -	45391
17 -	49893
18 -	52895

MODEL 1911 S.L., cont.

YEAR	APPROX. LAST NO.
19 -	57337
20 -	60719
21 -	64109
22 -	69132
23 -	73186
24 -	76199
25 -	78611

The Model 1911 was discontinued in 1925. However, guns were produced for three years after that date to clean up production and excess parts. When this practice ceased there were approximately 82,774 guns produced.

MODEL 52

YEAR	APPROX. LAST NO.
1920 -	None indicated
21 -	397
22 -	745
23 -	1394
24 -	2361
25 -	3513
26 -	6383
27 -	9436
28 -	12082
29 -	14594
30 -	17253
31 -	21954
32 -	24951
33 -	26725
34 -	29030
35 -	32448
1936 -	36632
37 -	40419
38 -	43632
39 -	45460
40 -	47519
41 -	50317
42 -	52129
43 -	52553
44 -	52560
45 -	52718
46 -	56080
47 -	60158
48 -	64265
49 -	68149
50 -	70766
51 -	73385
52 -	76000
53 -	79500
54 -	80693
55 -	81831
56 -	96869
57 -	97869
58 -	98599
59 -	98899
60 -	102200
61	106986
62 -	108718
63 -	113583
64 -	118447
65 -	120992
66 -	123537
67 -	123727
68 -	123917
69 -	E 124107
70 -	E 124297
71 -	E 124489
72 -	E 124574
73 -	E 124659

MODEL 52, cont.

YEAR	APPROX. LAST NO.
74 -	E 124744
75 -	E 124828
76 -	E 125019
77 -	E 125211
78 -	E 125315

This Model was discontinued in 1978. A small clean up of production was completed in 1979 with a total of 125419.

MODEL 53

The Model 53 was serial numbered in both its own series (1 to slightly over 15,000) as well as within the Model 1892 series. Early guns predominate the Model 53 serial number series with Model 1892 series serial numbers appearing more frequently mid to late production.
This Model was discontinued in 1932, however, a clean up of production continued for 9 more years.

YEAR	APPROX. LAST NO.	POLISHING ROOM SNA
1924-	1 to 1488	2458
25-	4350	6086
26-	6882	10302
27-	9180	10874
28-	11139	No further entries
29-	12873	
30-	13794	
31-	14416	
32-	14623	
33-	14727	
34-	14817	
35-	14976	
36-	15047	
37-	15078	
38-	15092	
39-	15099	
1940-	15109	
41-	15118	

Total Production Approximately 24,916. Records at the factory indicate the following serial numbers were assigned to guns at the end of the calendar year.

MODEL 54

YEAR	APPROX. LAST NO.
1925 -	1 to 3140
26 -	8051
27 -	14176
28 -	19587
29 -	29104
30 -	32499
31 -	36731
32 -	38543
33 -	40722
34 -	43466
35 -	47125
36 -	50145

MODEL 55

YEAR	APPROX. LAST NO.	POLISHING ROOM SNA
1924 -	1 to 836	1304
25 -	2783	3296
26 -	4957	6748
27 -	8021	11563
28 -	10467	12002
29 -	12258	No further entries
30 -	17393	
31 -	18198	
32 -	19204	
33 -	Clean up 20580	

MODEL 61

YEAR	APPROX. LAST NO.
1932 -	1 to 3532
33 -	6008
34 -	8554
35 -	12379
36 -	20615
37 -	30334
38 -	36326
39 -	42610
40 -	49270
41 -	57493
42 -	59871
43 -	59872
44 -	59879
45 -	60512
46 -	71629
47 -	92297
48 -	115281
49 -	125461
50 -	135461
51 -	145821
52 -	156000
53 -	171000
54 -	186000
55 -	200962
56 -	216923
57 -	229457
58 -	242992
59 -	262793
60 -	282594
61 -	302395
62 -	322196
63 -	342001

This Model was discontinued in 1963. For some unknown reason there are no actual records available from 1949 through 1963. The serial number figures for these years are arrived at by taking the total production figure of 342,001, subtracting the last known # of 115,281, and dividing the difference equally by the amount of remaining years available (15).

MODEL 62

YEAR	APPROX. LAST NO.
1932 -	1 to 7643
33 -	10695
34 -	14090
35 -	23924
36 -	42759
37 -	66059
38 -	80205
39 -	96534
40 -	116393
41 -	137379
42 -	155152

MODEL 62, cont.

YEAR	APPROX. LAST NO.
43 -	155422
44 -	155425
45 -	156073
46 -	183756
47 -	219085
48 -	252298
49 -	262473
50 -	272648
51 -	282823
52 -	293000
53 -	310500
54 -	328000
55 -	342776
56 -	357551
57 -	383513
58 -	409475

MODEL 63

YEAR	APPROX. LAST NO.
1933 -	1 to 2667
34 -	5361
35 -	9830
36 -	16781
37 -	25435
38 -	30934
39 -	36055
40 -	41456
41 -	47708
42 -	51258
43 -	51631
44 -	51656
45 -	53853
46 -	61607
47 -	71714
48 -	80519
49 -	88889
50 -	97259
51 -	105629
52 -	114000
53 -	120500
54 -	127000
55 -	138000
56 -	150000
57 -	162345
58 -	175223

MODEL 70

YEAR	APPROX. LAST NO.
1935 -	1 to 19
36 -	2238
37 -	11573
38 -	17844
39 -	23991
40 -	31675
41 -	41753
42 -	49206
43 -	49983
1944 -	49997
45 -	50921
46 -	58382
47 -	75675
48 -	101680
49 -	131580
50 -	173150
51 -	206625
52 -	238820
53 -	282735
54 -	323530
55 -	361025

MODEL 70, cont.

YEAR	APPROX. LAST NO.
56 -	393595
57 -	425283
58 -	440792
59 -	465040
60 -	504257
61 -	545446
62 -	565592
63 -	581471

1964 Model 70s began with the serial number 700,000.

YEAR	APPROX. LAST NO.
1964 -	740599
65 -	809177
66 -	833795
67 -	869000
68 -	925908
69 -	G941900
70 -	G957995
71 -	G1018991
72 -	G1099257
73 -	G1128731
74 -	G1175000
75 -	G1218700
76 -	G1266000
77 -	G1350000
78 -	G1410000
79 -	G1447000
80 -	G1490709
81 -	G1537134
82-	G1632872
83-	G1656883
84-	G1782457
85-	G1783276
86-	G1808838
87-	G1845122
88-	G1893903
89-	G1950701
90-	G1987984
91-	G2037985

The controlled round feed Model 70 was re-introduced in 1990 as the Model 70 Classic at serial number G15000.

MODEL 70 CLASSIC

YEAR	APPROX. LAST NO.
1990-	G16859
1991-	G23072
1992-	G26709

MODEL 71

YEAR	APPROX. LAST NO.
1935 -	1 to 4
36 -	7821
37 -	12988
38 -	14690
39 -	16155
40 -	18267
41 -	20810
42 -	21959
43 -	22048
44 -	22051
45 -	22224
46 -	23534
47 -	25728
48 -	27900
49 -	29675
50 -	31450
51 -	33225
52 -	35000

MODEL 71, cont.

YEAR	APPROX. LAST NO.
53 -	37500
54 -	40770
55 -	43306
56 -	45843
57 -	47254

MODEL 74

YEAR	APPROX. LAST NO.
1939 -	1 to 30890
40 -	67085
41 -	114355
42 -	128293
1943 -	NONE
44 -	128295
45 -	128878
46 -	145168
47 -	173524
48 -	223788
49 -	249900
50 -	276012
51 -	302124
52 -	328236
53 -	354348
54 -	380460
55 -	406574

MODEL 88

YEAR	APPROX. LAST NO.
1955 -	1 to 18378
56 -	36756
57 -	55134
58 -	73512
59 -	91890
60 -	110268
61 -	128651
62 -	139838
63 -	148858
64 -	160307
65 -	162699
66 -	192595
67 -	212416
68 -	230199
69 -	H239899
70 -	H258229
71 -	H266784
72 -	H279014
73 -	H283718

MODEL 100

YEAR	APPROX. LAST NO.
1961 -	1 to 32189
62 -	60760
63 -	78863
64 -	92016
65 -	135388
66 -	145239
67 -	209498
68 -	210053
69 -	A210999
70 -	A229995
71 -	A242999
72 -	A258001
73 -	A262833

WINCHESTER RIFLE AND SHOTGUN SERIAL NUMBER PREFIXES POST-1968

The following serial number prefixes are found on Winchester rifles and shotguns as a result of the Gun Control Act of 1968.

MODEL NO. (S)	S.N. PREFIX
Super X Model 1	M
Super X Model 1 (Ducks Unlimited)	IDU
12 Y	
12 (Ducks Unlimited)	DU
21 W	
22 WS	
23 PWK	
52 E	
60 (Cooey)	C
40-70A-770-670	G
88 H	
91 KS or WS	
94 No Prefix used	
94 Big Bore	BB
96 K	
100	A
101	K
101 Pigeon Grade	PK
Bolt Action Rimfires 121-131 & 141	Z
Rimfire 150-190-250-255-270 275 & 290	B
Rimfire 300-310 & 320	D
370 & 37A	C
490	J
1200	L
1300	LX
1400	N
1500	NX
1500 (European)	NE
9422	F

WINCHESTER SHOTGUNS

Records at the factory indicate the following serial numbers were assigned to guns at the end of the calendar year.

MODEL 1887

YEAR	APPROX. LAST NO.
1887 -	1 to 7431
88 -	22408
89 -	25673
90 -	29105
91 -	38541
92 -	49763
93 -	54367
94 -	56849
95 -	58289
96 -	60175
97 -	63952
98 -	64855

According to these records no guns were produced during the last few years of this model and it was therefore discontinued in 1901.

MODEL 1893

YEAR	APPROX. LAST NO.	POLISHING ROOM SNA
1893 -	N/A	7958
94 -	N/A	16985
95 -	N/A	24109
96 -	N/A	32908

MODEL 1897

YEAR	APPROX. LAST NO.	POLISHING ROOM SNA
1897 -	1 to 32335	46190
98 -	64668	63867
99 -	96999	90099
1900 -	129332	121740
01 -	161665	155949
02 -	193998	192780
03 -	226331	232089
04 -	258664	269816
05 -	296037	310112
06 -	334059	352757
07 -	377999	398919
08 -	413618	438586
09 -	446888	474392
1910 -	481062	514224
11 -	512632	544663
12 -	544313	574649
13 -	575213	609337
14 -	592732	621155
15 -	607673	634255
16 -	624537	645018
17 -	646124	673277
18 -	668383	705627
19 -	691943	713785
20 -	696183	744268
21 -	700428	748404
22 -	715902	760622
23 -	732060	780537
24 -	744942	793623
25 -	757629	806826
26 -	770527	816294
27 -	783574	829515
28 -	796806	845320
29 -	807321	857216
30 -	812729	865591
31 -	830721	875213
32 -	833026	885034
33 -	835637	885040
34 -	837364	885843
35 -	839728	886094
36 -	848684	895261
37 -	856729	901405
38 -	860725	905660
39 -	866938	909925
40 -	875945	918793
41 -	891190	930412
42 -	910072	950579
43 -	912265	965000
44 -	912327	968160
45 -	916472	968160
46 -	926409	975755
47 -	936682	981005
48 -	944085	985270
49 -	953042	989410
50 -	961999	995605
51 -	970956	1001930
52 -	979913	1007515
53 -	988860	1013730
54 -	997827	1017760
55 -	1006784	1021610
56 -	1015741	1024700
57 -	1024700	1024701

Records on this Model are incomplete. The above serial numbers are estimated from 1897 thru 1903 and again from 1949 thru 1957. The actual records are in existence from 1904 through 1949.

MODEL 1897 TRENCH/RIOT SHOTGUN

This information is provided by Mr. Pat Redmond, after many years of research and collecting. Reference a Winchester Repeating Arms Co. Memorandum dated September 1945. Trench, Riot, and Long Barrel Contract Dates 1/31/42 - 3/23/43, Contract Shipments 24829 shotguns.

YEAR	SER. NOS.	TYPE	CONFIGURATION
1937	902117-903762	Mil.	Long Barrel
1939	911788-911813	Mil.	Trench Gun
1940	914087	Com.	Trench Gun
1940	924312	Com.	Trench Gun
1941	920235-956126	Mil.	Trench Gun
1942	930537-956216	Mil.	Trench Gun
1943	956628	Mil.	Trench Gun
1944	965482	Com.	Trench Gun
1944	966144	Com.	Trench Gun
1944	967371	Com.	Riot Gun
1949	993750	Com.	Riot Gun

MODEL 1901

YEAR	APPROX. LAST NO.
1904 -	64,856 to 64,860
05 -	66453
06 -	67486
07 -	68424
08 -	69197
09 -	70009
10 -	70753
11 -	71441
12 -	72167
13 -	72764
14 -	73202
15 -	73509
1916 -	73770
17 -	74027
18 -	74311
19 -	74872
20 -	77000

MODEL 1911

YEAR	APPROX. LAST NO.
1911	1-3819
1912	27659
1913	30677
1914	40105
1915	43284
1916	45391
1917	49843
1918	52895
1919	57337
1920	60719
1921	64109
1922	69132
1923	73186
1924	76199
1925	78611
1926-28 parts clean-up ending at.	82744

MODEL 12

YEAR	APPROX. LAST NO.	POLISHING ROOM SNA
1912 -	5308	9266
13 -	32418	49344
14 -	79765	110370
15 -	109515	143142
16 -	136412	157861
17 -	159391	191510
18 -	183461	196269
19 -	219457	230343
20 -	247458	281302
21 -	267253	303678
22 -	304314	333678
23 -	346319	379021
24 -	385196	417326
25 -	423056	462132
26 -	464564	498101
27 -	510693	541109
28 -	557850	594589
29 -	600834	637335
30 -	626996	673015
31 -	651255	684476
32 -	660110	698596
33 -	664544	698662
34 -	673994	704074
35 -	686978	723448
36 -	720316	749429
37 -	754250	788635
38 -	779455	813810
39 -	814121	849225
40 -	856499	888006
41 -	907431	903580
42 -	958303	1002163
43 -	975640	1034440
44 -	975727	1042155
45 -	990004	1060683
46 -	1029152	1092085
47 -	1102371	1145110
48 -	1176055	1218845
49 -	1214041	1281025
50 -	1252028	1354540
51 -	1290015	1418315
52 -	1328002	1477650
53 -	1399996	1568660
54 -	1471990	1635300
55 -	1541929	1684790
56 -	1611868	1727280
57 -	1651435	1784325
58 -	1690999	1837879
59 -	1795500	1887319
60 -	1800000	1917780
61 -	1930999	1932638
62 -	1956990	1942598
63 -	1962001	1968260
64 -	N/A	1970885
65-	N/A	No further entry
1966 -	1970875	

A clean up of production took place from 1964 through 1966 with the ending serial # 1970875.

MODEL 12 TRENCH/RIOT SHOTGUN

This information is provided by Mr. Pat Redmond after many years of research and collecting. Reference a Winchester Repeating Arms Co. Memorandum dated September 1945. Trench/Riot and long barrel Contract Dates 4/1/42 - 3/21/44, Contract Shipments 61014 shotguns.

Blue Finish

YEAR	SER. NOS.	TYPE	CONFIGURATION
1941	926558–956504	Mil.	Riot & Long Barrel
1942	961934-1001014	Mil.	Trench/Riot/Long
1943	996899-1028856	Mil.	Trench & Riot

Parkerized Finish

YEAR	SER. NOS.	TYPE	CONFIGURATION
1943	1030000-1035214	Mil.	Trench Gun
1944	1035458	Mil.	Trench Gun
1945	1035525	Mil.	Trench Gun
1946	1071586	Com.	Riot Gun
1949	1740610	Com.	Riot Gun

NEW STYLE M/12

YEAR	APPROX. LAST NO.
1972 -	Y200 011-Y2006396
73 -	Y2015662
74 -	Y2022061
75 -	Y2024478
76 -	Y2025482
77 -	Y2025874
78 -	Y2026156
79 -	Y2026399

MODELS 120/1200/1300

YEAR	APPROX. LAST NO.
1972 -	L739617
73-	L828677
74-	L898065
75-	L967242
76-	L1063788
77-	L1163671
78-	L1202123
79-	L1235083
80-	L1269765
81-	L1320354
82-	L1434776
83-	L1567997
84-	L1755346
85-	L1894542
86-	L1983657
87-	L2075117
88-	L2178816
89-	L2306558
90-	L2386211
91-	L2498813
92-	L2599825

MODEL 24

YEAR	APPROX. LAST NO.
1939 -	1 to 8118
40 -	21382
41 -	27045
42 -	33670
43 -	NONE RECORDED
44 -	33683
45 -	34965
46 -	45250
47 -	58940
48 -	64417

There were no records kept on this model from 1949 until its discontinuance in 1958. The total production was approximately 116,280.

MODEL 36

Approximately 20,000 Model 36 single shot 9mm shotguns were manufactured 1920-1927. These shotguns were not serial numbered.

MODEL 37

Approximately 1,000,000 Model 37 single shot shotguns were manufactured 1936-1963. These shotguns were not serial numbered.

MODEL 40

YEAR	APPROX. LAST NO.
1939 -	1 to 2671
1940	10592
1941	13265
1942	18929

MODEL 42

YEAR	APPROX. LAST NO.
1933 -	1 to 9398
34 -	13963
35 -	17728
36 -	24849
37 -	30900
38 -	34659
39 -	38967
40 -	43348

MODEL 42, cont.

YEAR	APPROX. LAST NO.
41 -	48203
42 -	50818
43 -	50822
44 -	50828
45 -	51168
46 -	54256
47 -	64853
48 -	75142
49 -	81107
50 -	87071
51 -	93038
52 -	99000
53 -	108201
54 -	117200
55 -	121883
56 -	126566
57 -	131249
58 -	135932
59 -	140615
60 -	145298
61 -	149981
62 -	154664
63 -	159353

MODEL 50

YEAR	APPROX. LAST NO.
1954 -	1 to 24550
55 -	49100
56 -	73650
57 -	98200
58 -	122750
59 -	147300
60 -	171850
61 -	196400

WINCHESTER MODEL 101 SERIALIZATION

12 gauge

SER. NO.	MFG.MO.	YEAR
50,50,000	10	1959
50,500	3	1960
51,000	5	1960
51,500	6	1960
52,000	9	1961
52,500	3	1962
53,000	4	1962
53,500	5	1962
54,000	8	1962
54,500	9	1962
55,000	10	1962
55,500	12	1962
56,000	1	1963
56,500	2	1963
57,000	3	1963
57,500	3	1963
58,000	4	1963
58,500	5	1963
59,000	6	1963
59,500	6	1963
60,000	7	1963
60,500	8	1963
61,000	8	1963
61,500	11	1963
62,000	11	1963
62,500	11	1963
63,000	12	1963

12 gauge, cont.

SER. NO.	MFG.MO.	YEAR
63,500	1	1964
64,000	1	1964
64,500	2	1964
65,000	3	1964
65,500	3	1964
66,500	3	1964
67,000	5	1964
67,500	5	1964
68,000	5	1964
68,500	5	1964
69,000	6	1964
69,500	6	1964
70,000	7	1964
70,500	7	1964
71,000	8	1964
71,500	9	1964
72,000	9	1964
72,500	10	1964
73,000	10	1964
73,500	11	1964
74,000	11	1964
74,500	12	1964
75,000	12	1964
75,500	1	1965
76,000	2	1965
76,500	2	1965
77,000	3	1965

12 gauge, cont.

SER. NO.	MFG.MO.	YEAR
77,500	4	1965
78,000	4	1965
78,500	4	1965
79,000	4	1965
79,500	4	1965
80,000	5	1965
80,500	6	1965
81,000	6	1965
81,500	6	1965
82,000	6	1965
82,500	8	1965
83,000	8	1965
83,500	8	1965
84,000	9	1965
84,500	9	1965
85,000	10	1965
85,500	10	1965
86,000	10	1965
86,500	10	1965
87,000	10	1965
87,500	10	1965
88,000	11	1965
88,500	11	1965
89,000	11	1965
90,000	12	1965
90,500	12	1965
91,000	12	1965

MODEL 101, 12 gauge, cont.

SER. NO.	MFG.MO.	YEAR
91,500	1	1966
92,000	1	1966
92,500	2	1966
93,000	2	1966
93,500	2	1966
94,000	3	1966
94,500	3	1966
95,000	5	1966
95,500	5	1966
96,000	6	1966
96,500	7	1966
97,000	7	1966
97,500	7	1966
98,000	8	1966
98,500	8	1966
99,000	9	1966
99,500	9	1966
100,000	10	1966
100,500	10	1966
101,000	10	1966
101,500	11	1966
102,000	11	1966
102,500	12	1966
103,000	1	1967
103,500	1	1967
104,000	2	1967
104,500	3	1967
105,000	4	1967
105,500	5	1967
106,000	5	1967
106,500	5	1967
107,000	9	1967
107,500	10	1967
108,000	10	1967
108,500	11	1967
109,000	11	1967
109,500	11	1967
110,000	12	1967
110,500	1	1968
111,000	2	1968
111,500	3	1968
112,000	3	1968
112,500	3	1968
113,000	3	1968
113,500	4	1968
114,000	5	1968
114,500	5	1968
115,000	6	1968
115,500	6	1968
116,000	7	1968
116,500	7	1968
117,000	9	1968
117,500	10	1968
118,000	1	1969
118,500	1	1969
119,000	2	1969
119,500	3	1969
120,000	4	1969
120,500	4	1969
121,000	4	1969
121,500	4	1969
122,000	5	1969
122,500	6	1969

12 gauge, cont.

SER. NO.	MFG.MO.	YEAR
123,000	6	1969
123,500	6	1969
124,000	7	1969
124,500	7	1969
125,000	7	1969
125,500	8	1969
126,000	8	1969
126,500	9	1969
127,000	9	1969
127,500	10	1969
128,000	11	1969
128,500	11	1969
129,000	11	1969
129,500	2	1970
130,000	2	1970
130,500	3	1970
131,000	3	1970
131,500	4	1970
132,000	4	1970
132,500	4	1970
133,000	4	1970
133,500	5	1970
134,000	5	1970
134,500	5	1970
135,000	6	1970
135,500	6	1970
136,000	6	1970
136,500	8	1970
137,000	8	1970
137,500	8	1970
138,000	8	1970
138,500	11	1970
139,000	12	1970
139,500	12	1970
140,000	12	1970
140,500	1	1971
141,000	2	1971
141,500	2	1971
142,000	2	1971
142,500	3	1971
143,000	3	1971
143,500	4	1971
144,000	4	1971
144,500	4	1971
145,000	4	1971
145,500	5	1971

MODEL 101, 20 gauge.

SER. NO.	MFG.MO.	YEAR
200,000	3	1966
200,500	3	1966
201,000	3	1966
201,500	3	1966
202,000	4	1966
202,500	4	1966
203,000	4	1966
203,500	5	1966
204,000	6	1966
204,500	6	1966
205,000	7	1966
205,500	8	1966
206,000	8	1966
206,500	8	1966
207,000	9	1966
207,500	9	1966
208,000	9	1966
208,500	12	1966
209,000	2	1967
209,500	7	1967
210,000	10	1967
210,500	12	1967

MODEL 101, 28 ga. & .410 bore

SER. NO.	MFG.MO.	YEAR
211,000	1	1968
211,500	1	1968
212,000	10	1968
212,500	10	1968
213,000	10	1968
213,500	11	1968
214,000	12	1968
214,500	12	1968
215,000	1	1969
215,500	2	1969
216,000	5	1969
216,500	6	1969
217,000	9	1969
217,500	10	1969
218,500	12	1969
219,000	12	1969
219,500	12	1969
220,000	12	1969
220,500	1	1970
221,000	1	1970
221,500	2	1970
222,000	3	1970
222,500	7	1970
223,000	9	1970
223,500	9	1970
224,000	9	1970
224,500	9	1970
225,000	10	1970
225,500	10	1970
226,000	11	1970
226,500	11	1970
227,000	11	1970
227,500	12	1970
228,000	12	1970
228,500	4	1971
229,000	4	1971
229,500	4	1971